MONEY GOLF

Other Books by Michael K. Bohn

The Achille Lauro *Hijacking:*
Lessons in the Politics and Prejudice of Terrorism

Nerve Center:
Inside the White House Situation Room

MONEY GOLF

600 YEARS OF
BETTIN' ON BIRDIES

MICHAEL K. BOHN

Potomac Books, Inc.
Washington, D.C.

FOR MY SON, ERIK

Library of Congress Cataloging-in-Publication Data
Bohn, Michael K.
  Money golf : 600 years of bettin' on birdies / Michael K. Bohn.—1st ed.
    p. cm.
  Includes bibliographical references and index.
  ISBN-13: 978-1-59797-031-0 (alk. paper)
  1. Golf—Betting—History I. Title.
  GV979.B47B65 2007
  796.352—dc22

                            2006030803

Printed in the United States of America on acid-free paper that meets the American National Standards Institute Z39-48 Standard.

Potomac Books, Inc.
22841 Quicksilver Drive
Dulles, Virginia 20166

First Edition

10 9 8 7 6 5 4 3 2 1

CONTENTS

Illustrations

FOREWORD

THE GOLF GODS WANT US TO PLAY THE GAME with something at stake. I have always played informal rounds with some money on the line—a couple bucks when I was in high school but a little more after I turned pro. It's just the nature of the game. Sure, I still get a thrill from hitting an iron shot stiff on 18, but it's more fun winning $20 doing it. Besides, I can needle my friends with more gusto if I use their money to buy lunch for everyone after the round.

I learned about money golf when I was teenager in Richmond, Virginia. My father was an assistant pro at Meadowbrook Golf Club, and I loved the game from the start. When I was 13 years old, one of the club members, a local car dealer, asked me to partner with him in matches against his friends. At first I had no idea the men were betting, but I enjoyed the challenge of playing them. I soon began to appreciate the art of money golf, however, especially later, when my partner bought me my first car in 1965, when I was 15. It was a nice thank you for helping him win so many bets. I have liked playing for a little something ever since.

I turned pro in the fall of 1971 and had a good first season the following year on tour, when I broke the rookie earnings record. My career really took off in 1973, though, when I won twice and ended up fifth on the money list. Thinking back, the money games I played during practice rounds helped me improve my game. As Mike describes in chapter 6, Bert Yancey and I played Arnold Palmer and Tom Weiskopf almost every week in '73 with a little spending money at stake. Tom won the British Open that year and five other tournaments, but Bert and I beat the two of them like tom-toms. We kept playing those games for years, and I loved taking Arnie's cash whenever I had the chance.

Back in the 1970s, the PGA Tour didn't have the carnival of events now scheduled during the early part of each tournament week. Playing practice rounds for a friendly wager was fun, and we looked forward to those games. Nicklaus even sent me telegrams to make sure I was available for a game. He'd write, "I got Hale Irwin against you and Raymond Floyd."

I want to make one thing clear: I never bet during the actual tournament and no one should. Practice round matches, however, set professional golf apart from other sports. You don't see the Yankees and Red Sox playing a couple of casual innings before a three-game series. They are all business, all the time. We professional golfers, on the other hand, know how to separate business from pleasure in our sport.

At my home course, Preston Trail in Dallas, I have played money golf over the years with my friends, just as millions of other golfers do every weekend. The competition has always been more important than the money. But some of our "get-even" bets on nine and 18 were scary enough to make me glad to get back out on tour the following week.

I play golf by the rules, try my best to be a gentleman during matches, and always play for money—but I never bet more than I am comfortable losing. Just as Sam Snead once said, the game might be boring without something at stake.

Lanny Wadkins
Dallas, Texas

ACKNOWLEDGMENTS

MANY PEOPLE HELPED MOVE THIS PROJECT ALONG, especially in the beginning when I was struggling to define its scope and message. One in particular is Archie Baird, director of the Heritage of Golf Museum in Gullane, Scotland. He was the first to put betting on golf in a historical perspective, one that permitted me to follow the thread of gentlemanly wagering through the hundreds of years of the game's heritage. David Hamilton, a British golf historian, also helped, as did Dick Donovan, a noted American golf book collector and seller. Closer to home, I am indebted to Pete Van Pelt, PGA, the general manager and director of golf at Mount Vernon Country Club, for his interest and timely phone calls to contributors. Dick Johns, executive director of the PGA of America's Middle Atlantic Section, was very helpful, as were Donald Dell and Mike Milthorpe at SFX Sports.

I wish to thank Kevin Cuddihy and Sam Dorrance at Potomac Books for their help and support. I am also grateful to Sarah Flynn for her critical advice on the book's structure and narrative. Many thanks go to Dick Myers and Walker Merryman for reading the draft manuscript. Thanks also to my wife, Elin, for her unflagging understanding of my single-minded pursuit of a finished manuscript.

I interviewed too many people to name them all here, but I must single out a few for the important guidance and information they gave me at critical points in my research: Ben Wright, Peggy Kirk Bell, Charlie Mechem, and Bob Rosburg.

Thanks also to several golf professionals at my club, Mount Vernon Country Club of Alexandria, Virginia, for helping with the cover of the book: Bryan Armstrong, PGA, head professional; Ron Millner, PGA,

director of instruction; Terry Hummel, PGA, professional emeritus; and Liz
Cooper, PGA apprentice.

I must acknowledge the patience of my regular Saturday golf buddies
who grew weary of listening to the book's progress: Bill "Crawdad" Meares,
Steve "The Defender" Pickard, Allen "Answer Man" Benn, Bill "Pipeline"
Gute, Bud "G-Man" Small, Delaware Joe Resende, Classy Jack Burton,
"Woody" Wiedemer, and one of the nicest men I know, Lee Coogan.

At the cost of sounding crassly commercial, I must also praise the re-
sources of the used-book vendors at Amazon.com. The extraordinary range
of golf books available there allowed me to find hundreds of valuable sources.
Experts have always said nonfiction writers need their own library, and
Amazon now makes establishing a collection financially achievable.

As Archie Baird so rightly contends, the British refer to their preemi-
nent golf championship as simply "the Open." Despite his sound and valuable advice, I had to use the colonial term "the British Open" to minimize
confusion among U.S. readers.

1.

"Let's Make This Interesting":

An Introduction to Money Golf

"Kopplin," Arnold Palmer said to his playing partner Tom Kopplin, "$20 to whoever gets on this green in 2."

"Beautiful," Kopplin replied, "'cause there ain't no way you can get there."

The two men made this side bet on the 15th hole at Palmer's resort, the Bay Hill Club and Lodge in Orlando, Florida. The occasion was the daily "shootout," a fun combination of golf, betting, and incessant needling. Such proceedings are repeated at thousands of golf courses every day. But here's the man who put golf on the American map enjoying the sport just as common citizens do—playing golf for a little money.

Palmer fatted his 3-wood second shot, and his ball found the water in front of the green. After the round, Palmer pulled out his roll to settle the bet as well as others he made during the round. "Man, that's a stash," said Bill Damron, another member of the foursome. Damron, a 30-year shootout player and the father of Professional Golfers' Association (PGA) Tour member Robert Damron, gives Arnie the business just as he gets it from Palmer.

Most every day except during the annual PGA Tour visit there, a group of Bay Hill members gathers at noon for the shootout. The "commissioner" of the event arranges the day's players into fivesomes, each with golfers of differing skill levels, A through D. Palmer and visiting tour pros—such as Tiger Woods, Payne Stewart before his untimely death, Scott Hoch, or Steve Lowery—are the As, with 20-handicappers designated as the Ds. Team aggregate gross or three best ball scores determine the winner; so no handicaps, please. Each player puts $30 to $40 into the pool, which goes to the day's low team. Side bets are so numerous that special shootout scorecards include a blank page for recording the wagers.

1

The shootout group suspends a few rules of the United States Golf Association (USGA). For example, mulligans are allowed off number one, and there is no club limit. Palmer usually has two staff bags on his cart, a common practice among the group that leads to only one player in each cart. "Hit 'til you're happy," declares Palmer.

"I can assure you," Robert Damron said, "that the pressures of a tour event are nothing compared with trying to hit shots with my dad and Mr. Palmer sticking the needle in during every swing." Damron went on to say during his first shootout appearance at age 15, Palmer welcomed him to his team with his typical warmth. Palmer, however, did not wait long to start the hazing. "He let me have it on the first tee," Damron said. "My drive went way left, onto the range. So did my second. Two straight snap hooks."

Living at Bay Hill during the winter, Palmer joins the shootout as often as possible when he is not traveling. His love of the game and his friends pull him to the course—that and the action of a couple bucks on the line. His caddie at Bay Hill, Mike Sturgill, acknowledged the meaning of the shootout to Palmer: "This is more important to him than being on tour. He loves these people."

Palmer and his friends at upscale Bay Hill are not the only folks who bet on golf. Most every golfer, from U.S. presidents to the tank-top set at a dusty public track, turns to his group on the first tee and declares, "Let's make this interesting." There are 26 million golfers in America, and according to a 2002 *Golf Magazine* survey, 72 percent of them bet on their games. More recently, a 2006 *Golf Digest* online poll revealed 93 percent of the respondents bet at least some of the time when they played. Eighty-six percent believed they played either better or the same when betting.

Golfers have been betting on the sport since its beginning. The first known written reference to golf dates to 1457, when a Scottish government decree banned golf so men would spend more time on archery practice. Scotland was at war with England at the time, so good shots shouldn't have been wasted on the links. The earliest evidence of a golf bet followed shortly. Scotland's King James IV lost a 1503 match and 42 shillings to the Earl of Bothwell.

To arrange a fair bet between golfers of unequal skill, the Scots allowed a less talented player to take extra strokes during a match. That practice, as well as competitions between multiple clubs in the late 1800s, ultimately spawned the handicap system within golf.

Golf migrated permanently to the United States in 1888. Americans quickly embraced the sport and its unique relationship with wagering. As people formed clubs, they imported Scottish golf pros to design and build courses as well as to teach the game. The Scots showed new golfers both how to hit a mashie and to win their opponent's money.

Golf is the only U.S. sport people play—horse racing is another matter—that accepts wagering without its governing organization flinching and holding its nose. If Pete Rose had been a golfer, he wouldn't have been banned from his sport. Eight members of the 1919 Chicago White Sox team conspired with gamblers to fix the World Series between Chicago and the Cincinnati Reds, forever changing the game. Major League Baseball suspended New York Yankees majority owner George Steinbrenner for his dealings with a known gambler. The National Football League (NFL) suspended for a year Green Bay Packers quarterback Paul Hornung for betting, just as it did with Detroit Lions defensive tackle Alex Karras and Baltimore's Art Schlichter. The NFL also forced Joe Namath in 1968 to disassociate himself from his New York Bachelors III restaurant because gamblers ate there.

Gambling scandals have erupted regularly in college sports. Just since 1992, problems arose at Maine, Rhode Island, Northwestern (three separate incidents), Maryland, Boston College, Arizona State, and Fresno Sate. In 2003, the University of Washington fired its head football coach, Rick Neuheisel, for participating in a betting pool during the National Collegiate Athletic Association (NCAA) basketball tournament.

In other sports there is no parallel to golf betting. Tennis players don't gather at the net before a match to wager $10 for the first set, $10 on the second, and $10 for the match. You don't see NFL defensive tackle Warren Sapp peeling off a couple of $100 bills and settling up with Packers quarterback Brett Favre at the end of a game. Runners don't bet, and neither do hockey players. Fans of the "Sweet Science" bet on boxing and there have been plenty of fixed fights, but the participants don't wager among themselves. Some professional basketball players gamble—just ask Michael Jordan—but generally not on National Basketball Association (NBA) games. In 1990, Charles Barkley, then playing for the Philadelphia 76ers, had a friendly wager with New York Knicks guard Mark Jackson on the outcome of one of their games. The NBA commissioner fined each of them $5,000.

Today's means of measuring professional golfing prowess grew out of betting customs in the game. Terms like *$5 million purse, prize money,* and *leading money winner* are all extensions of betting practices. When Old Tom Morris competed for a £100 stake in the 1860s, his backers put up his half of the purse. Today television networks and tournament sponsors provide the prize money. There was no parallel in modern sports until the U.S. Tennis Association began its Open era in 1968. Track-and-field athletes didn't compete for cash purses until the 1980s.

Golfers bet, but there have not been any gambling scandals in organized golf. Wagering on the outcome of a match or tournament, either by the participants or onlookers, has not corrupted the sport, nor will betting undermine golf's future. Considering golf's long association with betting, what sets the game apart from those sports that vigorously attempt to keep wagering at arm's length?

One factor is where the game originated. The game developed away from the antigambling influences of puritanical America. U.S.-born sports—basketball, American football, and baseball, for instance—carry the social mores of the society in which they were created. With the exception of the years when Victorian standards quashed some forms of golf wagering, British golf has always embraced betting.

More important, the game's core is based on principle and etiquette. Golfers rely on an ancient and tested honor code to regulate matches by themselves, without the separate referees and umpires who are central to other games. This code, along with lessons about manners and standards of conduct that accompany instruction on the golf swing, steer the sport away from scandal and betting's frequent disreputable handmaiden, cheating. "Golf will never have a scandal," declared Lee Trevino, a man who grew up betting on the golf course. "Golfers are raised differently."

The guardians of the game, the USGA in the U.S. and Mexico and the Royal & Ancient Golf Club of St Andrews throughout the rest of the world, officially sanction betting between players during their game. Following is the USGA's stance on betting: "The USGA does not object to informal wagering among individual golfers or teams of golfers when the players in general know each other, participation in the wagering is optional and is limited to the players, the sole source of all money won by the players is advanced by the players on themselves or their own teams and the amount of money involved is such that the primary purpose is the playing of the game for enjoyment." In spite of the arduous, run-on sentence, the position is relatively straightforward.

LPGA player Karrie Webb can attest to the USGA's acceptance of betting on golf. Before the 2002 U.S. Women's Open, she bet USGA spokesman Craig Smith $5 she would shoot even-numbered scores in the first two rounds. Her 79-73 two-day total prevented her from not only playing on the weekend but also from collecting on the wager.

The women's professional tour, the Ladies Professional Golf Association (LPGA), openly acknowledges the presence of wagering in golf. It even permitted one of its members to sign a sponsorship deal with an Internet betting firm based in Great Britain. Victor Chandler, a big British bookmaker, has sponsored the British Masters, one of the regular stops on the European PGA Tour. Chandler is also the "official" bookmaker for the Ryder Cup. For a time, the Europeans allowed bookies to set up portable parlors on tournament grounds right next to the fish and chips counter and the beer tent.

The PGA Tour, the organization that sanctions the weekly professional tournaments in the United States, zealously works to keep organized gambling away from its organization. Its player handbook bans gambling at tournament sites. Tour pros, however, don't view betting on their practice rounds as gambling. It's just part of the competition on the golf course. Veteran player Brad Faxon and PGA Tour official Johnny Andrews demonstrated the benign role wagering has when they agreed to a bet of $286.67 during the 2005 Buick Championship. Faxon's first two rounds weren't that stellar, and he didn't think he would make the cut. Andrews, working the scorer's tent that week, was more optimistic. Faxon put up his meager winnings from the pro-am earlier in the week as the stakes. Surprisingly, Brad not only made the cut, but he also won the tournament in a play-off after a course record 61 in the final round. "I'll gladly pay him now," Faxon said later of Andrews.

However, when PGA Tour commissioner Tim Finchem says anything about betting at tournaments, he sounds like Claude Raines in Humphrey Bogart's cafe in *Casablanca*: "I'm shocked, shocked to find that gambling is going on here."

———•———

The custom of betting on golf has not changed in 600 years. The usual stakes—money, food, or drink—have remained the same through the sport's history. Early Scottish golfers bet animal pelts, and some believe that's the origin of the betting game called "skins." But golfers don't view this as "gambling" because gambling is risking something tangible on a game of chance. While every golfer welcomes Lady Luck to the golf course, a player is really betting on his ability to play better than his opponent plays. Chance has a role in golf. In an 18- or 36-hole match, however, skill almost always prevails over luck.

At the time of the 1744 founding of the Honourable Company of Edinburgh Golfers, the members assembled for dinner on Friday evenings during the winter golfing season. They also arranged matches and bets for the following day. Most were foursomes, with one two-man team playing alternate shot with one ball against another team. Later, at some clubs, four-ball matches appeared—one team matching their better ball against another team's better ball. The club recorded the matches and the outcome of the wagers in "Bett Books." Members also recorded side bets and propositions. In 1783, "Mr. R. Allen betts one guinea that he will drive a ball from the Castle Hill, without the gate of the palisade, into the Half-Moon battery over the parapet wall." Mr. Allen won the bet.

Harry Vardon, who popularized the overlapping grip, bet when he played during his historic tour of America in 1900. Young Francis Ouimet, the American amateur who shocked the golf world by beating Vardon in the 1913 U.S. Open, bet on his games. So did Walter Hagen, the first successful American professional. Christened "the Haig" by a flattering press for his splashy clothes, haughty demeanor, and high-rolling lifestyle, he chased the dollar through fairway and rough like hound after hare. Bobby Jones, the simon-pure amateur who won the 1930 Grand Slam, played for money in the manner of the old Scots—betting with his opponents even during amateur tournaments.

Every notable player since Hagen and Jones has also bet on his game. Sam Snead was the most active bettor in golf. "Show me a man with a fast backswing and a thick wallet, and I'll go get my golf clubs," he said. Arnold Palmer closely follows Slamming Sammy in bets per 18 holes. "We always play for something," said Jack Nicklaus of the hundreds of rounds he has played with Arnold Palmer. "We never play for much money," joked Palmer as he joined the conversation. "A $10 Nassau or something, because I don't want to hurt him."

Ben Hogan always bet, usually a $5 Nassau, a game that at its simplest involves three bets—$5 on the front nine, $5 on the back, and $5 on the entire match. Raymond Floyd and Lanny Wadkins relish a money match, even with stakes that might cause lesser mortals to choke like a dog. Tom Watson, Nick Price, Phil Mickelson, and dozens of other PGA Tour players always bet during informal rounds. Tiger bets on most everything that moves on a golf course.

Retief Goosen and Jason Gore were the final pairing on the last day of the 2005 U.S. Open. They both played poorly—Goosen shot an 81 to finish tied for 11th and Gore, an 84 to tie for 49th. By number 16 both were woefully out of the hunt, so they agreed to a $5 side bet on the remaining three holes. Gore double-bogeyed 18 to lose. The news media widely reported their wager, and no one thought a thing about it. It's just golf.

Goosen made a similar bet with Michael Campbell during the 2000 *Trophée Lancôme* European PGA tournament when both men lagged behind the leaders after 36 holes. Talking before the third round about the Ferrari sports cars each owned at the time, Goosen offered to sell Campbell his car cover for $1,000. "Let's play for it," Campbell proposed. Goosen agreed that if he won the tournament, Campbell would pay him $1,000 for the cover, but if Campbell won, Goosen would give him the cover for nothing. Retief shot 64–67 and won, with Michael posting 65–67 to tie for second. Campbell told the news media about the bet in 2006 as he described how a game within a game could take a player's mind off the more daunting task of making up ground on the tournament leader.

Tom Lehman has been a successful player on the PGA Tour since 1991 and won the 1996 British Open. He is a genuinely nice guy, and his peers respect his humility, devout Christianity, and family values. When not entered in tournaments that routinely pay the winner $1 million, Tom plays at his home course in Scottsdale, Arizona. He bets during these informal matches with his friends, usually a $10 Nassau, and often "presses" an opponent, by adding another $10 bet to the existing wager.

"It's a lot of fun when you get five or six presses going on a nine, and if a guy misses a 3-footer, you're riding him like crazy," Lehman said of his games. "You may lose only 40 bucks if you play lousy, but at least you're playing for something and you're having a great time. That's the way golf is meant to be."

Today, the overlap between golf and wagering is as complete as Vardon's grip. Players "gamble" by electing to hit a lengthy second shot into a par-5 green guarded by water and bunkers. Some of the stouthearted choose a high-risk, high-reward "flop" shot over a green-side bunker in order to land the ball near the hole instead of cautiously bumping the ball onto the fat part of the green. Tiger Woods attempted this shot in a play-off against Ernie Els to determine the outcome of the 2003 President's Cup. One of the TV commentators asked, "What are the odds on this shot?"

The risk and reward that define a wager extend into golf course design. Bill Love, the former president of the American Society of Golf Course Architects, attempts to place "gambling" holes toward the end of each nine, especially on the back. "If the topography permits, I try to offer a hole that can be played either safely or boldly," Love said. "If you elect to take the gamble of a long shot over a hazard at a critical point in a match, you should be rewarded. If you fail, I want the penalty to be a score worse than a bogey."

The Augusta National Golf Club always offered holes tournament leaders could play safely, while those trailing behind might gamble their way back into the hunt. According to several big-name players, the length the club added to several holes between the 2005 and 2006 Masters now has limited the player's choices.

A more direct connection between design and betting is a 19th hole—that is, a real one, not the Member's Grill. Several golf courses in the United States have an extra hole for settling bets. Reno's Wolf Run; Silverstone in Las Vegas; Knollwood Country Club in Elmsford, New York; and two Virginia clubs, Kinloch and Olde Farm, boast extra holes for players still tied after 18. At Idaho's StoneRidge, the 19th is a 236-yard par-4 called "the Gambler." Drive the green and win the bet. Congressional Country Club, near Washington, D.C., and most recently the site of the 1997 U.S. Open, had a betting hole on the original course.

Alister Mackenzie included a 19th hole in his initial design of Augusta National Golf Club, which Bobby Jones built and opened in 1933. Mackenzie laid out a 90-yard par-3, with its green where the practice green is now located. The *Augusta Chronicle* wrote about the extra hole in its January 4, 1933, edition. It didn't last long, however. Jones removed the hole, perhaps when he reversed the order of the nines in 1934. Several writers suggest Jones thought the extra hole disturbed the course's symmetry. In those days, golfers called an extra hole a "bye hole," taking the name from those holes not played after a match had been won. (If a player is three holes up with only two holes left, for example, he wins the match. He and his opponent either walk in or play for fun [or for a separate bet] the remaining, or "bye," holes, 17 and 18.)

Raymond Floyd followed Mackenzie's lead when in 2004 he designed Old Palm Golf Club in Palm Beach Gardens, Florida. The club calls the par-3 19th the "Bye Hole." It is only 103 yards long but has an island green. No pressure.

A number of golf courses in the U.S. have 19th holes to settle bets after completing a round. This is the "Bye Hole" at Old Palm Golf Club in Palm Beach Gardens, Florida. It's just over 100 yards long with an island green. "Double or nothing?" Johnson Design Golf Marketing

Betting is part of golf's lexicon. The late, esteemed sportswriter Jim Murray of the *Los Angeles Times* repeatedly used golf betting metaphors to describe how golfers react to pressure. He wrote in 1993 about Captain Tom Watson's selection of Floyd to the Ryder Cup team: "Raymond Floyd has been in enough $10,000 Nassaus not to get a lump in his throat and a loop in his swing when facing a par-3 that's 90 percent water and he's already one down." Of Vijay Singh's coolness during a 1997 tournament, Murray wrote, "You'd swear he was playing a $2 Nassau with the guys from the garage instead of a near-major tournament for a third of a million dollars."

Writers for the major golf magazines cannot put finger to keyboard without using the words *bet* or *wager* to express the strength of their predictions or analysis. Discussing which player might give the favorites a challenge during the 2004 U.S. Open, *Golf World's* John Antonini wrote, "Best bet to break through: Why not John Huston?" Regarding the possibility of Butch Harmon helping Tiger with his swing woes in 2004, Peter Kostis, a CBS television analyst writing for *Golf Magazine*, opined, "And if Tiger ever feels he needs Butch's help, I bet he'll be man enough to ask for it." Golf writers describe most any likely outcome as "best bets" and "decent bets."

Wagering even extends into golf industry marketing. In 1998, Spalding challenged other golf ball manufacturers to a $1 million bet that its Top-Flite System C & T balls would outperform balls from Titleist and Slazenger. Spalding's marketing angle was that they designed the "C" balls to play best with Callaway clubs and the "T" version for TaylorMade sticks. Nothing came of the bet because Callaway sued Spalding over the use of its name and images. The two parties settled, with Spalding withdrawing the balls from the market.

Famous golfers are not the only players with engaging anecdotes about money golf. Movie stars have great stories about golf betting. "I may have been a bit better than Hope," Bing Crosby said of his game and Bob's, "but he was a better bettor." Most U.S. presidents who played the game also bet on it. Warren G. Harding and John F. Kennedy (JFK) were the most spirited bettors, and the two who got in the most political trouble—Richard Nixon and Bill Clinton—bent the most rules.

Some folks play golf for large sums, but these men shun the spotlight, mostly for tax reasons. Las Vegas businessman Bill Walters once played a $100,000 Nassau. Professional gambler Doyle Brunson boasted of having $800,000 riding on a game. "A hunnert grand says you miss that putt" is not a phrase foreign to the likes of Walters, Brunson, Terrance Leon, Amarillo Slim, Leon Crump, Dewey Tomko, and Evel Knievel. Basketball superstar Michael Jordon lost $1.25 million on the golf course to Richard Esquinas in 1991.

Another element of money golf is a Calcutta, a betting auction held during tournaments. The Calcutta is common throughout golf, from six-figure events down to smaller affairs at a country club's annual member-guest tournament. Before play starts, oddsmakers rate participants in the event, whether individuals or teams, and then auctioneers sell them. The winning bids make up the pool. The bidder holding the tournament winner gets a majority share of the pot, with second and third place taking lesser shares. In many instances, the bidder sells a share to the players.

For years, Calcuttas accompanied most professional or open tournaments, with the pool at the Masters Calcutta dwarfing the official prize money between the 1930s and 1950s. Many of the nation's top sportswriters and newspapermen sat in on the Calcutta auction at the Bon Air Vanderbilt Hotel. Facing increasing pressure from the USGA and the PGA, the Masters Calcutta and many others went underground in the 1950s. Golf enthusiasts, however, still discreetly stage modern versions every April in Augusta.

Want to bet on Tiger to win the Masters? If you live in Las Vegas, you can place a bet at several sports books. Jeff Sherman, the golf oddsmaker at the Las Vegas Hilton, offers one of the most sophisticated books. ("Bookies" offer wagers, and their operation is called a "book.") He rates each player entered in a weekly PGA Tour event, offering odds on the highest-ranked 49, and then lumps the remaining players into the "field," posting about 8-1 odds for the group. He offers head-to-head or match-up odds so a bettor interested in wagering Tiger Woods against Phil Mickeslon at the Masters or U.S. Open can get a bet.

The United Kingdom is a bettor's delight. Golf wagering reaches its high point during the Open, and woe to anyone who calls it the British Open; after all, it is the oldest golfing championship. Touts and bookies abound, but big operations dominate golf bookmaking in Britain. Victor Chandler, William Hill, and Ladbrokes lead the way, offering an array of propositions and odds. Ladbrokes also offers odds on women's events on the LPGA Tour. Andy Clifton, head of communications at the firm, likes the women's game. "I've actually got a photo of Se Ri Pak on my desk playing out of the water on the 18th hole of a play-off for the U.S. Women's Open a couple of years ago that she went on to win," Clifton said. "Why? A little each way bet at 66-1." An "each way" bet involves a two-part bet—one to win, the second to place in the top four or five.

Rules prohibit gambling during a PGA Tour tournament, but when in the United Kingdom for the Open, some players wager on themselves. "I've bet on myself a few times," said five-time Open winner Tom Watson. Jerry Kelly, a lesser-known tour player despite winning twice on the PGA Tour during 2002, looked at the odds of his winning the Open that year. Seeing that books listed him at 80-1, he said, "Shoot, man, I got a better chance than that." He tied for 28th.

An important part of money golf history is the hustler. He occupies a unique position in golf's lore. Most knowledgeable golfers don't condone cheating, but they still admire hustlers for their creative abilities to gain an advantage over their pigeons and marks. Hustlers never arrange a wager unless they are sure of a win. If they cannot gain an edge, they will not play because that's just gambling.

Writers often overuse the "H" word, especially when describing folks who are just scrabbling their way through golf and trying to win rent money. Some called Trevino a hustler, but most of the time he just played golf for money during the years before he joined the PGA Tour. "As for me, I never hustled a soul," Trevino once said. "A hustler is a golfer who lies about his handicap. Hell, I didn't have a handicap. I always said I was a scratch player." He may have fudged a smidgen by saying that, because in 1961 Trevino hustled an unsuspecting golfer using a Dr Pepper bottle to hit the ball. The whole story is in chapter 6.

Many have hustled through golf's history, but only one man stands unchallenged as the best—Titanic Thompson. His real name was Alvin Clarence Thomas, and he astounded both bystanders and opponents during his career, attaining almost a mythical status in golf. There were others—Mysterious Montague, the Fat Man, Dandy Dick Martin, Dutch Harrison—and their exploits are almost as engaging as Thompson's.

Betting on the golf course has evolved with the sport. For hundreds of years, the Scots preferred match play foursomes (alternate shot). Whichever team won the most holes won the wager. As the nature of competitive golf expanded to include medal play, singles, four-ball (better-ball team play), and multiple-round tournaments, so have the number and kinds of betting

Informal wagers are an integral part of golf, and a bet between two comics page stalwarts is as common as Dagwood's sandwiches. KING FEATURES SYNDICATE

games. Now there are dozens of full-round betting games, with some classic in their simplicity and others more imaginative and complex. Golfers can propose myriad side bets during a round, adding both interest and reward for good play. "How 'bout a $10 Nassau four ways, automatic 2-down presses, with $5 Greenies and Sandies on the side?" Experienced golf bettors such as Sam Snead and Doug Sanders have offered betting advice, including determining the size and types of bets, spotting cheaters, and dealing with hustlers.

This book is not about scandal or the evils of gambling. It's about golf's long and healthy relationship with betting. It is a short history of golf, as told through anecdotes about betting on the game from Scottish kings to Tiger Woods and all the smooth-swinging flat bellies, movies stars, athletes, politicians, women golfers, Joe Six-Packs, hustlers, and sharks in between.

2.

"TEN GUINEAS A SIDE?"

THE EARLY YEARS, 1300–1887

GOLF IS AN OLD GAME. The first known reference to golf in Scotland is from 1457, but evidence suggests Romans played what might have been an early version of golf at the time of Christ. Some golf historians have suggested that golf arose in Scotland directly from the Roman occupation there. Others more rightly claim golf grew out of similar games played in what is now the Netherlands and Belgium, migrating over a period of years to Scotland's east coast.

Regardless of golf's precise geographic origin, hitting a ball from a starting point to a specified goal in the fewest strokes seems always to have been the source of a wager. The practice of betting on a golf match is as old as the game.

—●—

No one person invented golf as British major Walter Wingfield patented lawn tennis in 1874 and Dr. James Naismith created basketball in America in 1891. Rather, the game evolved from other similar sports, acquiring rules and customs along the way. As with human evolution, there have been a few dead ends. Some branches on golf's family tree are not connected to today's game; however, several games appear to be golf's ancestors or, at least, cousins.

A Greek sculpture from 500 BC depicts athletes playing a hockey-like game with curved sticks and a ball. Romans played *paganica*, also swinging wooden clubs at a leather ball stuffed with hair or feathers. Sportsmen in what is now northern France and Belgium were playing *chole* in the 1200s, a golf-like game with a touch of hockey. One team attempted to hit a ball overland to a target some distance away—perhaps miles. The team was allowed a succession of three-stroke sets. Between each sequence, the opposing team had one stroke to *dechole*, or hit the ball either away from the target or into a nearby pond or similar hazard. It was almost like your big brother hitting your croquet ball into the flower bed.

Played with iron-headed clubs and an egg-shaped, beech wood ball, chole was a betting game. In what seemed to be an auction, opposing players bid on the number of strokes they expected to use to advance the ball to the target. A wager was set on the bid and away they went. If playing on two-man teams, players alternated shots in a forerunner of the game now called foursomes.

The French also played *jeu de mail*, or *paille maille*, hitting a wooden ball along a fixed course. The elite played on a defined court or field, while commoners played across the countryside and along roads until they reached the goal, usually a rock in the road, or the "touchstone." The winner reached the touchstone in the fewest strokes. The English took to the game, anglicizing the name to pell mell and then Pall Mall. They initially played in London near St. James Palace on an open ground, or pitch, that became known as the "Mall." The goal was a wire hoop stuck in the ground, much like those used in croquet. Later, any open area that welcomed walkers and folks playing games became known as a mall.

The English also played *cambuca* in the 1300s, a game involving a curved stick and wooden ball that some view as a cousin to cricket. A similar game, *shinty*, migrated from Ireland to Scotland with Christian missionaries. Shinty players used sticks similar to golf clubs in a game still played in Scotland, especially in the Highlands. Several legendary Scottish golfers of the 1800s learned the game using "shinties" to hit their golf balls.

No clear records exist of how or when golf appeared in Scotland or from which of these several games it had descended. The current theory many golf historians favor ties Scottish golf, the progenitor of the modern game, to the game of *colf* played in what later became the Netherlands, Belgium, and Luxembourg.

Called *kolven*, *colve*, *kolf*, and other similar names, the game of colf appeared to be a children's game played in town streets. They used wood enshafted clubs with iron heads that were double sided, sort of a 5-iron for both left- and right-handers. The ball had a leather cover stuffed with hair or wool. Participants played "short" colf in roads or on ice when the canals froze and usually with a post or hole as the target. Adults occasionally played "long" colf along a cross-country course of 5,000 yards or so, much as in chole.

The Dutch played colf at Loenen aan de Vecht in northern Holland as early as 1297. A 1387 governmental decree in the Dutch city of Brielle banned gambling except in four instances, one of which was playing "the ball with the club." There were even references of colf in the Dutch settlements at Fort Orange and Albany, New York, during the 1650s. Nevertheless, colf declined in popularity and generally disappeared later in the 1600s both in the Netherlands and its New World colonies.

Archie Baird, director of the Heritage of Golf Museum in Gullane, Scotland, asserts golf came to Scotland from the Low Countries. "Several groups of people could have brought the game to Scotland," Baird said in a recent interview. "Scottish wool merchants traded with the Dutch, and their frequent travels gave them an exposure to the Dutch game. Also, people fleeing Dutch religious persecution brought their sports with them to Scotland. Scottish soldiers, fighting for the Dutch as mercenaries in the Hundred Years War against England, married Dutch girls and brought home both their wives and Dutch games." The words *golf*, *golfand*, and *golfing* are ancient Scottish verbs that mean "to strike."

Sometime before 1400, golf landed at Scotland's east coast ports—Dunbar, North Berwick, Aberlady, Leith, and St Andrews—which would later form the brightest stars in the constellation of celebrated Scottish golf courses. According to British golf historian David Hamilton, two versions of golf arose, probably following the distinction in the Low Countries—short and long golf. The Scots played short golf in churchyards and streets using a wooden ball and one club. Played mostly on Sundays, medieval Europe's day for sport—at least after church services—short golf was a game for the common folk.

Hamilton believes that both commoners and noblemen played long golf on the seaside grasslands that were a feature of almost every town and seaport on Scotland's east coast. Without rules or a defined routing of play, they played toward targets hundreds of yards away. "Grip it and rip it," as John Daly would say many years later. At some unknown point, those targets became rabbit scrapes (holes) in the ground, most likely because of the many critters that inhabited the grassy areas.

—●—

A 1457 Scottish Parliament decree is the earliest available record of golf in Scotland. Faced with yet another war with England, the parliament issued a ban on recreation that might interfere with archery practice, a warrior skill needed on the battlefield: *"Item it is ordaynt and decretyt . . . [th]at ye futbawe and the golf be utterly cryt done and not usyt and [th]at the bowe markes be maid at all parochkirks apair of butts and schuting be usyt ilk Sunday."* Translation: "Item, it is ordained and decreed . . . that football and golf be utterly condemned and stopped and that a pair of targets be made at all parish kirks [churches] and shooting be practiced each Sunday."

Golf historians surmise that by at least 1457, the Scots were also playing "long" golf on the sandy, seaside land that the Scots called "links," or "links land." Over millions of years, rivers deposited alluvial soil as they flowed into the North Sea, while storms pushed sand ashore. A line of dunes protected the area. Native grasses, mostly fescue and bent as well as heather and gorse, further stabilized the links. There were links near each coastal town—Dunbar, North Berwick, St Andrews, and others. The word *link* is derived form the Anglo-Saxon word *hlinc*, meaning a ridge.

The Scots treated the links as common land. Shepherds used it as pasture, and it was a field for games and horse racing. People washed their clothes in the creeks, or burns, that ran through the links. Townspeople often removed strips of sod to roof their houses. The Scots called those strips "divots." Seriously, that's the origin of the term. (Remember, a divot is the displaced patch of soil and grass, not the hole left behind. "Please replace your divots" is the rule.)

The Scots originally played golf on the links without designated tees, fairways, and greens. Grazing rabbits and sheep kept parts of the links shorn, and golfers played their ball through those areas of shorter grass—"fairways"—and hopefully stayed clear of the "rough," or the heather and gorse. Sheep settled into scattered depressions and cavities to escape wind and weather, gradually enlarging these areas over time into the sand-filled bunkers that torment novice golfers around the world.

Historian Robert Browning wrote that Scots played with boxwood balls until about 1600. Comparable to those used in chole and Pall Mall, they were brittle and easily shattered. Similarly, golf clubs in the fifteenth and sixteenth centuries were all wooden. Golfers met on the links and arranged matches between individuals or two-man teams. From the beginning, the game was a contest between players with something at stake.

Archie Baird contends the custom of wagering on the outcome of chole and colf matches on the continent followed the game to Scotland. Scottish merchants, who traded with the Dutch, were the likely importers of the betting custom.

The earliest record of a golf bet in Scotland was in 1503, only 46 years after the oldest existing written reference to the game. The treasurer to Scotland's King James IV noted an expense of 42 shillings on February 3 of that year, with the annotation: "Item to the King to play at the golf with the Erle of Bothuile" [Bothwell]. The king lost his match and his stake to Bothwell.

Besides James IV, the first Scottish golfer known by name in history was Sir Robert Maule (1497–1560), a sportsman and a betting golfer. "*He had gryt delight in haukine and hountine . . . Lykwakes he exercisit the gowf, and oftimes past to Barry Lynks, quhan* [where] *the wadsie* [wager] *was for drink.*" (The links at Barry are located just south of the Carnoustie Golf Links, host to the 2007 British Open.)

—•—

Many Scottish royals, especially the Stuarts, were avid golfers. King James IV, who issued another wartime ban on golf in 1491, made peace with England in 1503 by marrying Margaret Tudor, the daughter of England's King Henry VII. The peace eased both the need for archery practice and restrictions on golf, not that the king couldn't bend the rules if he wanted. James's treasurer recorded a golf expense shortly before his marriage—14 shillings for new clubs. His son, James V, golfed at Gosford in East Lothian after setting up a private golfing layout there.

Mary Queen of Scots, who succeeded her father James V in 1542, was a sporting woman who was ahead of her time. She bet on cards and dice and played backgammon and billiards. Outdoors, she enjoyed Pall Mall and golf.

Another Stuart, King Charles I of England, carried on the family tradition. Shortly after his coronation in 1625, Charles was golfing at Leith links when notified of the Irish Catholics' rebellion. Some historians maintain Charles immediately left for his palace at Hoylrood to prepare for a challenge to his throne, but others say he finished his round. Golf historian Sir W. G. Simpson supports the former version, largely because of the wager involved. Simpson wrote in 1887 that Charles "acted on this occasion with his usual cunning—that at the time the news arrived he was beaten, and that he hurried away to save his half-crown rather than his crown." (A half-crown—an eighth of a pound—was long the usual golf bet in Britain.)

Charles's son James, who sat on the joint English and Scottish throne, avidly played "at the golf" in Scotland before his coronation. In 1681, James disagreed with two Englishmen who claimed golf originated in their country. The three arranged a match to settle the matter. James chose a local shoemaker and worthy golfer, John Patersone, to be his partner. The cobbler and the future king won both the match and bragging rights about golf as well as a considerable sum on the wager. Patersone's share enabled him to build a fashionable house in Edinburgh. Above its door is a crest displaying a hand grasping a golf club and the motto "Far and Sure." James's selection of the merchant as a partner may have been the first use of a ringer in a golf match.

The shift from wooden to leather-covered golf balls around 1600 may have been the origin of golf's reputation as a sport for the elite. The "feathery" was expensive—four to five shillings apiece, or more than clubs—and hard to make. A skilled ball maker produced only two or three a day. He stitched wet cowhide into a sphere and turned it inside out, leaving part of one seam open, through which he stuffed boiled feathers. Legend has it the ball required enough feathers to fill a top hat. The artisan inserted the final feathers with a metal ram attached to a breastplate for more leverage. With his hands free, he then stitched the ball closed. He hammered it round and painted the ball after it dried. Golfers of the day not only steered clear of ponds and streams, as we do, but also puddles, because a feathery was troublesome to control once wet.

Golfers did not have sets of clubs; instead, each player commissioned the manufacture of individual clubs, usually no more than four or five. The heads were more elongated and narrower than those found on today's clubs. Some also had concave faces, a shape that gave rise to the term *spoon*. Craftsmen made the heads of beech or thorn wood and the shafts of ash; hickory came into use only in the 1800s. The elite bought two-piece, or jointed, clubs, while the less fortunate carved one-piece sticks from a suitable tree branch. Irons were rare because of the damage they wrought on the leather ball. A golfer might use a lofted iron for getting the ball out of deep sand or a small-headed club for extracting a ball from a wagon rut on the links. Play it as it lies.

Match play was the only competitive game for hundreds of years in Scotland. Golfers favored foursomes in which two-man teams competed. Each team member alternately hit the ball, with the winners determined by which team won the most holes. Match play seems sensible in retrospect, since the game was played over the links in a casual, almost free-form manner. Besides, dumping a feathery into a burn or burying it in a cow pie would only mean the loss of a hole. A few such disasters could ruin your round in stroke play.

Aside from church decrees or royal records, insights into the Scottish golfing life during the 17th century generally come to us through golfers' diaries. Starting in 1671 Sir John Foulis of Ravelston, near Edinburgh, recorded all his matches, dining expenses, club and ball costs, coach fare, and, of course, his bets. Foulis had a bad day on November 19, 1672. He not only lost £5 to several cronies—Chancellor Lyon, Master of Saltoune, and others—but also a few balls, for he paid 12 shillings for new ones.

Historians also turn to poems about the game, since newspaper accounts of the sport are unavailable through the early 1700s. James Arbuckle published *Glotta* in 1721, glorifying golf on the green and referring to the ever-present wager.

> *In winter, too, when hoary frosts o'spread*
> *The verdant turf, naked by the mead,*
> *The vig'rous youth commence the sportive war,*
> *And, arm'd with lead, their jointed clubs prepare:*
> *The timber curve to leathern orbs apply,*
> *Compact, elastic, to pervade the sky:*
> *These to the distant hole they drive;*
> *They claim the stakes who thither first arrive.*

The first news account of a golf match came in 1724 when Alexander Elphinstone played Capt. John Porteous of the Edinburgh City Guard. The two competed for a huge sum at the time, 20 guineas a side, with Elphinstone winning the bet. (A guinea was a coin worth £1, one shilling.)

—•—

Golf in Scotland during the early 1700s began to take a shape we might recognize today. That evolution occurred as interest in "short," or churchyard, golf and other stick-and-ball games in Europe declined. For the next 150 years, the sport focused on long golf played exclusively on Scottish links by men using a feathery ball and multiple clubs.

The links are often long, narrow areas on the shoreline. This shape eventually led to the custom of laying out holes in succession away from town and then returning to the start by playing holes that ran the opposite way. The Scots referred to the first half of the holes as "out," or out from town, just as we now play "out" on the front nine. Players returned "in" on the second series, or back to town.

Initially, they set no standards for the number or length of holes. Edinburgh's Leith links boasted only five holes, but they were brutes for the time, ranging from 414 to 495 yards. These distances would not pose much of a challenge for Tiger today, but back then, a five on any of them made a golfer gloat. Three turns of the five holes constituted a round. The number of holes increased to seven a few years later. North Berwick started with seven, and the original layouts at St Andrews and Prestwick had only 12 holes. The Prestwick men generally played three "rounds" of their circular layout, with 36 holes considered to be a good day of golf. That number generally carried over into the early tournaments years later.

St Andrews had 12 holes with 10 sharing greens. Golfers played 11 out and back for a 22-hole round. In 1764, the Society of St Andrews Golfers (later the Royal & Ancient Golf Club) deemed the first four holes, which were also the last four, to be too short. They converted them into just two holes, thus leaving 10 holes, with eight played twice. The golf world gradually adopted the resulting 18 holes as the standard.

Players often hired a servant or a boy to carry their clubs as well as to run ahead to mark the flight of the ball. Some have suggested that the term *caddie* (or caddy) is derived from "cadet," a French term for the youngest son of a family. Hamilton, however, argues caddie arose from a Scottish term for multipurpose messengers and porters who hung about Scottish towns looking for work. Records refer to these men as "caddies." Hamilton concludes golfers hired caddies to carry their clubs, just as gentlemen hired them to carry luggage in town. The caddie did not use a bag at first. He simply carried the clubs in the crook of his arm.

The caddie also fashioned a clump of sand upon which he placed his master's ball to start each hole. Later, the caddie filled a metal, cone-shaped form with moist sand and plopped it, open end down, on the ground. After removing the form, he balanced the ball on the sand cone. The keeper of the green placed wooden boxes at each tee to store the sand, hence the term *tee box*.

An egalitarian mix of noblemen, merchants, and regular folks played golf on the Scottish links during the 1700s. Golfers from every social class walked on the links and teed it up. Nevertheless, players of similar economic means gradually congregated among themselves. Golfing clubs arose in the mid-1700s. At first they played on the still public links, but later they built their own courses. Historians generally peg the date of a club's formation as the year of its first recorded tournament, an event that reflected golf's maturation beyond singles and foursomes matches.

A group who played at the public Leith links near Edinburgh held a championship on April 2, 1744. They called themselves the Honourable Company of Edinburgh Golfers. The Edinburgh town council donated £15 for a trophy, and the competition was open to all Scottish golfers, a condition that necessitated creating rules governing play. During routine matches on the links, the group's members dealt with contingencies easily, for all were accustomed to the course's hazards and eccentricities. Strangers, however, needed to know how to deal with difficulties or problems as they arose. The resultant set of 13 rules governing play at Leith marked the start of organized golf.

Twenty-two men formed the Society of St Andrews Golfers, which held its first open tournament in 1754, although golfers had played on the St Andrews links for hundreds of years before. In 1834, the club renamed itself the Royal & Ancient Golf Club of St Andrews (R&A), one of several clubs in town. While the R&A briefly owned the famous Old Course in the 1890s, the Links Trust now maintains and operates the six, soon to be seven, courses laid out on the land.

The winner of each club's annual tournament became captain for the following year. A member attached a silver golf ball to a ceremonial silver club in honor of his victory. New club members had to touch the trophies with their lips, a ritual that actor and R&A member Sean Connery called "kissing the captain's balls."

The R&A adopted the Leith rules for its first championship. The club later became the governing body for golf throughout most of the world.

The clubmen gathered weekly in the evening at local taverns to arrange matches and wagers and then to celebrate after the following day's rounds. The company patronized Luckie Clephan's inn, while the St Andrews golfers went to Bailie Glass's, each to "pay a shilling for dinner, absent or not." As these groups grew and coalesced, they built their own clubhouses, and some ultimately laid out their own golf courses. The members heightened their club's exclusivity by wearing a club uniform—usually a coat, often red, with the club's seal affixed. The clothes also helped define golf as an upper-class—or, at least, expensive—sport. Golf on the public links continued, but the game's lingering connection to private clubs dates from these associations' formations in the mid-18th century.

The formation of golf clubs in Scotland during the 1740s and 1750s intensified the custom of betting on golf matches. Men began to arrange multiple matches for their weekly golf outing. Within the Honourable Company, the members met on Saturdays, or what they called "play" days. Matches were almost always alternate-shot foursomes, games they could play quickly, usually in an hour and a half for a round. Golfers of similar skill were matched in pairings that would both speed play and ensure a fair wager. While St Andrews held its first stroke play competition in 1776, the Edinburgh Company resisted until 1837.

After the matches, members dined and applauded good play and chided the losers, some good naturedly and others with barbs sharpened with brandy and gin. During multiple after-dinner rounds of claret, the Honourable Company members arranged matches for the following week. They referred to the games as the "Dinner Matches." Early on, the Honourable Company played the matches at Leith, then at Musselburgh starting in 1836, and later at Muirfield, the course the company laid out in 1891.

Members recorded all the wagers in the company's "Bett Book," starting in 1776. The most common bet was "100 merks," or about £5 at the time. The Bett Book contains references to "100 merks a corner and dinner for the Company," indicating that the losing team owed each of the opponents 100 merks plus the meal after the match. Side bets and propositions were recorded too. In 1783, Mr. Robertson wagered that he could "compleat the round [five holes at Leith] in 35 strokes for 12 guineas. Taken by Mr. Guthrie and lost by Mr. Robertson by one stroke." Mr. Armstrong beat Mr. Dunbar in 1801, using only one hand. Players make these same bets today.

The company found fault with any member who agreed to a bet but didn't play on the appointed day. The captain fined such miscreants "a pint of wine for each guinea unless he gives sufficient excuse." This assessment in kind reflects the friendly nature of the betting, a characteristic that persists in today's game. Winning the money during the Dinner Matches was not the focus of the events; a congenial time at golf with friends was the goal. One of the Bett Book recorders, the company official chosen to document the wagers, guessed in the 500 matches he played over the years, he had won as many as he had lost.

Wagers or not, members enjoyed the same ribald humor seen in many a Men's Grill since then, at least judging by the company's motto "Stiff Shafts and Hard Balls." That line remained on club stationery until the temperance movement exerted its influence in the late 1800s, a time when "Pussyfoot put its paw in Scotland," according to the R&A's professional at the time, Andra Kirkaldy.

Not much is new in golf today, for every part of our game seems to have a historical precedent. One of the company's keenest observers offered the following advice in the late 1700s for those playing alternate shot, something you may have to do one day with your spouse. (To foozle a ball is to badly miss-hit it.)

> When playing a foursome, do not remind your partner about his bad shots until the game is over. You may rest assured that he did not foozle his ball on purpose; and even a gentle reminder is only apt to increase his anxiety, and you never know when you may be guilty of a similar error yourself. An anxious player never makes a good foursomes partner; he only irritates both himself and his partner, and his irritation is fatal to a successful combination.

—●—

As the 1800s and the Industrial Revolution in Great Britain began, interest in golf declined. Throughout this period, however, the moneyed leisure class continued golfing, wagering large sums all the while. They ate and drank on the same scale. Historian Browning called the time "the golden age of foursomes play." Not tied to the land or a shop, they played often, not just on Saturdays, and even during the summer.

George Carnegie, sportsman and poet, wrote *Golfiana* in 1833, capturing the excesses of the class. Carnegie described a large-stakes match, including a £5 side bet on the last two holes at 15-1 odds. In the poem, Carnegie described one of the golfers, John Campbell of Saddell, as he played his new featheries (made by John Gourlay) in front of his club members clad in their red uniforms:

Saddell, dress'd in blue coat plain,
With lots of Gourlays, free from spot or stain,
He whirls his club to catch the proper swing,
And freely bets round the scarlet ring.

The sporting gentlemen also created the professional golfer. The elite employed jockeys and trainers for their racehorses as well as huntsmen to mind their hounds. It was only natural for them to hire permanent caddies to assist them on the links. These partnerships, as well as the patrons arranging for the caddies to play on their own, gave rise to a budding class of expert golfers who formed professional golf's foundation: Allan Robertson, Willie Park, Old Tom Morris, and others. St Andrews held the first caddies tournament in 1819.

As the caddies progressed from servants to professionals, they not only aided their gentlemen on the links but also gave the game a fundamental competitive form for years to come: challenge matches between professionals. Gentlemen backers arranged matches between their respective caddies, with each side wagering on their man. The winning golfer shared in only a fraction of the pot, but he supplemented that take with a side bet with his opponent. This custom ultimately led to the modern method of measuring a pro's success by the amount of money he wins.

The gentlemen also tried their own hand at high-stakes matches. In 1829, for example, Major Cruickshank and Captain Bertram had a go at John Wood and James Hay at the Montrose links for £100 a side. Historian Hamilton credits Cruickshank with what would become another common golf wager, playing at night. Using servants with candles to show the way, he and Lord Kennedy played three holes at Montrose for £500 a hole. No small potatoes here, m'Lord.

Charles Lees captured both the spirit and realism of daytime play in his 1847 painting, "The Golfers." It colorfully depicted a match between some of the same golfers described in *Golfiana*—John Campbell and the wonderfully named Maj. Hugh Playfair, among others—and a gallery full of bookmakers, bettors, and wenches bringing drinks to all.

Golf's fortunes were again on the rise by the 1840s. Some credit both the growing middle class and the Victorian era's emphasis on the healthy aspects of outdoor leisure activities, especially such seaside endeavors as golf. "Golf was not violent and no animals were hunted or killed," Hamilton

Charles Lees's 1847 painting of a golf match on the links at St Andrews captured the essence of the game in the mid-1800s. Sir David Baird and Sir Ralph Anstruther are playing a foursomes match against John Campbell and Maj. Hugh Playfair. The gallery includes several men holding notebooks for recording the many bets on the match.
SCOTTISH NATIONAL PORTRAIT GALLERY

wrote in his 1998 book, *Golf: Scotland's Game.* "Golf gave a good day out, and a little betting on the side was not discouraged, and helped the excitement. The game was healthy, cheap and innocent; ministers of religion could and did play." One development ultimately broadened the appeal of golf to all social classes in Great Britain, a cheaper ball.

—●—

The gutta percha ball, made from latex drawn from the Malaysian gutta tree, arrived in 1848. Completely waterproof and used to cover underwater telegraph cables, gutta percha softened when warmed in hot water, allowing the formation of the first truly round golf ball. During the 50 years following the gutta's introduction, golf exploded in popularity. Baird said there were 17 golf clubs in the world in 1850, most on the east coast of Scotland; 34 in 1870; and 387 in 1890. While the advent of the British railroad system during those years helped golfers travel to golf courses and thus expand the game, the new ball was the ticket to popularity.

Golfers did not fully accept the gutta at first. Although clearly more durable, the ball's smooth surface made it almost uncontrollable. Its most likely trajectory was a duck hook. Some golfers realized after the ball had been roughened and scored by iron clubs it performed better. Ball makers began adding cross-hatching to the surface as well as mixing in other ingredients to the gutta. The new variant, called the "gutty," was vastly superior. More important, the gutty allowed players to use more iron clubs. Fearing damage to the feathery, golfers had always run the ball onto the green with wooden clubs. With the gutty, a player could hit down on the ball with a lofted iron and fly it to the green.

Club makers responded to the new ball by producing iron clubs with a greater variety of lofts, fashioning all of the cleeks, mashies, and niblicks that are so confusing to the modern player. A cleek, equivalent to a 2-iron today, derived its name from the Old Scottish *cleke* or *cleik*, which is a metal hook. A mashie was a mid-iron and its name came from the downward stroke. The Old Scottish word for sledgehammer was *mash*. Niblick is the diminutive of the Scottish word for nose, or *nib*. The term *short nose* referred to the club's small head. Similar to our 9-iron, the Scots used it for playing out of ruts and tight lies. "Playing" clubs (drivers) and spoons (lofted fairway woods) continued to be made from wood, but hickory became the favorite for shafting both woods and irons. The whippy motion of ash shafts, so needed for the featheries, was unsuited for the new irons.

During the decade of the gutta ball's introduction, most in Britain regarded Allan Robertson as the game's greatest player. The first true professional golfer, he started at St Andrews as a caddie but rose to what amounted to head professional, a position that had not yet been defined. He also employed several craftsmen to make clubs and balls, including Tom Morris before he became old. In 1844, Robertson's shop produced 2,500 featheries. Further, he also may have been golf's first hustler.

Morris described Robertson as a "kindly body, wi' just a wealth o' sly, pawky fun about him."(*Pawky* is a Scottish term meaning shrewd or artfully cunning.) Robert Browning said Robertson used his demeanor to hustle his opponents: "Kindness and pawkiness combined to make him adept at nursing his matches against amateur opponents and just 'snodd'n them' at the Burn [the creek on 18]. By such a narrow victory he avoided wounding his opponents' pride, and at the same time made it impossible for them to ask for increased odds at the next encounter!"

The first tee in a money game in 1859. These men were among the best Scottish golf pros that year—James Wilson (left), Bob Andrew, Willie Dunn (addressing his ball), Willie Park, Allan Robertson, Daw Anderson, Old Tom Morris, and Bob Kirk. Robertson was the father of the profession, and Morris and Park won eight British Open championships between them. UNIVERSITY OF ST ANDREWS

In 1849, Robertson and Old Tom Morris played the Dunn brothers, Willie and Jamie, for £400 during a three-course match played over St Andrews, Musselburgh, and North Berwick. At their home green of Musselburgh, the Dunns won the first 36-hole match easily, 13 and 12, but the St Andrews team squared the match at their home course. On the 35th hole at North Berwick, the Dunns found their ball on the wrong side of a boulder near the green and "lost all judgment and nerve," according to a spectator. They continued "hacking recklessly at the ball instead of knocking it backwards." Robertson and Morris won that hole and then the last for the victory at North Berwick. Since the entire match hinged on the number of "greens" (courses) won, versus the aggregate number of holes, Robertson and Morris prevailed 1-up. The Bank of England advises that £400 in 1848 would be worth about $37,000 today.

During an 1858 match, just a year before his premature death, Robertson shot a 79 at St Andrews, an extraordinary score when compared to a winning total of 100 during medal competitions of the time. R&A members sought out Robertson as a partner in foursomes, teaming to play a match against another amateur and professional. In 1853, Robertson partnered with Mr. Erskine against Musselburgh's pro Willie Park and Mr. Hastie for a match at St Andrews. In the third and last round, Park and Hastie were

1-up on the 17th, the Road Hole that's known to millions of television viewers. A large wager rode on the match, with Campbell of Saddell, the golfer from *Golfiana*, offering a £15 to £5 side bet within the gallery on the leaders. Erskine, playing the second shot onto the green, left Robertson on the road. The "model player," as the press called Robertson, pitched the ball onto the footpath, where it bounced once onto the green and rolled downhill into the cup. Browning picks up the narrative:

> If ever there was a shot that turned the tide of a battle this was it, for Mr. Hastie went bald-headed for the hole and ran a yard and a half past, and Park was unforgivably short with the return, so that Allan and his partner won the hole that seemed irretrievably lost. What was worse, Park, in his vexation, topped the ball off the eighteenth tee into the Burn, with the result that his side lost that hole as well, and with it the match.

Browning credits Robertson for introducing iron approach shots to golf. Faced with a shot over a bunker with a feathery, golfers previously used a wooden baffing spoon. They attempted to hit, or "baff," the ground behind the ball, thus drop-kicking the ball and hoping for elevation without much distance. Robertson, using the gutta ball he initially scorned, pitched over the hazard with a niblick. He also introduced putting with an iron, using his cleek for lag putts and reverting only to a wooden putter to hole out.

—●—

Although golf's popularity in Britain waned during the first half of the 1800s, those sporting clubs that did not fail during the downturn kept the game alive. As the gutta ball helped renew interest in golf after its introduction in 1848, the clubs and their competitions reinvigorated the game on a national level. The most tangible product of this revitalization was the Open Championship.

Col. J. O. Fairlie, a founding member of Prestwick Golf Club on Scotland's west coast, established a stroke play championship for professionals in 1860 to be decided over three rounds on the 12-hole Prestwick layout. This first Open Championship had only an eight-man field, with Willie Park from Musselburgh winning with a score of 174, two shots clear of Prestwick's Tom Morris. There was no prize money that year, nor for the next two; instead, the champion won a red leather Challenge Belt. Prestwick hosted the first 12 Opens, a fact often obscured by reverential attention to the St Andrews links.

The stroke play tournament prompted little interest among the sporting gentlemen in Scotland. Challenge matches between professionals were the most exciting form of competitive golf at that time. "Stroke play makes for dull wagering," wrote one observer. So two days after the first Open, backers arranged a "friendly" match between Park and Morris over the same 36 holes. Morris won 7 and 6 as well as a £20 side bet he made with the Open winner. The gentlemen's wager was considerably larger.

Staged money matches—or "challenges," according to the attentive British press—were central to the golfing world during the second half of the 1800s. Allan Robertson's exploits marked the start of the phenomenon, but the bewhiskered, pipe-smoking Tom Morris was the iconic face of money golf during the period. "Old Tom" and his son, "Young Tom," provided good copy and most of the era's surviving images, despite their opponents' often equally skillful play. Most of the Morrises' popularity was likely because of the spreading science of photography, a news feature Robertson largely missed. Every coffee table book about the R&A and St Andrews links has photos of Old Tom in his rough woolen jacket and vest, with a sensible cap shading his weathered face. With a wooden club in hand, he is usually presiding over his own tee ball or a match of lesser golfers and aspirants.

Son of a letter carrier, Tom was born in 1821 in St Andrews and apprenticed as a young man in Robertson's shop. In 1851, Morris left Robertson's employ after a spat over the new gutta ball. Playing a match with Campbell of Saddell, Morris exhausted his supply of featheries and played on with a gutta Saddell offered. Robertson, who made his living making the leather balls, initially scoffed at the new balls and called them "filth." Seeing his assistant with one irritated Robertson to the point Morris had to find another job.

Colonel Fairlie immediately recruited Morris to be the professional keeper of the Prestwick links, home to the new Prestwick Club. Tom worked there until returning to St Andrews in 1863, four years after Robertson's death. The R&A paid Morris to maintain the public golf course. During his tenure, Morris separated the green of the first and 17th holes and changed the direction of play to counterclockwise. He also pioneered the use of separate teeing areas, breaking with the long custom of teeing the ball within a few club lengths of the cup after finishing a hole. As a rule, not much had been done to maintain the links until the mid-1800s. Morris observed "neither broom nor scythe" had been used at St Andrews until then. While many argued for keeping the St Andrews links in their primitive state, Morris began to sweep the putting greens, cut new holes every Saturday, and defined bunker edges to prevent erosion.

He died in 1908 after falling on the stairs of the New Club, where he was an honorary member. (There are five golf clubs in St Andrews, with the R&A and the New Club being the oldest.) Morris did not carry the complete reputation of the gruff, whiskey-fueled Scottish professional golfer. He did enjoy a nip of the malt, but who wouldn't after two rounds in St Andrew's quickly changing weather?

Only one or two challenge matches occurred annually between 1840 and 1858, but 10 took place in 1865, 20 in 1869, and so on. The winning golfer or team got a cut of the stake, and the players generally made a bet among themselves to keep things interesting. News reports often described the stakes to be so many pounds "a side." The term meant that the backers had bet that amount on their golfer or a two-man team, as opposed to the modern Nassau and its separate bets on each nine (front side, back side) and the match. Gallery members also bet among themselves during the game.

Neither the spirited competition nor the money wagered resulted in foul play during the period. "Not a single allegation of nobbing, cheating, or throwing a match can be found," wrote Hamilton, "in spite of the public interest and intensity of play." The sport's ability to keep cheating at bay despite the wagering is an enduring hallmark of the game.

In a contest typical of the time, Willie Park challenged Morris in 1862 to a match consisting of 36 holes played at each of four greens: Musselburgh, Prestwick, North Berwick, and St Andrews. The stake was £100, to be taken home by the backers of the golfer who won the most holes over the four rounds. They played on November 21, 25, 28, and December 2, with Morris winning 17-up.

Morris won four of the first eight Opens but lost to his son in 1869. Young Tom was the Tiger Woods of his time, winning his first of four straight Opens at age 17. He retired the championship belt, and a new trophy was created, the silver Claret Jug that is still in use today. Young Tom's star shone brightly but not for long. The lad died when he was only 24 years old.

Just before his death in 1875, Tommy offered £50 of his own money to any amateur who could beat him, even tendering the odds of "a third" to any taker—giving a stroke every three holes. Capt. Arthur Molesworth, a gentleman golfer from the first modern English club, Westward Ho! accepted the challenge. The wager called for 12 rounds at St Andrews over a week, with £25 going to the winner of the most holes and £25 to the golfer who won the most rounds. Molesworth usually played with only three clubs: his play-club (driver), a lofting iron, and a putter, calling them "Faith," "Hope," and "Charity," respectively. Morris won 11 and 10 on holes and 9-3 on rounds, despite playing the last day in a snowstorm.

Matches between gentlemen amateurs and professionals were common. More often, however, a club member partnered with a pro against a similar team in foursomes. Even though gentlemen played among themselves for small cash pools called "sweepstakes"—more of a betting pool than prize money—their social standing and not the exchange of money on the links determined their amateur status. If you made a living keeping the green, caddying, making clubs, or giving lessons, you were considered a professional, or a working man in those days. (They were barred from the clubhouse well into the 20th century.) Everyone else was an amateur.

Gentlemen bet on many sports and activities then, and golf took one of its prominent terms from a favorite of the time, betting on running events and especially on handicapped sprints. The slower runners had a head start of a few yards. The fastest man, however, took his mark on the "scratch," a line drawn in the ground. The best runner, one who started at the line, became known as a "scratch sprinter," a term that migrated into golf about 1860 to denote a top-notch player.

—•—

Why has betting on golf matches been a part of the game since its origin? "Early golf betting follows very much the habits of sporting gentlemen in general," answered David Hamilton. He noted those gentlemen bet also on horse racing and prize fighting, suggesting wagering on golf was merely an extension of their other pastimes.

British golfer and former CBS TV announcer Ben Wright traced the association between golf and wagering to his homeland's social nature. "Brits are betting daft," he explained. "We are a nation of gamblers; no question about it." Wright also agreed with the supposition that the sports' participants accepted betting because the game grew and matured in Scotland and later in Great Britain as a whole. "Betting was the established tradition."

"Wagering is part of the golf culture," declared Archie Baird of Gullane, Scotland. "The game was never exposed to the puritanical attitudes about gambling in the States. You Yanks are too straight-laced about betting on sports."

Professor Wray Vamplew of Scotland's University of Stirling said wagering large sums on golf in Great Britain in the 1500s and later was a sign of wealth. "It was conspicuous consumption at a time when there were few consumer goods to spend money on. It demonstrated wealth by showing that they had enough money to risk a thousand pounds on a sports event; winning the bet was less important."

Golf began in Europe about the same time as court tennis, an indoor sport. The ancestor of modern tennis was also called "real" or "royal" tennis, because the noble class played the game. James I, King of Scotland (1406–1437) and progenitor of all the golfing Stuart kings and queens, had his own tennis court. Both the players and the gallery bet on the outcome of royal tennis matches.

"Generally speaking, betting was common, if not the rule, in all sorts of medieval games," said Professor Heiner Gillmeister of Germany's University of Bonn. Gillmeister maintained that at the start, tennis players always competed for money. In support of his claim, Gillmeister referred to the tradition of keeping score in tennis by counting by 15s, with the winner being the first to reach 60 points. (Players count 15, 30, 45, and game; 45 is contracted to 40, and since you have to win by two points, deuce and advantage points are played between 45 and game.) During the 1300s in France, a coin known as the Great Penny of Tours, or *deniers*, was worth 15 pence. Gillmeister pointed to evidence tennis players bet one of these coins on each point, with 60 pence equaling game. Sixty, Gillmeister argues, may have declared the end of the game because regulations of the time forbid stakes over 60 *deniers* on games played for money.

Both tennis and golf developed as games subject to wagering. Yet at some time between the reign of King James I and the invention of lawn tennis in 1874, betting on the outcome of tennis matches essentially disappeared. A bettor can assuredly put £5 on the outcome of the All England Lawn Tennis Championships at Wimbledon each summer, but casual tennis players don't bet between themselves as golfers do. No one is quite sure why.

—●—

CHIPS AND PITCHES

Bulger driver. Willie Park, Jr., is credited with inventing the bulger driver in 1885 and using it in that year's Open. Its rounded or bulging shape, in contrast to the older wooden clubs' tapered design, has carried over to modern golf clubs. Some years later, Sir Henry Lamb, a prominent amateur, challenged him with claims of having invented the bulger in the same time frame. In the end, the pair established they had both devised similar clubs concurrently without knowing that the other was involved in the endeavor. Because Willie was a club maker and a professional continuously in the public eye, he received most of the popular acclaim for the bulger.

Fore! Several theories abound on the origin of this warning to other golfers, and Robert Browning advances the best. Two cannon guarded Leith's east gate in the 1500s, and before firing them in the town's defense, the gunners shouted, "Ware before!" This warning was a contraction of "Beware before!" or "Look out in front!" Browning surmised that "Fore!" migrated to the nearby Leith links as the game developed.

Golf bags. The first golf bag appeared in 1880, an innovation that eased the problem of carrying a bunch of sticks under your arm.

Golf beyond Scotland. The first British golf course outside the United Kingdom, the Royal Calcutta Golf Club in India, opened in 1829. The first club to open on the European continent was in Pau, France, a resort destination for Brits, and play began in 1856. The Royal Montreal Club in Canada opened in 1873.

Women golfers. Besides reports of Queen Mary's golf game in the 1560s, early references to women golfers are limited to a 1592 Edinburgh ordinance extending golfing bans on the Sabbath to women. The next appearance of women's golf in available records is in 1810, when the Musselburgh Golf Club's minutes discussed an annual women's tournament. St Andrews formed the Ladies' Golf Club (later called the Putting Club) in 1867, and shortly thereafter women's clubs started at North Devon, Wimbledon, Carnoustie, and Westward Ho! There was no prohibition of women's golf in the 18th century. Historians assume they played informally on the public links, but it was not well documented.

3.

BEST BETS:

OUIMET, HAGEN, AND JONES

AN AMERICAN GOLFING BOOM, 1888–1930

JOHN REID, A BUSINESSMAN LIVING IN YONKERS, New York, bent over and placed a brand new gutty ball on a mound of moist earth. He then addressed the ball with his new driver, feeling stiff on a chilly February day in 1888. Surrounding Reid were five friends whom he had enlisted for the outing: John B. Upham, Henry O. Tallmadge, Harry Holbrook, Kingman H. Putnam, and Alexander P. W. Kinnan. Since there was only one set of clubs, they decided Reid and Upham would play, sharing the clubs. After a nod to all, Reid reared back and then gave the ball a good whack. The result was not particularly far and sure. But with that shot in a pasture across from his home, John Reid became the father of American golf.

Reid, an immigrant Scot from Dunfermline, West Fife, was an executive with the J. L. Mott Iron Works in the Bronx. Looking for a sport beyond tennis and hunting, Reid decided on golf, recalling the game he had seen as a youth. The previous year, Reid asked his fellow Scot, Robert Lockhart, to buy clubs and balls during one of Lockhart's periodic business trips to Scotland. His friend accomplished his mission with style, going straight to Old Tom Morris's shop in St Andrews to buy a driver, brassie, spoon, cleek, sand iron, a putter, and two dozen gutties.

The conversion of Reid and friends to enthusiastic golfers was immediate. As soon as the weather permitted, they laid out three rudimentary holes in the field. They quickly moved to a larger venue, and on November 14, 1888, the six men founded the first permanent U.S. golf club, St. Andrew's. They tried to distinguish their modest undertaking from the historic Scottish links by adding the apostrophe and a period after the abbreviation for "Saint." The club relocated a third time to an orchard in 1892, where the golfers became known as the Apple Tree Gang. One particularly large tree served as the clubhouse. They hung their coats on the limbs and relaxed in the shade after matches, eating sandwiches and tasting the musky wonders of another Scottish export.

Starting from John Reid's humble beginnings, golf grew quickly in the United States. The *New York Times* reported the trend in an October 1891 article headlined "Golf Is Growing in Favor": "Young or old can play it and it may be played by men or women in any number above two. The players are called 'golfers.'" By 1895, the *Times* declared no other sport "has advanced so rapidly in this country." Just 12 years after Reid's first pasture play, golfers had formed 1,040 golf clubs in the United States.

Dr. W. S. Rainsford, rector of New York City's St. George's Episcopal Church, was a member at St. Andrew's. He extolled the game's beauty in an 1896 interview with the press. While he favored golf's social attributes and respected its code of honor, the sporting parson disagreed with another part of the game that found its way across the Atlantic in short order. "I consider it detrimental to the best interests of the game for contestants to play the game when they know that their friends have made wagers on them, as it is for the players to back themselves individually for a money purse."

Rainsford's comments clearly show betting on golf matches was an integral part of the game in the United States from the start. Expatriate Scottish golf pros brought with them the game's customs, techniques, and etiquette to the States. St. Andrew's hired such a man, Samuel Tucker, in 1894 to be the greenkeeper and professional. Either Tucker introduced the Yonkers men to wagering on golf, or they took to it spontaneously. They may have even caught the bug when they first touched the leather grips on Reid's set of Tom Morris clubs.

Brief references to golf in the United States appeared before 1888, but there is no evidence that the game took permanent hold. As early as 1788 the *Charleston City Gazette* carried notices about the South Carolina Golf Club, but no information survives about its golfing activities. Similarly, the *Georgia Gazette* in Savannah printed an invitation "to a Ball to be given by the Golf Club of this city," But again, no further information exists.

In 1884, Bostonian Russell Montague and several friends created a golf course in White Sulphur Springs, West Virginia, a few miles from the Old White Hotel, a resort that later became the Greenbrier. They named the course Oakhurst Links, but by 1910, play had ceased there and the golf course returned to nature. Oakhurst was indeed America's first organized golf club; however, its remote location and short life deprived the club of the status it might have otherwise deserved. Current owner Lewis Keller hired golf course architect Bill Cupp to restore the nine-hole layout and opened it to the public in 1994. Keller commissioned the manufacture of replicas of 1880 clubs and balls and limited play to golfers using that equipment.

Tuxedo Park built a golf course in 1889. (The exclusive sportsmen's colony north of New York City gave its name to the dinner jacket.) In Rhode Island, Theodore A. Havemeyer, along with Cornelius Vanderbilt II, John Jacob Astor, and others, was the driving force behind the creation of the Newport Golf Club in 1890. Havemeyer later became president of the USGA and donated the championship trophy for the U.S. Amateur Championship.

Shinnecock Hills opened in 1891 in Southampton, Long Island, and the venerable course has hosted seven USGA championships since then. Start-ups of other notable early clubs included the Chicago Golf Club in 1892; The Country Club in Brookline, outside of Boston, in 1895; and Baltusrol Golf Club in Springfield, New Jersey (1895).

Tournaments arose naturally during the first years of the American golf experience. Newport hosted the first "national" event in 1894, when 20 golfers from clubs in the Northeast gathered for a 36-hole tournament. Newport's own William G. Lawrence won with a 188. The runner-up was Charles Blair Macdonald, the designer of the Chicago club. He felt he should have won, complaining stroke play was not a true test of golf. His whining prompted another event later in the year at St. Andrew's, a match play tournament with a field of 27 from eight clubs. Macdonald was second again.

Macdonald's peevishness, plus disagreements between players and clubs at these first two tournaments, prompted a discussion about the golfers' need for a governing body. Henry Tallmadge of St. Andrew's invited delegates from four geographically dispersed clubs—Chicago, The Country Club, Newport, and Shinnecock—to help him found the Amateur Golf Association of the United States in December 1894. As president, the group elected Havemeyer, a businessman whose family founded the American Sugar Company. The men soon changed the name to American Golf Association and then again to United States Golf Association.

The USGA sponsored its first U.S. Amateur Championship in 1895, with MacDonald finally winning. Reverend Rainsford, the non-betting parson, lost in the quarterfinals.

—●—

On the day following the 1895 Amateur, the USGA conducted the first U.S. Open at Newport. Ten professionals and one amateur played in the tournament. Newport's young assistant professional, Horace Rawlins, won the 36-hole stroke play event with a 173. Newport's head pro, Willie Davis, and Willie Dunn, Jr., the designer and pro at Shinnecock, had been the favorites in pre-tournament betting. Most of the money backed Dunn.

Dunn's father was the greenkeeper first at Blackheath Golf Club in England and later at North Berwick in Scotland. He and his twin brother, Jamie, played Allan Robertson and Old Tom Morris in the well-publicized, £400 money match in 1848. Willie, Jr., was giving golf lessons at the French resort Biarritz when vacationing H. K. Vanderbilt saw him play. Vanderbilt convinced the Scot to come to America and lay out the original 12 holes at Shinnecock.

African-American John Shippen was a member of the crew who constructed the Shinnecock Hills golf course under Dunn's supervision. He also became a caddie, and as his golf skills quickly improved, Dunn hired him as his assistant. Club members urged the 16-year-old Shippen and another young golfer, Oscar Bunn, a Native American, to enter the 1896 U.S. Open at Shinnecock. While other entrants objected to Shippen's and Bunn's participation, Havemeyer ensured their inclusion in the field. Shippen had a bad second round but finished a respectable seven shots back of the winner, Scot James Foulis. Shippen is believed to be the first American-born golf professional.

With new golf courses being built a yard a minute, the clubs turned to Great Britain for professionals. The colorful Scots intrigued the Yanks as much as the game did. The Americans equated a barely intelligible brogue with golfing prowess. Most assumed the gibberish contained valuable nuggets of golfing advice heretofore known only to the Scots. The character Shivas Irons in Michael Murphy's books comes to mind. Besides Tucker at St. Andrew's and Davis at Newport, Chicago hired Foulis. The Country Club imported Willie Campbell, and his matches with Dunn in 1894 seemed to be the first games between professionals in the United States. St. Andrew's hosted the first professional tournament later that year.

Members at St. Andrew's paid Willie Park, Jr., to travel to the United States and play a series of challenge matches in 1895. Park, a two-time British Open winner and son of its first champion, played his initial match at St. Andrew's against Willie Campbell. Park won the $150 stakes. His three matches with Shinnecock's Willie Dunn, however, were the highlight of Park's tour. The two went at it Willie-Nillie for $200 a round. Members at the clubs hosting each match—Shinnecock, Meadow Brook on Long Island, and Morristown Golf Club in New Jersey—contributed the stakes. Prior to the first game, the *New York Times* reported bettors favored Park at 5-3 odds, and several $100 bets had been struck. Park won all three matches.

During a second visit to America in 1896, Park found himself in a money game at Shinnecock. One of the members, B. Spaulding Garmendia, offered a wager of $1,000 that he and Park could beat St. Andrew's member Arthur Livermore and Willie Tucker, the brother and assistant to the St. Andrew's pro, Sam Tucker. The Yonkers team accepted, and they played on a scorching August day. Park carried a bucket off the first tee, with members assuming it contained a cool beverage. The gallery soon discovered that clever Scot, knowing that excessive heat deformed the latex balls, had iced his gutties in the bucket. His gamesmanship did not help, though, as Livermore and Tucker won handily.

Park's fellow British professionals won the first 16 U.S. Opens. Early on, some of those men carried on the Scottish customs long associated with both their predecessors and peers at home, drinking and gambling. Fred Herd from St Andrews won the Open in 1898, the first contested over 72 holes. Despite winning $150, Herd had to fork over a deposit for the trophy. The USGA, aware of his drinking habits, was concerned Herd might pawn it to fund his longing for the malt.

As further evidence that wagering on golf followed the Scottish golfers' westward movement, the *New York Times* reported two increasingly familiar bets at the end of the 1800s—cross country and night golf. Marion Wright bet two fellow gentlemen $1,000 he could cover the ground between downtown Newport and the seventh green at the golf club in less than 103 strokes. Observers estimated the distance at about 6,700 yards. Wright made it in 99 shots. In addition, Fred McLeod, a Scot working as a pro in the Chicago area, accepted a bet that he could shoot lower than 45 on Onwentsia Country Club's front nine at night. McLeod, who won the 1908 U.S. Open, shot a 38 by the light of a half moon and won the money.

—●—

Coincident with golf's dramatic expansion in the States was an equal boom in the game's popularity in Great Britain. Golf historian David Hamilton credits several developments for the increased interest, foremost of which was the growing middle class. Real wages increased 60 percent in Britain between 1870 and 1890, and more people sought the leisure activities long the province of the elite. The number of golf courses increased from 58 in 1870 to 1,571 in 1900.

A flood of new magazines told the game's story. *Golf* started in 1890, followed quickly by *Golfing*, *The Golfer*, *The Golfer's Magazine*, and *Irish Golfer*. (*Golf Magazine* started in America in 1898.) Robert Clark's landmark book, *Golf: A Royal and Ancient Game*, published in 1875 (a collector's item today), launched a new line of sports books. The news media covered the increasing number of tournaments as well as high-stakes challenge matches.

The British press lavished coverage on Sir Arthur Balfour (later Earl of Balfour), a politician whom many call the "father of English golf." He took up the game seriously at age 36, lamenting the fate of those like himself who "threw away in their youth the opportunity of beginning golf." He was a splendid sportsman as well as an articulate and respected public official. The press reported endlessly on Balfour's pursuit of the game, leading Robert Browning to call him "golf's greatest publicity agent."

The first grass mowers helped ease the construction and maintenance of inland golf courses that lacked the patches of naturally short turf on the links. Tin cups replaced the holes fingers or an old cleek used to dig. For those clubs still using sheep to cut the grass, they installed flagsticks with springs that would bend against a grazing ewe's flank.

Golf's explosive growth at the end of the 19th century produced viable jobs for the supporting cast—professionals, greenkeepers, course designers, and caddies. Willie Park, Jr., was a prime example of those pursuing the emerging vocation, one that Browning called "the original businessman professional." He was first a championship player, but he shrewdly exploited his on-course achievements to attract other opportunities. Park was the first professional to publish a golf book and designed courses in both Europe and North America. Not every Willie from Scotland—or for that matter, a PGA Tour player today—can broadly capitalize on his game, but Arnold Palmer, Jack Nicklaus, and a few others certainly followed in Park's footsteps.

Andra (Andrew) Kirkaldy, who succeeded Old Tom Morris as the professional at the R&A, was a contemporary of Park's. While he never won the Open, he was a fine storyteller. Born in St Andrews in 1860, he placed sixth in his first Open at age 18. After an eight-year hitch in the British Army, Kirkaldy returned to the game in Scotland. His memoir, *My Fifty Years of Golf* (rare and expensive), gives the reader a front-row seat on money golf at the turn of the nineteenth century.

"Andrew, were you nervous playing before so many people for so much money?" asked an R&A member after one of Andra's challenge matches.

"What was there to be nervous about?" Kirkaldy answered. "Nervous men should never back themselves. It would be like pickin' their ain pockets. I never gave the crowd a thocht, and the money only made me stick to the lead when it came my way."

Kirkaldy answered Willie Park's 1889 challenge to play a four-green match for £100. (Park's father offered a similar £100 challenge in 1855.) Kirkaldy and Park played 36 holes each at Musselburgh, Prestwick, Troon, and St Andrews. The match gained considerable press attention, and golf's growing fan base responded. A gallery of 16,000 cheered for Kirkaldy at St Andrews for the final round. Betting among the onlookers was, um, energetic when the two teed off, with Kirkaldy holding a 3-up lead after playing the first three courses.

"Andra, I'm backing you," announced his friend, Willie Fernie, winner of the 1883 Open. "I have a good bit of money on you. You can win, and mind you do."

"There's nae doot aboot that, Willie, I'm goin' to win."

And win he did, 8 and 7. Fernie was nearby as the golfers walked back to the clubhouse.

"Hoo muckle did ye mak', Willie?" asked Andra.

"Enough to cover my expenses, Andra."

"Nae doot," Kirkaldy replied, "and pay yer hoos rent for a year into the bargain."

Kirkaldy's backers gave him a share of the £100, and several gentlemen who won side bets pressed their thanks into Andra's palm. In Kirkaldy's terms, they were "verra mindful, verra mindful."

Kirkaldy said challenge matches were the "life of golf" at the time. Alternative events—exhibition matches—were gaining favor in Britain in the late 1800s, and the best players had more opportunities for a good payday than the youngsters or lesser players did. "I wouldn't give a button for an exhibition game," Kirkaldy said. "Man against man, and pocket against pocket, in deadly earnest is the thing."

Caddies benefited immensely from the golf boom. While Park, Jr., employed his own aggressively protective caddie, nicknamed "Fiery," courses usually maintained a gang of men and boys to carry for the players. The large number of neophyte golfers needed someone to offer clubbing advice, read the greens, follow the flight of the ball, and clean the clubs. As every golfer knows when playing one of the old Scottish links courses for the first time, caddies are a must. Save for team competitions, the Rules of Golf reflect a caddie's special status, allowing only him to advise his player.

Caddies have always sought to supplement their fees. During the latter half of the 1800s in Britain, three or four shillings were the norm, and the player usually charged the caddie three pence for a lost ball. The fine helped deter the caddie from declaring a ball lost, then pocketing it, and selling it back to the pro. Some caddies hung out upstream near the Swilcan Burn at St Andrews, stirring up mud in the stream to obscure any balls hit into the water. Once the golfers passed by, the boys retrieved the balls and sold them. Others trained dogs to find lost balls in the gorse. Kirkaldy called them "dog caddies."

Kirkaldy, who had a story about everything in golf, told a few about caddies, including their nicknames. "'Hole in 's pocket' got his name when his player lost his ball," Kirkaldy said. "He would drop one down his trouser leg and say, 'Here it is; and no such a bad lie after all.' That would only be when the caddies and players were betting on the match and 'Hole in 's pocket' had been promised perhaps a sovereign if his employer won."

Andra also told of two caddies named Jock and Hutchie who looped during a match between an American and an Irishman at Musselburgh. The Yank promised his caddie Hutchie a sovereign (a gold £1 coin) if they won. With the players all square on the final hole, Jock picked up a rock from the green on the way to remove the flag. "Lost hole," cried the American, citing the rule at the time that prohibited removing impediments within 20 yards of the hole. Thus losing the morning round, the Irishman promised Jock £5 if he won the afternoon game.

The two golfers were again all square on the last hole, and both bunkered their drives. "What is he givin' ye this time?" Jock whispered to Hutchie as they walked toward the hazard.

"A sovereign again," answered Hutchie, "if he wins."

"I'm getting £5 if my man wins," Jock said. "Let's hurry up to the bunker. Gi'e me the sovereign you won this mornin', and I'll drop it next to the

Yankee's ba'. He'll pick it up, of course, and I'll be on him like a hawk for breakin' the rules. My man'll be the winner, and we'll run halves wi' the money."

Just as Jock figured, the American pounced on the coin, and Jock shouted, "Lost hole!"

—●—

Golf's rapidly expanding popularity in the late 1800s led to two fundamental facets of the game in Britain that we take for granted today—handicaps and the concept of par golf.

The game started with two or four golfers comparing the number of holes won to determine the winner of both the match and the bet. Early on in Scotland, the participants knew many of the players on the links, with a golfer more often playing another of equal skills. As golfing societies began to organize play, the club captain or another officer—the "adjuster of the odds"—paired golfers of roughly the same ability to guarantee a fair wager. In a pairing where one had a clear advantage, the lesser player started the match a specified number of holes up. A slightly more complicated system gradually developed in which the more skilled player granted strokes throughout the round. "One more" stroke a hole was just that, but a "third-one" meant the underdog got a stroke every third hole, and a "half-one" advantage granted a stroke every other hole.

Until the latter decades of the 1800s, most called the process of leveling the playing field "assigning the odds." As the sport grew, the game adopted the term *handicap* from a practice in horse racing, where track authorities made faster horses carry weights in addition to the jockey. The term also grew out of the custom of placing bets in an up-turned cap. Horse owners reached into the hat— "hand-in-cap"—and either left the money there to signify acceptance of the odds or retrieved it to indicate their dissatisfaction and withdrawal from the race.

British professionals played each other at scratch, but as more amateur golfers from different clubs and courses entered tournaments, how to match them evenly became confusing. One approach that started in the 1860s was to group the golfers in flights according to skills, just as is done today. The handicap system we use now, however, grew out of an idea that Hugh Rotherham proposed in 1890. Players would play a match against a hypothetical perfect golfer, one who never flubbed a shot or made mental mistakes. To make the scheme work, Rotherham had to determine what the ideal player would shoot, or what he called the "ground score." He and his fellows determined the perfect score for each hole at their home course, and the first such tournament was a success in 1891.

As other clubs staged similar tournaments, Dr. Thomas Browne of the Yarmouth Club in Norfolk, England, coined a name for the perfect player, "the bogey man." Browne drew upon a popular ditty of the day: "Hush! Hush! Hush! Here comes the bogeyman! He'll catch you if he can!" If the perfect golfer was right behind you on the links, you better hit 'em straight.

By 1892, Browne had introduced the concept of a bogey score to other clubs. The term was soon accepted throughout Great Britain as a standard score on a hole. At the United Services Club at Gosport, England, the military officers there assumed if a player of the bogeyman's skill were a soldier, he would certainly be a high-ranking officer, probably a colonel. *Colonel Bogey* became a common term and even made it into a popular musical composition, "The Colonel Bogey March." Actor Alec Guinness and his fellow prisoners of war whistled the melody while marching in the film *The Bridge on the River Kwai.*

Using the term *bogey* to describe the score that a scratch player should make on a hole didn't last long. As the average player's overall skill level in the game improved through better equipment, instruction, and course grooming, a score of one less than bogey became the standard for each hole. Soon, players used the term *par* to describe this new level of excellence. Former USGA official Dean Knuth said the term was taken from the stock market and its reference to the normal, or par, value of a stock.

But a nationwide system needed more than just a scratch score as a basis for assigning handicaps to golfers. Then, as now, each course offered extreme differences when testing golfers' skills. A bogey score on one course could not be equitably compared to another. Two members of the Royal Wimbledon Golf Club and Issette Pearson of the British Ladies' Golf Union (LGU) solved the problem in 1898. The amateur golfing community adopted a uniform method of gauging, or "rating," the difficulty of every course. Early handicap chairmen could then calculate a handicap number—generally the difference between your score and the scratch player's score, as adjusted for the course rating—that might be accepted beyond a golfer's home course.

Several years passed before both the British and the USGA eliminated shortcomings in the first handicapping system. But as Robert Browning notes, the women of the LGU achieved what the men had failed to accomplish: they established a system that was reliable from club to club.

—●—

The gutta ball made the game more affordable, but 50 years later, another golf ball innovation made the game more fun. In 1898, two men in Cleveland, Ohio, patented a new, rubber-cored ball. Coburn Haskell, an avid amateur golfer, worked with a friend, Bertram Work, an engineer at the B. F. Goodrich rubber company, and created a new ball by winding thin threads of rubber around a rubber core. Although they covered the ball with gutta percha, it was still distinct from the old, solid gutta percha ball.

The Haskell ball was an immediate hit. Most golfers gained an extra 25 yards off the tee, but its liveliness, especially around the green, earned it the nickname "Bounding Billy." Walter Travis won the 1901 U.S. Amateur with a Haskell, and that publicity further stimulated sales. Scot Sandy Herd won the 1902 British Open with the new ball, beating Harry Vardon who was still clinging to the gutty.

Various cores were used in the early versions, even compressed air. Goodrich's "Pneumatic" was prone to accidental explosions either in play or in your pocket. Spalding introduced a wound rubber ball in 1903 with a cover of balata, a natural latex from the South American tree *Manilkara bidentata*.

To help control its flight, Haskell used a "bramble" system of bumps on the ball's surface, similar to those on the gutties. Englishman William Taylor soon reversed that technique and molded dimples on the cover. Spalding bought the U.S. rights for the process, and by the 1930s its dimpled, balata-covered, wound rubber ball became the standard for many years to come. (The dimples produce a turbulence layer around the ball that reduces air friction and results in greater distance and control.) Other improved manufacturing techniques made approach shots to the green more manageable, overcoming the excessive bouncing.

The Haskell allowed mediocre golfers to advance the ball, even if it were sliced, hooked, or topped. A poorly hit gutty never made it past the women's tee. The new ball allowed golfers to use more compact swings and employ more lofted clubs to create the backspin needed for control. "The rubber-cored ball turned an ordinary clumsy golfer overnight into a moderate performer," declared Englishman Henry Cotton, a three-time winner of the British Open. Golf was fun!

From the Haskell's introduction until 1921, no one had established standards for golf balls. A wide variety of sizes, weights, cores, and covers appeared as manufacturers brought the technology of the 20th century to golf ball production. The USGA and the R&A later specified joint standards, but they soon disagreed about its size.

—●—

"I recall an incident which occurred on the evening before the beginning of the great match," said Harry Vardon as he described his famous £100 challenge game with Willie Park, Jr., in 1899. "I was taking a walk with my brother when Big Crawford, possibly the most famous of all the North Berwick caddies, appeared around a corner. As he saw us, he threw a big horseshoe at me, which, although it missed me, very nearly brained my brother. He explained that he was tossing the horseshoe over my head for luck, as he had backed me to win with every penny he possessed." It was not unusual for side bets to abound during these very popular money matches, just as it was not unusual for a seasoned caddie to bet on Vardon, a true pioneer in the game and the first international golf star.

He won the British Open six times—the tournament's all-time winner—was runner-up four times, and won the 1900 U.S. Open. Vardon won half of his British Opens with the gutty ball and half with the Haskell, a remarkable adaptation. The Englishman's upright swing was a smooth and efficient improvement over the flat, lunging sweep his contemporaries used. His more vertical plane enabled Vardon to hit the ball higher and farther, and his swing was the prototype for the great golfers of the 20th century. He also disdained the traditional baseball grip. One wag quipped the overlapping "Vardon grip" that he popularized did for golf what Marilyn Monroe did for the cocktail dress.

Vardon's 1900 tour of America demonstrated skillful golf to the country's burgeoning golf population for the first time. Hired by Spalding to promote their Vardon Flyer, a gutty ball, he played 88 matches on the tour and lost only 12 against the better ball of his opponents and only one in singles games. His appearances drew thousands at each stop, and he packed a department store in Boston while hitting balls into a net.

Born on the Isle of Jersey, young Vardon and his brother, Tom, played a few surreptitious holes of golf at night on the Royal Jersey Golf Club. But his first serious introduction to golf came when he was 17 and working as a gardener for one of the club's members, Major Spofforth. Before long Spofforth began helping Vardon learn the game, and the two of them soon were winning stakes matches at the club. The major gave Vardon part of the winnings and reduced his gardening duties so that Harry could practice more. The story sounds like something Titanic Thompson would say later: "I'll take my gardener and play any two of you blokes for £10 a side."

Vardon became a pro at the age of 20 and started playing in tournaments. In 1894, he entered a major competition at Portrush, Ireland. Vardon said a syndicate bought most of the players in the "selling sweep," or Calcutta, with the unknown Vardon going for a measly shilling. When he made the semifinal, the syndicate sent some muscle to talk with the kid. "You must win this match," the man urged. "Whatever you do, don't allow yourself to be beaten."

"It was an exceedingly stupid thing for anyone to say to a young player," Vardon said later, acknowledging the pressure the warning produced. Up early by four holes, Vardon soon lost three back. "The members of the syndicate were extremely anxious, and again I was told on no account must I lose the match." Vardon did indeed win, but then he lost in the finals to Sandy Herd.

Many of the good and great golfers of the 20th century—for example, Gene Sarazen and Byron Nelson—learned valuable lessons as youngsters when playing for money. Later chapters describe how others used betting to understand pressure golf. Vardon's teenage money matches with Major Spoffort helped him deal with the demanding high-stakes challenge matches later in his career.

"One of the most important events in my life and the greatest match I ever played against anyone, was my contest with Willie Park," Vardon wrote in his book *My Golfing Life*. Vardon beat Park by a stroke in the 1898 Open, and the Scot wanted revenge. He challenged Vardon to a home-and-home match at £100 a side, but they didn't agree on the terms until after the 1899 Open, which Vardon also won. Vardon refused to play at Park's home course, Musselburgh, because of its rowdy crowds. Instead, they played 36 at North

Berwick in Scotland and 36 at Ganton, England, where Vardon was the pro. They ponied up their own money instead of allowing backers to fund the stakes.

Vardon said 10,000 people were in the gallery at North Berwick. The crowd was so large members hoisted a white flag with a *P* on it when Willie won a hole; a red *V* flag meant a Vardon win. Vardon beat Park by two holes at North Berwick, and he was confident of his chances at Ganton. Park hit a low hook that he used on the Scottish links courses. The first three holes at Ganton required a long carry off the tee. Vardon handled them easily with his high ball flight, but the holes severely tested the Scot. Vardon indeed won those holes and then coasted to an 11 and 10 win for the £200 (about $20,500 today).

Another high-profile challenge match involving Vardon was the "Great Foursome" match in 1905. The wager was for £200, with George Riddell backing the Scots—James Braid and Sandy Herd—and Edward Hulton betting on the English team of Vardon and James Taylor. Vardon, Taylor, and Braid were so dominant in British golf at the time that the press called them "the Great Triumvirate." Combined, they won 16 Opens between 1894 and 1914. Expectations ran high about the match. It was as if Tiger Woods and Phil Mickelson played Ernie Els and Retief Goosen for a sizable sum today.

They played 36 each at St Andrews and Troon and then again at St Annes and Deal in England. Vardon and Taylor demolished the Scots at Troon, winning 14 holes, and left for England 12-up at the halfway point. The English eventually won 13 and 12. Bernard Darwin, grandson of evolutionist Charles Darwin and an eminent golf writer of the day, said the match equaled the legendary four-green challenge between Robertson and Morris versus the Dunn brothers in 1848. Darwin also lamented the decreasing frequency of challenge matches as golfers concentrated instead on the purses at stroke play events.

"I cannot help regretting the passing of these contests," Vardon wrote in 1933, agreeing with Darwin's disappointment in the dwindling number of challenges. "In a way it is a pity as a stern struggle between two leading players in a real money match is something going a long way to see."

——●——

Golf fans in Britain avidly followed the exploits of professional golfers, especially those in high-stakes challenge matches. But aside from the occasional touring Brit in the States, U.S. fans had few local pros to follow in the press or to cheer for on the course. Amateur play received a great deal of attention in American golf's early years, but some confusion persisted about who was an amateur.

The initial distinction lay in Britain's class system. Gentlemen "belonged," but caddies didn't. Playing for money didn't classify a golfer as a professional, because gentlemen also wagered on their game. Prior to the first British Amateur championship in 1884, organizers created artificial obstacles to keep working men—"fishermen and weavers"—out of the increasing number of tournaments. In Scotland, according to Hamilton, a high entry fee screened out many. In England, entrants had to be members of established golf clubs, and weekday tournaments made it hard for working amateurs to play.

By the second British Amateur, the Brits finally defined an amateur as a player who did not accept prize money—wagers between fellow amateurs didn't count—nor did he make money in the golfing trade. This distinction migrated to the United States in 1897, but America's priggish attitude about amateurism's sanctity exacerbated the matter. U.S. attitudes about money have drained the life out of many sports and athletes. One egregious example is the U.S. Olympic Committee's seizure of legendary Jim Thorpe's track medals from the 1912 Olympics because he had played minor league pro baseball prior to the games.

At any rate, several U.S. amateurs caught American golf fans' interest. Charles Blair Macdonald, the winner of the first U.S. Amateur in 1895, was one of the first. He was good enough to routinely bet his partners he could hit a ball off the crystal of a watch without cracking the glass. He always won that money.

Macdonald also designed a number of courses. His signature work was the National Golf Links in Southampton, Long Island, which opened in 1911. There he replicated famous holes from British courses, and the National went on to become a landmark precursor to modern American golf courses. Herbert Warren Wind said the National "dramatized for Americans what a real golf course looked like."

Macdonald made a $1 million bet at the National with his nephew, Peter Grace, who later became president of W. R. Grace, Inc. Story has it that while a college student, Grace played the National with his uncle and told him the course was too easy. "Take the first hole," Grace said, "par-4. But a good drive can reach the green."

"Nonsense," said Macdonald, who quickly escorted Grace to the number one tee to settle the matter. With a helping wind, Grace drove the green on the 310-yard hole. Macdonald was reportedly so mad he wrote Grace out of his will that night, a sum Grace later said amounted to a million bucks.

The first great moment in American golf was Walter Travis's victory in the 1904 British Amateur, then second only to the British Open in prestige. He took to golf late, at age 34, so he deserved his nickname of the "Old Man."

Travis complained loudly of what he considered shabby treatment by the Brits in 1904, especially by the tournament committee, who assigned him a dim, cross-eyed caddie. The locals certainly didn't view Travis as a favorite, eagerly offering bets against him. An American named W. W. Burton accepted all the wagers out of patriotism.

Travis nevertheless beat the long-driving Ted Blackwell in the 36-hole final 4 and 3. The British were aghast at the Yank's victory and pointedly said so. "Never since the days of Caesar has the British nation been subjected to such humiliation," harrumphed Lord Northbourne at the trophy ceremony. Travis took most of the slights good naturedly, saying, "A reasonable number of fleas is good for a dog. It keeps the dog from forgetting that he is a dog."

Meanwhile, Burton cleared $3,000 by defending Yankee golf.

Travis putted wonderfully during the tournament with a radically new club design—the Schenectady, a center-shafted, mallet putter with an aluminum head—that was new to Great Britain. Most golfers there used heel-shafted putters that were not much more than a cleek. Arthur T. Knight of Schenectady, New York, invented the club in 1902. Travis used it in that year's U.S. Open but then discarded it until the day before his first match in Britain. The R&A subsequently banned the club until 1952, when the members reportedly permitted its use to entice Ben Hogan, who used one, to play in the British Open.

As with Vardon and many others, Travis, a three-time U.S. Amateur winner, found himself in a pressure betting situation. In the 1902 U.S. Open, someone bet heavily that Travis would beat two professionals, Stewart

Gardner and Willie Smith. (The bet is similar to a "match-up" bet today.) "I knew of the bet," Travis said, "and was much chagrined at my poor showing the first day. So the next day I 'girded up my loins' and made up my mind that that I would give of my best." On the last hole, Travis had a comfortable lead over Smith, but he needed a birdie to tie Gardner's score. His head was filled with his own feelings plus with what he guessed was going through the bettor's mind. "All of these thoughts flashed through my mind in the brief space of a few seconds." Travis made the putt but didn't explain if the tie won the bet.

Sportswriter Grantland Rice later asked Travis to explain the basis for his mental toughness. "I never hit a careless shot in my life," Travis said. "I bet only a quarter, but I play each shot as if it was for the title. I concentrate as hard for a quarter as I do for a championship."

The amateur player who garnered the most attention in America before Bobby Jones's time, in the 1920s, was 20-year-old Francis Ouimet. Three things led to golf's lasting popularity in the United States. The first was the 1898 invention of the lively Haskell ball, and the second was Harry Vardon's 1900 tour of the country. The third development, however, had the most impact: Ouimet unexpectedly beat Vardon and another Englishman, Ted Ray, in the 1913 U.S. Open at The Country Club in Brookline, Massachusetts.

Ouimet grew up in a house across the street from The Country Club's 17th hole. He and his older brother were hooked on the game early and laid out three holes in an adjoining pasture, using tin cans for cups. Francis began caddying at the club at the age of nine. Like so many boys who followed, he wagered with his friends as they played his homemade course. The usual bet was a ball drawn from the hoard each accumulated by rummaging about for lost balls in the club's rough. While caddying, his rapidly improving game gained him the opportunity to play with the members. He quit caddying at 16 to maintain his amateur status. (The USGA struggled with how to cope with golf's growing class of professionals.) In high school, he led Brookline to the state championship, and he won the individual title in the Boston Interscholastic Championship.

Inspired by reading Vardon's book *The Complete Golfer*, Ouimet began winning local tournaments. His only victory of note, however, was the 1913 Massachusetts State Amateur, staged just before the Open.

Ouimet's caddy deserted the young man for another player the day before the first qualifying round at the Open. Francis ended up with a

10-year-old neighborhood kid named Eddie Lowery, who skipped school to loop for Francis. The photograph of Ouimet and the four-foot-tall Eddie taken during the tournament is one of golf history's iconic images. Ouimet easily qualified, finishing four strokes behind the medalist, Ted Ray, and one behind Vardon.

Former president William Howard Taft watched Ouimet and Vardon during their qualifying round. Afterward, he mentioned to a friend that bookmakers in London were offering 2-1 odds on Vardon and Ray against the rest of the field, with a minimum bet of $5,000. After watching Ouimet's excellent play that day, Taft advised his friend to get part of that action but to take the field.

As many know, Vardon, Ray, and Ouimet were tied for the lead after 72 holes and faced an 18-hole play-off the next day. The local bookies posted 5-4 odds that either Ray or Vardon would beat Ouimet. Francis shot a splendid, even-par 72 to win the Open, fives strokes clear of Vardon and six of Ray.

America had its first golf hero. More important, as a player he was neither a privileged society swell nor a professional; instead, he was like the polite young man who lived next door. Americans opened their arms to Ouimet and rushed to adopt his game. The ranks of U.S. golfers grew from 350,000 in 1913 to 2 million just 10 years later.

Tied for fourth behind Ouimet was another American youngster, a brash pro from upstate New York. Before the tournament's start, the 21-year-old player strode into the locker room and announced, "The name is Hagen. I've come down from Rochester to help you fellows stop Vardon and Ray." A disastrous triple bogey at 14 on the final day cost him a spot in the play-off, but Walter Hagen would soon make his own mark in golf as well as gain legendary status in money golf's history.

—●—

Defending champion Johnny McDermott tied Hagen for fourth place behind Ouimet, Vardon, and Ray. It was a bitter disappointment for the young professional, the first player born and reared in the States to win the U.S. Open. British golfers had won the first 16 Opens, but McDermott not only won in 1911 at age 19 but the next year as well. He was the first to win the Open under par, and he remains the tournament's youngest winner.

After his first Open victory, the slightly built former caddie offered a standing challenge wager of $1,000 to any taker. Only three golfers took the bet, and Johnny beat them all. In November 1912, an unidentified golfer wearing a mask turned the tables by issuing his own $1,000 challenge to McDermott. While "the masked marvel," as the press called him, practiced at the public golf course in New York City's Van Cortlandt Park, his spokesman, British Army captain C. Alston Tyrer spoke to reporters in hopes of stirring up interest in a challenge match. McDermott declined two days later and identified the masked man as William Horne, a journeyman English pro. Horne and Tyrer had previously approached McDermott directly, but the American had declined, citing both the wager's unfavorable conditions and Horne's lack of stature. Horne then set up the publicity stunt to gain the news media's attention.

McDermott's two U.S. Open wins should have garnered the public favor that befell Ouimet, but his relative obscurity reflected the position professionals occupied in American golf's hierarchy. Golf writer George Peper observed the American professionals faced formidable obstacles to success: "the British pros, the American amateurs, and disregard and poverty." McDermott beat the Brits, but the odds were stacked against him. One town alone, Carnoustie, Scotland, sent 250 Scottish pros to work at U.S. clubs.

Amateur players got most of the ink until Bobby Jones retired in 1930, in part because the public didn't always view professional athletes as the media gods who are worshipped today. The Americans expected purity in their amateurs and all that. Plus, Peper contends, some amateurs were as good as the pros.

Another factor affecting the professional golfers' public status was the lingering feeling they were tradesmen, a perception inherited from the class-obsessed English. They were not permitted in the clubhouses at events open to pros until 1920. The fans enjoyed watching them play, much as they might like circus performers, but their attitude still was, please, go around back for your dinner.

Most historians of the U.S. professional game point to a tournament in Lakewood, New Jersey, on January 1, 1898, as the beginning of what later became the pro tour. Ten hardy souls battled the course and the weather for a purse of $150. Golf writer and editor Al Barkow suggested the competition was meant to entertain and to attract attention to the hotels in the resort towns between New York and Philadelphia. It was a commercial event rather than the serious play seen in the national or regional tournaments administered by the USGA or other amateur golf organizations. Each year brought a few more pro tournaments, but they were haphazard without any coherency to their scheduling or relationship to one another.

Organizers founded the Professional Golfers' Association of America in 1916, not as a trade union, but as a means to organize the pros' activities. The initial emphasis was the pros' responsibilities at clubs; the PGA did not sponsor a tour. The PGA held its first championship the same year, with Jim Barnes defeating Jock Hutchison, 1-up.

In those early years, the few professional tournaments offered such small purses the players turned to more lucrative events—exhibitions. Descendents of the big money challenge matches, exhibitions entertained the fans as tour events would later. Exhibitions also offered gallery members chances to bet on their favorite players, a custom they openly pursued on the course.

During World War I, a time when the public gave up many leisure activities in deference to the troops' sacrifices, U.S. golfers kept at the game by raising money in tournaments. Players bought war bonds as their entry fees, and organizers paid purses in bonds. The Red Cross charged the gallery $1 each for the exhibitions, using the money for their operations overseas. The public became used to paying to see the pros, and later the gate receipts became a big part of the purse at golf tournaments. Although the pros earned fees for the wartime events, the fans admired their participation, which also helped raise their social status. In addition, donating net proceeds from professional tournaments to charity, a common practice with the PGA Tour today, arose from these wartime fund-raising events.

Upon this humble scene of U.S. professional golf appeared—no, burst— the country's first celebrity professional player, Walter Hagen. "The Haig" brought money golf to America.

—●—

"Miss this little bit of a putt for $1,000?" mused Hagen as he lined up a 12-footer. "Not a chance!"

The occasion was a match Hagen and partner Joe Kirkwood had against two local pros in New Orleans in 1929. Organizers were paying Hagen and Kirkwood for an exhibition match, but Hagen wanted to rustle up a side bet to add interest to the game. Not finding one, he asked about the course record. "Sixty-nine," someone said.

"I'll bet $1,000 I break it," Hagen said. A group raised its side of the bet and later watched anxiously as Hagen eyed a putt on 18 for a 68 and the money. He stroked it smoothly, and as the ball headed for the hole, the Haig turned to the gallery, held out his up-turned palm, and said, "Gimme."

Walter Hagen won 70 or so tournaments around the world. He won 10 majors—four British Opens (his 1922 victory was the first by an American), two U.S. Opens, and four straight PGA Championships. He was also the playing captain of the first five U.S. Ryder Cup teams (1927–35).

Born in 1892, Hagen grew up in Rochester, where his father was a blacksmith. Walter started caddying at the age of nine at Rochester Country Club, but he was skilled in other sports, especially baseball. Hagen talked often about his tryout with the Phillies. As his game improved, he first became an assistant to the Rochester pro and then head pro later.

His swing was not classic, even for the time. He swayed to and fro rather like a rocking horse, according to fellow competitor Mike Brady, instead of pivoting as Vardon did so ably. Hagen's iron play was first rate, and many considered him the best pressure putter during the 1920s until his age and lifestyle brought hesitancy to his stroke. "Whiskey fingers," Wind said of Hagen's malaise.

Hagen's swing demanded exquisite timing. When it was off, he sprayed shots like a duffer. His reputation as a great scrambler didn't come from hitting fairways and greens. Many contend, however, some of his inaccuracy was a ploy to sweeten the bet or to get into his opponent's head. Nevertheless, Wind said Hagen made the game look hard to the gallery because several times a round, he had to execute an amazing recovery shot just to halve or tie the hole. The British writer Henry Longhurst said the fans appreciated Hagen because "his golf was fallible." Hagen coped with his mistake-prone golf through his ability to put a bad shot behind him, thus keeping his confidence intact.

How he played championship golf was but one-half of the Hagen persona. The rest was his style, both on and off the course. He was a glib and self-assured man who chatted up a pretty woman in the gallery as easily as he made small talk with royalty on the course. He was a flashy dresser. His silk shirts, fine gabardine plus fours, and patent leather golf shoes set him apart from his colorless competitors. He was a show horse out in front of the draft animals. Married and divorced thrice, Walter chased women like a "free-range rabbit," according to one writer.

"Walter broke 11 of the Ten Commandments," quipped Fred Corcoran, an early director of the PGA tour. In many scenes, all seemingly stolen from the movies, Hagen would arrive in a limo just before his tee time. Still clad in the previous evening's tux, he would blow a kiss to a slim blonde in the back seat and then walk to the first tee as if he were entering a ballroom. He used this showmanship to enhance his brand, using today's terminology. Grantland Rice called Hagen a "dazzling ornament to the history of sport."

Late in his career, at the 1940 PGA, Hagen's mood was as gloomy as the weather. "It was raining hard, the course was muddy, and I needed a little nip or two for my health's sake," he said. His opponent that day, Victor Ghezzi, wanted to start their match and was impatient with the Haig's pre-round lubrication. "I suggested that Ghezzi begin play and I would join him on the third hole, conceding him wins on the first two," Hagen later recalled. Hagen knew he couldn't miss the starting time, but his offhandedness irritated the younger man. Ghezzi indeed won the first two holes, but Hagen rallied, winning 2 and 1.

Hagen's pursuit of the sporting life benefited the many pro golfers who followed. He didn't want to change clothes in the caddie yard or eat a boxed lunch, so he forced the snobbish Europeans to accept pros in the clubhouse. He succeeded through the brilliance of his golf and the force of his personality. Hagen and Gene Sarazen sat down for lunch in the 1920s with Britain's Prince of Wales at Royal St. George's clubhouse, and their presence ruffled the club's staff. "Golfing professionals are not allowed in the dining room," they whispered to the Prince. "You stop this nonsense or I'll take the 'Royal' out of St. George's," declared the future King Edward VIII. Just before Hagen's death in 1969, his PGA friends honored him at a dinner. "If it were not for you, Walter," toasted Arnold Palmer, "this dinner would be downstairs in the pro shop and not in the ballroom."

Hagen's cockiness—he walked onto a course as if it were his—was part of his game, and he usually delivered. In a tournament on Santa Catalina Island off California in the 1920s, Hagen trailed Horton Smith with three holes left in the final round. On the 16th tee, he saw Smith, who had finished his round, in the gallery. "Well, kid, I can tie with a three-two-one!" Hagen said. Walter indeed shot a three on 16 and a two on 17, but he still needed an ace on the par-3 18th. Alas, his tee shot hit the stick and ended up a foot from the hole. During an exhibition match, he bet $10 with no odds that he could make a hole in one and then did. "The idea, when betting even money on a 100,000-to-one shot," Hagen explained haughtily, "is to recognize the one time when it comes along."

The purses were so small during Hagen's salad days he never depended on prize money alone to support his lifestyle. After winning his fourth and last British Open in 1929, Hagen gave the £100 winner's check to his caddie, Ernest Hargreaves. His real money came from his fees for exhibition and challenge matches.

Some of the better-known golfers, including Hagen, arranged tours during the winter through the South and West in the United States, playing matches against local pros at each stop. The events attracted large galleries, and organizers used the gate receipts to fund the prize money. To hype a match in the press, either the touring pros or their opponents issued side bet challenges. While the touring pros usually won the stakes, the chance to play against the international stars also benefited the growth and development of the increasing number of homebred pros.

Hagen was the best draw for these matches because of his flair, and he commanded a minimum fee of $1,000 for an exhibition. He played more than 3,000 of them between 1912 and 1939. Typical was a 1920 match with Jim Barnes, who later won the U.S. and British Opens and the PGA. "The long-awaited and important Hagen-Barnes match will be played at New Orleans this morning and afternoon, at thirty-six holes for a fifteen hundred dollar side bet," announced the *New York Times*. That a northeastern newspaper would dedicate eight inches of type to an exhibition match 1,300 miles away reflected the growing interest in these events. Hagen won on the 37th hole.

Before the match with Barnes, someone mentioned to the two golfers that $1,500 might be too large a wager (about $15,000 today) and asked if they would consider splitting the pot. Barnes was willing, but Hagan said, "Oh come on, Jim. Let's play for it."

In October 1922, the Haig agreed to an unofficial "international championship" match with the young Sarazen, who won the U.S. Open that year. Since Hagen was the reigning British Open winner, the organizers hyped a trans-Atlantic angle, even though both players were Americans. For a $3,000 purse, they played 36 holes each at the Oakmont Country Club near Pittsburgh and the Westchester-Biltmore Country Club in Rye, New York. Hagen tried to mess with Sarazen's mind before the match by sending him a new tie and a flirtatious note from a fictitious female admirer. Sarazen showed up on the first tee wearing the tie and kept looking in the gallery for the lady. The younger Sarazen prevailed, however, 3 and 2. Fortunately, instead of the winner-take-all deal Hagen had made with Barnes, he and Sarazen had decided to divvy the stakes 55-45, with the winner getting the larger sum.

During the winter of 1923, Hagen and Joe Kirkwood, who was also a trick shot artist, toured the Sun Belt and played 150 challenge matches, losing only 20 of them. In the locker room in Agua Caliente, Mexico, after their exhibition match, Hagen challenged Kirkwood to a $50 cross-country wager. They started at the clubhouse and set the finish a mile away in the toilet of their hotel room. A crowd of locals followed the two as they hit their balls along the main street, onto the hotel's lawn, through the lobby, and down the hall to their room. The match was all square by that time, and members of the gallery were making their own side bets. "In the end I won," Kirkwood wrote later, "because Walter had trouble picking his approach off the tile floor in the bathroom. On the first try my pitching wedge picked the ball clean, and it ended the contest with a polite splash right into the white bowl."

A perfect venue for Hagen's money matches was Great Britain, and he scheduled them coincident with his travel to play in the Open. Two games garnered the most notoriety. The first was in 1926 against a Brit named Abe Mitchell, thought to be the world's best match player at the time. Mitchell challenged all comers to a 72-hole match for £500. Hagen accepted but uncharacteristically passed on putting up his own money. Mr. A. W. Wallace, a Detroit businessman, financed Hagen's end of the bet. The press reported that the £1,000 wager was the largest ever offered a professional golfer in England.

Mitchell had four holes in his pocket after the first 36 at St. George's Hill in Weybridge, England. Hagen kept Mitchell waiting at the start of the third round at Wentworth Country Club in Sussex. He finally arrived 20 minutes late and was chatting with the gallery when the referee "drew his attention to the fact that the match in which he was concerned was in progress." Hagen was at his scrambling best that day or perhaps his ball-striking worst. He missed five fairways in the morning round as well as on the first four holes in the afternoon. Relying on his short game—Hagen got up and down from the green-side rough 12 times over 35 holes—he won the match 2 and 1.

Two years later, Hagen was not so lucky. During the winter before the 1928 British Open, Englishman Archie Compston issued a challenge to any American traveling to Britain for the championship. He proposed stakes of £750 a side, which was about $3,750 then and $36,000 today. Walter accepted, fronting his own money that time. The match was scheduled only two days after his arrival, and Hagen tried unsuccessfully to have the match postponed.

They played at London's Moor Park. Organizers limited the gallery to 1,500 people and charged each attendee 15 shillings, the highest-priced ticket then for a golf match in Britain. Hagen, who had irritated the Brits with his tardy arrival for the Mitchell match two years earlier, hired an off-duty Scotland Yard policeman to get him up each morning and to the course on time. Hagen and his manager made sure the press knew of the arrangement, demonstrating their savvy public relations skills.

Compston, a strapping young man with a full head of tousled blonde hair, absolutely drubbed Hagen on the first 36, winning by 14 holes. Archie shot 67-66 for a 133 total or, as the Brits said then, "11-under fours." (Shooting "fours" meant averaging four shots per hole for 18 holes, or 144 for 36.) Hagen never recovered, with Compston dormie 18 at the start of the final round on the second day. He won on the next hole, 18 and 17. The English press headlined Hagen's lopsided loss: "American Gets His Own Medicine! Hagen's Ghost Is Laid!"

Hagen laughed last when he won the British Open a few weeks later. His 292 was three shots clear of Compston and two of runner-up Sarazen. The papers then reversed course: "Hagen's Great Victory! A Bonnie Golfer!"

As the news of Compston's stakes match win over Hagen reached the United States, MacDonald Smith, head pro at Lakeville Country Club in Long Island, issued his own challenge to Compston. Smith, a transplanted Scot from Carnoustie, offered to play Compston for $5,000 when the Englishman arrived in the States for the U.S. Open. Compston declined. Members at Lakeville then tried another angle to attract an entertaining match at their club. They offered a $10,000 wager to any pair of golfers who would take on Smith and Gene Sarazen; none accepted.

Walter Hagen was the first golf professional who made a living by playing golf. He quit his club job in 1919 after winning his second U.S. Open and hit the road in search of a payday. He claimed he was the first player to make $1 million, but he seemed to spend $2 million on his lavish lifestyle.

At the 1933 British Open at St Andrews, one of money golf's foremost raconteurs, Andra Kirkaldy (white shirt and tie), talked with English golfer Archie Compston. Perhaps they were recalling Archie's challenge match against Walter Hagen in 1928, which they played for £750 a side, about $36,000 today. Compston dusted Hagen, winning the 36-hole match 18 and 17. University of St Andrews

While many applaud Arnold Palmer for bringing television's money to the professional game, the Haig paved the way for all who followed. He succeeded because of his championship-level golf as well as his pizzazz. "Golf had never had a showman like him," Sarazen claimed later. "All the professionals who have a chance to go after the big money today should say a silent thanks to Walter Hagen every time they stretch a check between their fingers. It was Walter who made professional golf what it is."

Hagen's prime coincided with what many called the golden age of American sports. Babe Ruth's Yankees rose to prominence in the 1920s, and Red Grange, the Galloping Ghost, lit up the gridiron for Illinois and then the fledgling NFL. Jack Dempsey attracted thousands to his prize fights, and the great thoroughbred Man O' War was the betting public's favorite. Hagen raised golf's status in America just when professional sports became a formidable and moneyed part of American life.

The Florida real estate boom in the 1920s aided Hagen's success and the professional tour that followed. Developers built golf courses to attract buyers and then paid professional golfers to play the courses to gain publicity in northeastern papers. These exhibition matches gradually grew into the tournaments that became the winter swing through the South and West.

Many of America's classic golf courses came to life during this period. Their names echo through modern golf history: Oakland Hills (1918), Pebble Beach (1919), Winged Foot (1923), Olympic Club (1924), Cypress Point (1928), Medinah #3 (1928), and Seminole (1929). Three great golf course architects practiced during the era, and their names are linked to landmark courses: Donald Ross, A. W. Tillinghast, and Alister Mackenzie.

Some say Scottish golf died along with Old Tom Morris in 1908. In addition, Wind maintained the game's leadership passed from Great Britain to the United States after Hagen won the British Open in 1922. He also wrote American golfers "completely altered the complexion of international golf" by the early 1920s. Harold Hilton, one of only three amateurs to win the British Open (1897), agreed and said at the time, "To put the matter in the very plainest of language, American players of the present day are better golfers than their British cousins."

—●—

Another group of professionals played golf in the 1920s, Al "Scarface" Capone and his band of gangsters.

Timothy Sullivan cowrote a *Sports Illustrated* article in November 1972 about his youthful days as a caddie at Burnham Woods, a nine-hole golf course near Chicago. According to Sullivan, the Capone gang had spread into the Chicago suburbs, building breweries and opening roadhouses that offered booze, broads, and betting in Burnham.

Al and the boys liked to relax over a round of golf. At lunch one day at Burnham Woods in 1926, Capone chatted up Tim's older sister, Babe, who was a waitress in the clubhouse restaurant. Capone, who later had a, uh, relationship with Babe, headed for the first tee.

"Kid, I need a good caddie," Capone said to Sullivan, one of several boys vying for the loop. "Your sister here tells me you're very good. Think you can carry all those clubs?" Sullivan, needing Depression era income, nodded yes, regardless of the size of Al's bag.

"Machine Gun" Jack McGurn partnered with Capone that day, playing against Fred "Killer" Burke and Capone's right hand man, Jake "Greasy Thumb" Guzik. The bet was $500 a hole. After nine holes and numerous side bets, Sullivan said $10,000 changed hands. Al tipped Timmy $20, a bill rarely seen in the Sullivan household in those days.

During the four years Sullivan caddied for Capone at Burnham Woods, he learned the nuances of the caddying art. He always carried a few extra balls in his pocket so when Capone lost one in the woods, Timmy could secretly drop another. "You're O.K., kid," Al told him. One of Al's guys, whom everyone called Banjo Eyes, once spotted Sullivan fishing for another ball and yelled, "The boy's cheating." In the ensuing argument, Banjo Eyes called Capone a liar, who bellowed back and told Eyes to get on his knees. Al pulled a gun from his golf bag to reinforce he issue. When Sullivan admitted cheating, Capone calmed down.

"Al once shot himself in the foot," Sullivan said. "I saw him do it. He was lifting his golf bag when the revolver inside went off." Capone's boys took him to the local hospital. The doctors, not knowing how Capone was wounded, sent him packing after a day, because they feared a rival gangster might come to the hospital to finish the job. The incident brought new meaning to the phrase "shooting a low round."

If Walter Hagen ushered in the beginning of professional golf, then Bobby Jones celebrated the end of amateur golf's reign as the game's dominant part. And it was a glorious finish at that.

In one of the greatest athletic achievements of the 20th century, Bobby Jones won all four of the era's major tournaments in one year, 1930: the match play British Amateur, the medal play British Open, the similarly formatted U.S. Amateur, and the U.S. Open. In the purple prose of the day, the press called Jones's feat the "impregnable quadrilateral." O. B. "Pop" Keeler, Jones's friend and biographer, dubbed it the "Grand Slam" after the similar clean sweep in bridge.

Books and magazine articles about Jones's Grand Slam ballyhooed the fact Jones played for the love of the game rather than for money. That's not exactly true. Bobby Jones bet on his golf games just like the rest of us but not a great deal of money, just a few bucks here and there. Jones understood and accepted betting between golfers was a customary part of the game.

Born in 1902, Jones started paying serious attention to golf at the age of six after his lawyer father bought a summerhouse on the grounds of the Atlanta Athletic Club's East Lake golf course. He formed his game on his own by observing the club's pro, Stewart Maiden, on the course and tagging along with his dad. He dropped all other sports at age nine. Two years later, he was betting ice cream sodas on matches with his buddy, Frank Meador. He won the inaugural 1916 Georgia Amateur at the age of 14 and then entered the U.S. Amateur for the first time that same year, losing in the third round. As a young teenager, Bobby Jones was a national golfing prodigy.

It wasn't until 1923, however, that Jones won his first national tournament, the U.S. Open. He described the intervening period as the "lean years." Ultimately, Jones won four U.S. Opens, five U.S. Amateurs, one British Amateur, and three British Opens.

The public did not take to Jones because he was an amateur slaying professional dragons, a context of pro dominance that didn't evolve until later; instead, they were drawn to him more by his style and personality. Wind wrote Jones was "the model American athlete come to life. Everybody adored him—not just dyed-in-the-wool golfers, but people who had never struck a golf ball or had the least desire to." Wind believed fans enjoyed Jones's true modesty, humor, and demeanor. "They liked the way he looked, this handsome, clean-cut young man, whose eyes gleamed with both a frank boyishness and a perceptiveness far beyond his years." Although his friends called him "Bob," the press wanted to keep him perpetually young and always referred to him as "Bobby." The newspapers also christened him "Emperor Jones" after a 1920 Eugene O'Neill play by that name.

Not all was honey and cream with Jones, though. He smoked incessantly, often drank bourbon with a deep thirst, and loved off-color jokes. He also had a terrible temper, one he struggled to control on the golf course as a teenager. Bobby often played practice rounds with Sarazen in the 1920s, a sometimes lively event because both threw their clubs when frustrated. In an attempt to limit their explosions, Jones and Sarazen made a wager that called for the thrower to pay the other $10 each time one of them let loose. In their first round under these conditions, Jones hit a particularly bad shot. Sarazen warned his caddie, "There goes his club and here comes my 10 bucks." But Jones didn't throw his club and never had to pay Sarazen.

Bobby's competitiveness, which outlived his club throwing, made him Hagen's favorite. A reporter asked Hagen whom he would choose as a partner to take on two other golfers with $10,000 of his own money at stake. Hagen answered, "That's easy—Bob Jones. He is the best competitor I've ever seen."

After graduating from Georgia Tech and earning another bachelor's

Amateur Bobby Jones (left) had more in common with pro-fessionals Gene Sarazen, Bobby Cruickshank, and Walter Hagen than a love of the game. They all played for "a little something" during matches, even when appearing together during a war bond exhibition during World War II. Dick Johns, Middle Atlantic Section, The PGA of America

degree from Harvard, Jones spent two winters in Sarasota, Florida, selling real estate for Adair Realty and Trust, a firm owned by a family friend. A salesman Jones was not, but it brought him in contact with Hagen, who was in St. Petersburg playing exhibition matches to publicize a real estate development there. By Jones's second Florida winter (1925–26), Hagen proposed a match with Jones, who had just won his second straight U.S. Amateur. The press called it the "Battle of the Century." The leading amateur and professional players of the decade would fight it out on the golf course. They agreed to play 36 holes at a course in the Whitfield Estates development Jones was publicizing. A week later, they would play another two rounds at Hagen's Florida home course, Pasadena Country Club. One of Hagen's friends Benjamin Namm put up the $5,000 stake. Since Jones wouldn't take any money, the bet became Hagen's appearance fee. All the gate receipts for the March 1926 match also went to Hagen.

Hagen thrashed Jones on Bobby's home course, 8-up, and then won the match 12 and 11 at Pasadena. After donating part of his winnings to charity and buying a set of diamond and platinum cufflinks for Jones—"I bought the kid a little something," he told Sarazen—Hagen netted $6,800. Some talked about a rematch, but the USGA warned Jones it would jeopardize his amateur standing.

It was an extraordinary win for the Haig, but Jones's fortunes didn't exactly sag afterward. Later in the year, Jones became the first golfer, amateur or professional, to win the Double Open, winning both the British and U.S. events in the same year. Hagen and Jones made a bet after their match about their performance during the upcoming 1926 season. They wagered a new hat. Jones had the better record, but neither spoke of the payoff.

Jones showed both his spirit and sense of humor in another exhibition against Hagen about the same time. Following the lead of Andra Kirkaldy's caddie friends, Jock and Hutchie, Bobby pulled Walter's string when Hagen bunkered his ball. Jones had his caddie toss a crumpled $20 bill into the sand when Walter wasn't looking. As Hagen walked into the bunker, he picked up the money as if it had his name on it. Lost hole!

Jones tuned up for his Grand Slam season by playing in two tournaments in the southeastern United States. He twice broke the course record in the first event, although he eventually lost, and then won the second by 13 strokes. A pro named Bobby Cruickshank was astonished with Jones's play in those tournaments. He said to Pop Keeler, "Bob is just too good. They'll never stop him this year." Cruickshank was so impressed he bet $1,200 with 50-1 odds that Jones would win all four majors in 1930. Another version of this story has Cruickshank sending $500 to Great Britain for his father-in-law to bet on Jones with 120-1 odds. Either way, he saw a helluva payday.

At a tournament in England just before the slam's first leg, Jones shot a disappointing 75 in the first of two scheduled rounds. Something must have inspired Jones during lunch with his pairing partner, Dale Bourne, because Bobby bet Bourne £1 he could break par in the afternoon. Jones shot a course record 68 and won the tournament by one stroke. He and Bourne, the 1926 English Amateur winner, had a similar bet during a practice round before the last stop on the Grand Slam tour, the U.S. Amateur at Merion.

Jones's friends and admirers in Atlanta were just as confident as Cruickshank was of Bobby's chances at winning all four majors. The Associated Press reported members of the Lloyd's of London insurance consortium gave 50-1 odds to several Atlantans who sent $2,500 to London. There was no confirmation of the $125,000 payout.

Jones retired from competitive golf after winning the slam. He continued to play informal rounds with friends and carried on his practice of a friendly wager during his games. Harold Saunders played with Jones regularly at East Lake, and their usual bet was $1 a round. "He always played hard," Saunders said of their matches, "he was a competitor." Tommy Barnes, another old-timer at East Lake, said he and Jones played a $1 Nassau with a $4 limit. "You'd think he was playing for the U.S. Open," recalled Barnes. Golf writer John Derr played a four-ball match with Jones during World War II, and Derr and his partner, a pro named Johnny Bulla, took $4 each off of Jones and his partner. "I wish I had saved those four dollar bills Jones paid me that day," Derr said. "I should have had them framed, but I was still in the service and they amounted to folding money then."

During two practice rounds before the first Masters tournament in 1934, Jones set the pace for friendly wagers among the thousands of golfers who would play in Masters since then. Jones and Ed Dudley, the Augusta National's first pro, played a $1 Nassau with Paul Runyan and Horton Smith. "It was a great thrill," Runyan said after losing both times.

Jones didn't bet much. But that the greatest amateur player in the game's history always wanted to make "things interesting" again confirms that betting between golfers is part of the game.

—●—

Scottish women played golf regularly on the links through much of the game's history. In England and the rest of Great Britain, however, women's participation in the sport grew slowly. Social mores in the 19th century limited women's involvement in athletics, regardless of the game. Men enjoyed the boost Victorian ideals had on outdoor activity, including golf, but women had to wait a bit longer.

Issette Pearson and other pioneer women golfers formed the Ladies Golf Union in 1893, and they held their first British Ladies Amateur Championship that same year. Lady Margaret Scott won the first three tournaments.

Reflecting the social status of young, unmarried women, her father, Lord Eldon, gave her acceptance speech after her third victory in 1895. He also announced she would not play in any more championships, declaring three titles were quite enough for a young lady.

Except for brief references to the affinity of Mary Queen of Scots for betting, little information is available about ladies wagering on golf in Great Britain before the 20th century. One known anecdote, however, is about men betting on the women. In an auction pool before the 1895 ladies' championship, Lady Scott, the prohibitive favorite, sold for £30. Enid Wilson described the auction in *A History of Golf in Britain*, but she didn't say whether the purchaser was male or female. Presumably, it was a man, based on women's general absence from the sporting life in 1895.

Women did catch the wave of golf's growing popularity at the turn of the 20th century, with clear evidence coming from a challenge match that

A 1920 British cigarette advertisement illustrated golf's comfortable acceptance of a friendly wager, even in mixed company. TIME & LIFE PICTURES

Old Tom Morris played in 1899 against Rhona Adair. An Irish lass from Portrush, the red-headed Adair beat the aging Morris 1-up over 36 holes at St Andrews. She also won the British Ladies in 1900 and 1903.

Cecil Leitch played a more widely reported challenge match in 1910 against a noted British male amateur, Harold Hilton. Leitch, whose given name was Cecilia, was only 19 years old at the time, but she later went on to win four British Ladies' Amateurs. She proposed the match to gain publicity for women's golf, and the *Ladies' Field* magazine sponsored the event.

"For weeks before, the match was widely discussed, opinions greatly differing as to the probable result," she wrote later. "Perhaps I was given some confidence by the wise and encouraging advice of that wonderful judge of form, James Braid, who during a friendly round at Walton Heath told me just to play my own game and I would come through."

Golf writers of the time said Leitch was the first women to "hit" the ball, rather than "sweep" the club head through the ball. Hitting down on the ball with her irons enabled her to generate more height and control. She and other women in the 1920s enjoyed playing in much less restricting clothes than their predecessors did 15 years earlier. Those long dresses over voluminous petticoats, and their blouses' leg-of-mutton sleeves were certainly fashionable, but they constricted women to the point that a sweeping swing was all they could muster.

Leitch and Hilton played 36 holes at Walton Heath in London and another two rounds at Sunningdale. Hilton, who had earlier won both the British Amateur and Open, gave Cecil a half-one handicap—nine strokes per round—and they played from the same tees. A boisterous gallery of 3,000 crowded the course, and many bet heavily on the match. Under blue skies at Walton Heath, Hilton won the first day, 1-up. In a dreadful rain at Sunningdale two days later, Leitch drew even and eventually won the match 2 and 1.

In the United States, the *Ladies Home Journal* urged American women in 1894 to play golf, especially those "in middle life." Shinnecock opened a 12-hole separate course for women in 1892, and in Morristown, New Jersey, several women built a ladies-only course, Morris County Golf Club. The USGA held its first Women's Amateur Championship in 1895 at Meadow Brook; four of the 11 entrants were from the Morristown club. Mrs. Charles S. Brown (née Lucy Barnes) won, shooting 132 over 18 holes.

From 1910 through the 1920s, several attractive and talented young women golfers caught the country's attention as well as many a young man's eye. The first was Alexa Stirling, a childhood friend of Bobby Jones. The two teenagers played exhibitions during World War I to raise money for the Red Cross, collecting $150,000 in 1917 alone. Alexa also won three U.S. Women's Amateur Championships and two Canadian.

Glenna Collet won six U.S. Women's Amateurs, starting in 1922, and many considered her to be the Bobby Jones of women's golf in America. But it was a contemporary of Collet's, Edith Cummings, who captured the most press attention. Cummings, who beat Stirling for the 1923 Amateur, was strikingly beautiful and prompted one reporter to declare, "No handsomer girl ever graced an athletic contest." She also made an impact on F. Scott Fitzgerald, who modeled the female character Jordan Baker in his 1925 book *The Great Gatsby* after Cummings.

Just as in Britain, little information is available about the betting habits of this period's women golfers. Two nuggets, however, give us a tiny insight into women's wagering.

The first showed up in the society column of the *New York Times* in 1896, a few days before the second U.S. Women's Amateur at Morris. The paper named the leading contenders and what clubs they represented—Newport, Baltusrol, Westchester, Morristown, and others—as well as speculated on the outcome.

> The men golf players are almost as much interested, if possible, in this tournament as the women themselves, and there will be delegations present of both men and women at Morristown from the clubs that are represented there, to cheer on the individual players. Betting has already begun in the New York clubs on the result of this tournament, and it is safe to say that the women themselves who are to play, or who are interested in the game, are laying some quiet wagers among themselves.

In 1921, Stirling met Leitch in the semifinals of the Canadian Amateur, with Leitch winning 2 and 1. The press reported they played the bye hole, 18, for a bet, and Stirling won. No one mentioned the nature of the wager.

—•—

CHIPS AND PITCHES

Boo! The Hoylake links, across the Mersey River from Liverpool, was the site of a 1914 bet that seemed like a lock to the mark. A man playing to a 6-handicap challenged a scratch player, proposing that instead of strokes, he be allowed to shout Boo! three times during the match. The better golfer thought his considerable powers of concentration could withstand such verbal taunting, so he accepted to the tune of a couple hundred pounds. On 13, the 6 shouted his first Boo! on the scratch's downswing. Having grown taut waiting for the first one, the shout had its desired effect. Now knowing two more were coming, the scratch lost his composure and stumbled his way to a loss.

Club names. Baltusrol Golf Club in Springfield, New Jersey, has hosted 15 USGA national tournaments since it opened in 1895. The club also welcomed the 2005 PGA Championship. Members named the club after a man named Baltus Roll, who once owned the golf course land. Winged Foot Golf Club takes its name from the New York Athletic Club's logo—the winged foot of Mercury, the Roman god of merchants and travelers. Although there is no formal connection between the two clubs, many of the first 200 members of Winged Foot also belonged to NYAC.

In their cups. First held in 1927, the Ryder Cup competition matched teams of professionals from the United States and Great Britain. The Brits only won two of the biennial events over the next 46 years, so they invited players from Ireland to join in 1973 and then from all of Europe in 1979. The amateur equivalent is the Walker Cup Match, first contested in 1922 at the National Golf Links between a U.S. team, which included Jones and Ouimet, and players from Great Britain and Ireland. The American side won 8-4. The trophy is named for George Herbert Walker, a former president of the USGA and namesake of former U.S. president George H. W. Bush.

Standardized golf balls. In 1920, the R&A and the USGA agreed all golf balls should be 1.62 inches in diameter and 1.62 ounces in weight. The USGA strayed from that standard in 1932, mandating a larger and lighter ball of 1.68 inches and 1.55 ounces. The "Balloon Ball" only lasted a year, and the USGA reverted to the 1.62-ounce weight but kept the 1.68-inch size. The R&A sanctioned the smaller ball until 1990, when it adopted the American standard.

Steel shafts. Jones won all his tournaments with hickory-shafted clubs. The Chicago-based Western Golf Association permitted steel shafts in 1922, and the USGA approved them in 1924. The R&A would not allow play with steel shafts until 1929. The new shafts resisted much of the twisting common to hickory, allowing golfers to generate greater club head speed and yet still bring the club face back square to the ball. Billy Burke was the first player to win the U.S. Open with steel shafts in 1931. Johnny Fischer was the last one to win a national tournament, the 1936 U.S. Amateur, with hickory shafts.

Tees. African-American dentist George F. Grant patented the first wooden tee in 1899, but he didn't market the idea. Another black dentist, William Lowell, invented the first successful all-wooden, cone-shaped tee in 1922. He painted them red and formed a company, Reddy Tee, to market them. He also hired Walter Hagen and Joe Kirkwood to use them on one of their exhibition tours.

4.

Titanic Thompson Stays Afloat:

Tough Times, Tough Bets, 1930–38

"A MAN'S TRUE COLORS WILL SURFACE QUICKER in a $5 Nassau than in any other form of peacetime diversion that I can name." When Grantland Rice penned this assessment of money golf, he was one of the preeminent sportswriters of the 20th century, and his prose remains the standard of the time. In addition to describing Notre Dame's Four Horsemen and producing memorable lines as "It's not whether you win or lose, it's how you play the game," Rice wrote about golf hustlers, pricey Calcutta auctions, and high-stakes matches. A fixture in golf during the 1930s, he understood the place betting plays in golf, especially during the Great Depression and the early years of the PGA Tour. (Initially, the PGA did not call its yearly collection of tournaments the "tour," nor did it have a separate division within the association for touring players until 1968. That situation changed again in 1974, when touring players split from the PGA and formed a completely separate organization, the PGA Tour. While that name is not technically accurate before 1974, it is used throughout the book for simplicity.)

The abdication of Emperor Jones left American golf without a star for some years. Other skilled golfers graced the links, but none had Jones's good looks and appeal, which shone so brightly in the wire photos, newsreels, and ticker-tape parades. Golf fans would have to wait until Arnold Palmer charged across their flickering, black-and-white television screens for an engaging player who could seemingly win at will.

"Golf without Jones would be France without Paris," suggested Herbert Warren Wind. He said Bobby's retirement hurt championship golf, leaving tournaments unpredictable and "colorless." Jones's 1930 Grand Slam, and his subsequent immediate withdrawal from golf's spotlight, was an important point in the sport's history by itself, but it also coincided with a larger event, the Great Depression. The two even might have been connected.

Until Jones's retirement, many saw golf as a sport for gentlemen and their ladies. Amateur golfers, playing only for the fun and challenge of the sport, save for the ever-present friendly wager, occupied the upper levels of golf's hierarchy. In both the United States and Great Britain, golf professionals were treated like tradesmen, such as cobblers and blacksmiths. Both the British and U.S. national amateur tournaments equaled the respective Opens in appeal and skill level. Announcers on the first tee referred to amateurs as "Mister" but did not allow the pros any title. After Jones retreated from formal competition, however, the national amateur tournaments lost their status. Professional golf soon overshadowed the amateur game. Only later, when young Tiger Woods won six straight national amateur titles—three junior and three adult—did America pay much attention to amateur golf. Some still view golf as a sport for the moneyed because of high equipment costs and green fees, but since Jones's time, golf's glitterati have been the pros.

Within weeks after he won the Grand Slam, Jones signed a deal with Warner Brothers to make 12 golf "shorts." They were 10-minute films that, with cartoons, usually preceded the main movie feature in theaters. Jones earned $120,000 up front plus 50 percent of the net receipts. Estimates at the time suggested Jones earned between $250,000 and $500,000. He announced his retirement on November 17, forsaking his amateur status, because the USGA certainly would have considered Jones a professional for accepting Hollywood's money.

Each film included movie stars who volunteered to act without pay in order to get a game with Jones. The films' thin plots showcased the swing instruction and advice Bobby gave to the rest of the cast. The 10th film *Trouble Shots* reflected both the custom of the day and Jones's comfort with golf wagers. Comedian Joe E. Brown bet actor Edward G. Robinson that Brown could beat Jones under the right conditions. The script has Jones and Brown play each other's drive, a betting game now called "Bobby Jones" (see chapter 9 for the details).

Jones and his biographers maintained he quit the sport because of the physical and mental stress of playing championship golf. Obviously, both his amateur status and his retirement at the peak of his game burnished

Jones's reputation and legend, but millions of people were out of work in 1930 and times were tough. It was expensive to play golf as an amateur. George Von Elm, who beat Jones to win the U.S. Amateur in 1926, turned pro in 1930 a few weeks before Jones retired. Von Elm's expenses ran $10,000 a year, or more than $116,000 today.

No one has suggested Jones retired for the money, but the Great Depression changed golf as much as every other aspect of life in both America and the rest of the world. The Depression forced many golf courses to close, undercut equipment sales, and slowed the professional tour's development. "Brother, can you spare a dime?" was a question heard on the golf course too.

Two legendary money golfers—Dutch Harrison and Sam Snead—believed the modern art of golf hustling was a product of the Great Depression. "After the stock market crash in 1929, half of the 6,000 golf courses went broke," said Harrison, an 18-time PGA Tour winner and member of the PGA Golf Hall of Fame. "Who'd want to become a golf pro? It was the day of the hustlers hustling the hustlers, and anyone else."

Snead agreed: "The total [annual] PGA purse wasn't much over a $100,000, leaving the starving pros no way out but to drive a jalopy or even hitchhike from club to club, making money matches with the members. The danger was that you had to handicap yourself too many strokes. A good amateur could jump up and win your last dime. So the pros took to playing under assumed names."

For the hustle to work, both sides of the wager must think they have the upper hand. The hustler is sure of it, but his opponent is convinced the odds or the proposition favors himself, largely because of some misrepresentation by the hustler. "Who in the world could play golf standing on one leg? I'll take some of that!" Also, a powerful human tendency—an urge to get in on a good deal, maybe even one that is slightly illegal—helps the hustler as he sets up the "con," or confidence game. A stock market tip, inside dope from the race track, and a sure thing at the golf course all play to the larcenous corner of every man's soul.

Damon Runyon captured the feel of hustlers, card sharks, and other celebrants of the sporting life in New York. He wrote "The Idyll of Miss Sarah Brown," a short story, that later became the basis for the 1950 Broadway play *Guys and Dolls*. In both the story and the play, Runyon introduced the character Sky Masterson, who gained his nickname from betting as high as the sky, by writing about the advice Sky's father game him as a youngster.

"Son," the old guy says, "no matter how far you travel, or how smart you get, always remember this: Some day, somewhere," he says, "a guy is going to come to you and show you a nice brand-new deck of cards on which the seal is never broken, and this guy is going to offer to bet you that the jack of spades will jump out of this deck and squirt cider in your ear. But son," the old guy says, "do not bet him, for as sure as you do you will get an ear full of cider."

Runyon knew the man holding the cards had an edge. He modeled Sky Masterson on a real-life character who also always had an advantage, Titanic Thompson.

—●—

"Of all the hustlers that lived in my time, I was the best. I was smart, which is better than lucky in some ways, and I was cool and steady and a fine athlete, so I usually had the edge in most games." Thompson claimed his hustling supremacy in a 1962 *Sports Illustrated* article cowritten with Bud Shrake. Stories of Thompson's exploits abound in the world of golf, with every noted golfer who played between the 1920s and 1960s seeming to have a Titanic anecdote. Some tales get taller with each telling, but plenty of true stories remain.

Harrison recalled his first contact with Thompson, a meeting in 1928, when Harrison was a 19-year-old assistant pro at the Willow Beach Golf Club south of Little Rock. "At dinner, Mr. Ti explained that he was arrangin' a golf match that would pit him an' me against the top-rankin' professional golfers in Arkansas, Paul Runyan and Julius Ackerbloom." Thompson had set up a $4,000 bet on the match, promising a cut to Harrison. "If we won, I would receive $400. 'Course I knew he had a shadowy reputation—an' he sure had the sharpest, most penetratin' eyes I've ever seen. The eyes just bored a hole right through ya."

Just before the game, Thompson heard Harrison might have been bought off and was going to throw the match in favor of Runyan and Ackerbloom. "It really shook me when Mr. Ti backed me up against a car in the parkin' lot beforehand and poked a .45 revolver in my belly," Harrison recalled. "He gave me that penetratin' eye." Dutch assured Thompson no one had gotten to him, so Titanic went to the first tee and inveigled a stroke and a half from their opponents by offering to play left handed. Ackerbloom sank a 60-foot putt on 18 to halve the match, but neither team wanted to go to extra holes, so they called it a draw.

The game was typical of Thompson's hustling on the golf course. He recruited an unknown yet skilled player, added to that edge by concealing his natural left-handed dexterity, and then intimidated young Dutch into remaining "honest." Intelligence, nerves, self-assurance, and golfing prowess—Thompson had the whole hustler's package.

Born Alvin Clarence Thomas in Rogers, Arkansas, in 1892, "Titanic" grew up in a three-room log house watching his relatives play cards, checkers, and dominoes. His gambler father left the family when Alvin was four months old. With only a few years of school, the youngster left home at age 16, promising his mother he would never smoke or drink.

Along the road Thomas learned the finer points of gambling on dice and pool. Blessed with a keen eye and a steady hand, he also won money in turkey shoots and target matches. Parlaying that skill into a job, Thomas signed on with a medicine show run by one Capt. Adam Beaugardus. While gaining an education as a hustler during his travels, Thomas was also searching for his father. When he was 18 years old, Thomas found him in a card game in Oil City, Louisiana.

"I saw several men playing stud poker," Thomas recalled. "One of the men was tall and slim like me and had long, slender fingers that riffled the cards gracefully and laid them out neatly across the table just the way my six uncles did. He had all the same motions." Thomas not only found his father but also joined the game and took $3,600 off his old man.

By 1912, Thomas was shooting pool in Joplin, Missouri, a few months after the sinking of the Titanic. After winning $500 off a man named Snow Clark, Thomas offered double or nothing that he could jump across the pool table without touching it. After placing a mattress on one side, Thomas got a running head start and then dived headfirst over the table. When others asked about this nimble hustler's name, Clark said, "Beats me, but it ought to be Titanic, the way he's been sinking everybody around here." Shortly thereafter, he registered at a hotel as "Titanic Thompson," because he like the way the name sounded.

Titanic was a nomad most of his life, moving from one game to the next. He was married five times, in each instance to a woman younger than 20 years of age and one of whom was 16 years old when she married Ti. He put one child up for adoption, but he stayed in touch with another, Tommy, as well as Ty Wayne, his son by his last wife, Jeannette. Ti was tall, dressed well, enjoyed expensive cars, and frequently carried a pistol that he used with conviction. He never did smoke or drink.

In the 1920s he stopped long enough in San Francisco to learn the game of golf. In town with Nick "the Greek" Dandolos to play poker for several months—Titanic won $960,000—he started taking lessons in secret. "I kept out of the sun so I wouldn't get a tan because I didn't want anyone to know I was a great natural-born golfer until it was worth something to me." Within a year, Titanic won $56,000 on the first full round of golf he played. He claimed he became a scratch player, either left- or right-handed.

He was indeed good. In 1933, bettors arranged a $3,000 match between Titanic and golfing great Byron Nelson at Ridglea Country Club in Fort Worth. The oddsmakers gave Thompson three strokes, an advantage Nelson felt was unfair. Young Byron shot a 69 to Titanic's 71, so with his strokes Thompson won the match. Regardless, Ed Dudley, the first head pro at Augusta National, said Titanic was "one stroke better than anybody else in the whole goddamn world."

Titanic spurned the PGA Tour, not wanting to take a cut in pay. He often made in a week's hustling what the tour's leading money winner made in a year. "I didn't care about the championships," he said. "I wanted the cash."

Titanic generally did not play singles matches, as he had against Nelson; instead, he arranged four-ball games with Dutch Harrison or another young gun. He enlisted Herman Keiser, who later won the 1946 Masters, as one of his partners. Arriving at a local course, Titanic sought his usual edge by offering to pick a caddie to play as his partner. The marks couldn't resist. With an innocent-looking Keiser standing in the caddie pen, Titanic "selected" him and then went off to take everyone's money.

Pioneering African-American player Lee Elder caddied for Titanic, frequently serving as the *ringer*, a term to describe a golfer whose skills are unknown to an opponent. Titanic boasted he and his caddie could beat a club's two best players, knowing Elder gave him the edge in the match. Sometimes Elder wore chauffeur's clothes to reinforce the con. "Heck, I'll take my chauffeur as a partner and play anybody at this club," Titanic would say. In other instances, Elder prowled the caddie shack, setting up games for Thompson through the caddies. "Ti was a great friend," said Elder. "He was the first white golfer who ever treated me with respect and dignity. I will never forget him."

Thompson also sought an edge in a match through shrewd betting and impeccable timing of those bets. "See, when it's the other man's turn to shoot, especially on or around the greens, then I push him into a big bet," he said. "Make it so damn high that his hair stands on end." Sam Snead said Titanic also confused his opponents by adding side bets at a dizzying pace. "Every time he lifts his club, your man is involved with figures," Thompson told Snead. "The thing gets more complicated than a math equation, until his confusion licks him down the line."

One classic Titanic story epitomizes his understanding of people and how golf affects them. In 1952, he arranged a game at $1,000 a hole with a big, long-hitting man, giving him three drives off every tee; the pigeon could pick the best. Thinking he had a lock, the hefty guy swung away, winning the first seven holes. Titanic won the last 11 and $4,000. "See, a big hitter, he's got maybe 20 swings in his system," Thompson said. "After that his game is just a prayer and a stagger. I 'spect that big fella learned hisself a good lesson out there today. If he hadn't been so greedy, he'd have figured out what he was lettin' himself in for before we started playing."

Despite his sterling play on the course, Titanic's cleverly crafted proposition bets are recalled more often than his golf matches. None was a spur-of-the-moment wager, although he made it seem as such; instead, each was the culmination of practice and careful preparation. Whether it was bouncing a golf ball into a water glass (he practiced) or guessing a hatcheck girl's weight (he had asked her the previous day), one had to admire his ingenuity.

Many of his props involved throwing something. Although he was an excellent athlete, he relied more on the edge than just a great arm. He bet Al Capone $500 he could throw an orange over a building, and he won but only after deftly trading the orange for a smaller, heavier lemon. In another story he bet he could throw an unshelled peanut from the stands behind home plate at Yankee Stadium to second base. The mark didn't know Ti had opened the shell, replaced the nut with lead shot, and glued it back together, making it heavy enough to throw it that distance. (Other variations of this trick feature pecans and walnuts.) Yet another bet had him throwing a pumpkin over a building. Once the wager was made, Ti went to a vegetable vendor he had seen the day before who sold all sizes of pumpkins. He bought a softball-sized gourd and won the easy money.

In Joplin, he noticed workmen installing a sign that read "Joplin, 20 miles." He dug it up that night and moved it five miles closer to town. Later, he bet his fellow gamblers Hickory McCullough and Beanie Benson the sign's mileage was wrong.

Another distance con was a horseshoe match he had with world horseshoe pitching champion Frank Jackson. Ti built a 41-foot horseshoe court— one foot longer than regulation—practiced hard, and then challenged Jackson to a $10,000 winner-take-all game. "Jackson couldn't figure out why his throws were falling short . . . I think I could have beaten him anyhow, but why take the chance?"

Thompson sometimes purposely lost a golf match to set up an opponent for a prop for the real money. He would offer the match's "winner" double or nothing that he could hit a silver dollar with his pistol eight out of eight times from 20 feet. Thompson, a four-time Arizona State champion trapshooter and former sideshow sharpshooter, collected those bets regularly.

"I won $1,000 by betting I could drive a ball 500 yards, which I did by knocking it onto a frozen lake outside Chicago," Thompson claimed in 1962. "The ball went about a mile." Some said a young Franklin Roosevelt won a similar wager from a school classmate before polio changed his life.

In 1939, Thompson bet Texan Johnny Moss that Moss couldn't break 46 using only a 4-iron at the nine-hole Meadowbrook golf course in Lubbock, Texas. He goaded Moss, whose poker and golf skills were almost equal to Thompson's, into an $8,300 bet, which Titanic knew to be Moss's entire roll at the time. Hundreds of spectators, including many of their fellow hustlers, crowded around Moss as he teed off.

"On the first hole, a 420-yard hole," Moss recalled, "I knocked that ball a whack and I was alayin' about three feet from the hole in three shots. A cinch. I stroked the ball and that putt rolled straight for the hole and then just before droppin' in like it should've, it bent off." Moss went to the second hole thinking his ball had hit a pebble in front of the hole. When the same thing happened on number two, Moss suspected foul play, especially since he had paid the greenkeeper $100 to leave the cups in the same location as they had during his practice rounds.

"Then it dawned on me. Couldn't be but one thing. Someone had crept out there early and raised them cups, raised them just an eighth of an inch or so, so's the ball would kick away." Moss sent his caddie on to the third green to stomp the cup liner back down, but someone raised the cup liner on number four. This to-and-fro continued to five, when Thompson admitted to being behind the hustle. "Ti just grinned, the way he does," said Moss, "and I told him if he calls off his man I'd call off mine. We agreed to that and when I'd done with them nine holes, I'd shot a 41 and took all the bets."

Thompson and a gambling acquaintance, Hubert Cokes, set up some marks in Oklahoma City by teaching an illiterate pool hall regular named Goody how to spell *rhinoceros* and *Mississippi*. Ti and Cokes then staged a mock argument about Goody's intelligence, setting up the bet that the man could spell any word. "Somebody suggested Goody spell *restaurant,* but we ruled that out because it was on the wall," recalled Titanic. "*Cacciatore* was another possibility, but we decided against it because Goody ate Italian food a lot." Thompson and Cokes finally steered the crowd to *rhinoceros*, with Cokes asking Goody to spell the word.

"Sure, Hubie. M-i-s-s-i-s-s-i-p-p-i. How's that?"

While Thompson occupies a special place in golf's kingdom, he was no saint. He admitted killing five men, all allegedly trying either to rob or to kill him. Many suspect he killed a sixth, Arnold Rothstein, a man accused of fixing the 1919 World Series and disgracing baseball with the Black Sox scandal. In 1928 Titanic found himself in a card game with Rothstein in New York. Thompson and several others, including Nathan Raymond and George McManus, won about $475,000 from Rothstein. Arnold claimed the men cheated him and refused to pay. He was shot to death a few weeks later, and the police hauled in Thompson, Raymond, and others for questioning. "I know plenty of people thought it was me who killed Rothstein," explained the always-confident Thompson. "I ask you why would I have killed a guy who owed me a quarter of a million dollars?"

Thompson died in a Texas nursing home in 1974. Legend has it he was hustling his fellow patients out of their Social Security checks until the end. "His whole life, Titanic got up every morning looking for action," his son Tommy recalled. "The money was just the way of keeping score. He lived for that action until the day he died."

—•—

The Great Depression did not turn every professional player into a hustler, but the severe economic downturn almost halted many sports activities. Gene Sarazen recalled that every pro "approached the dwindling number of jack-pot tournaments in a very serious frame of mind, for there was no knowing whose home club would next fold up." Walter Hagen and Sarazen were about the only pros not dependent on a club or off-season job to feed their families during the early 1930s.

The tournament purses that were too small to sustain the pro ranks before the Depression became even skimpier soon after the 1929 crash. The Los Angeles Open, one of Sarazen's jackpots, reduced its once sumptuous purse of $10,000 to $7,500 and then again to $5,000, a sum available only when actor Richard Arlen pledged his own funds in 1932. The Miami Open offered but $400 to the winner, and organizers had to use player's entry fees and corporate donations to help finance the meager purse. With prize money falling faster than the stock market, many tournaments simply folded. To some of the older pros, the dire situation was exacerbated by Prohibition, a social experiment in nationwide behavior control that lasted from 1919 to 1933. What's a poor man do when he can't get a wee nip to ease his pain?

Many pros searched for ways to supplement their income from a club job or infrequent tournaments. "Wild Bill" Mehlhorn, who won 20 PGA tournaments during his career, sold subscriptions to *Golf Illustrated* magazine. He also looked for money matches. "One fella, a rich guy from New York, wanted to back me on the golf course," Mehlhorn said. "We'd be partners, you see, and he'd put the money up. Wanted to play for $10,000 against anyone who'd have us." Mehlhorn knew prize money wasn't going to help him. "I quit playing tournaments in the 1930s because there wasn't any money in it."

Jackie Burke, Jr., an icon in professional golf, recalled how he made it through those lean years: "I really didn't play much amateur golf when I was a kid, I just gambled a lot. That was the only way to make money in the Depression. I never played a round of golf that I wasn't gambling. The early professionals, that's all they were was gamblers. That's the way they were brought up, in the caddie yards." Burke won the Masters and a PGA Championship during his career, and he founded Houston's legendary Champions Golf Club with Jimmy Demaret. The USGA gave Burke its 2004 Bobby Jones Award for distinguished sportsmanship, demonstrating golfers who bet on the game are considered good guys.

Chandler Harper remembers the time. "You could finish third and win $100," said Chandler, who had eight tour titles, including the 1950 PGA

Championship. "What you did was gamble. On those early days on the tour, I guess we all gambled."

Harper, a Virginian nicknamed "Old Bones" for his thin frame, recalled one of his money games in the 1930s. Paired with Lloyd Mangrum and Joe Ezar during the Sacramento tour stop, Harper said they were playing the final two rounds on the last day. None of them had a chance to finish very high, plus the weather was awful—rain and sleet. "So Ezar says, 'Let's play $2 cuts.' Skins. He called them cuts." Because Ezar owed Harper money from a bet five years earlier, Harper insisted they play whip-out, that is, paying off after each hole. After shooting 68-68, Harper won most of the money. "Making him pay after each hole, I end up with a pocket full of $1 bills that are wet as hell." Sadly, Harper's final score only earned him a three-way tie for last in the tournament.

Ezar, more known for his trick shot routine than winning tour events, looked for extra money everywhere. He gambled often, and legend has it he never stayed higher than a hotel's second floor so he could make an easy getaway out the window. While performing his show after the second round of the 1936 Italian Open, Ezar made a bet with a wealthy Italian who was in the gallery watching Ezar. Joe wagered he could break the course record, 67, set that day by Henry Cotton. The Italian offered 5,000 lire if Joe shot a 66 and double that for a 65. When Ezar asked how much for a 64, the man said, "40,000 lire" (roughly $2,500 at the time).

"That's very generous of you," Ezar said. "Now, I'll tell you what I will do. I will write down the score I will make on each of the 18 holes for my 64."

After a rowdy night of partying, a shaky Ezar nevertheless posted a 64, matching his hole-by-hole predictions except on 10 and 11. Cotton won the tournament, and Ezar finished second.

Tommy Armour figured in another bet with the gallery. In the 1930 U.S. Open, Ralph Guldahl had a 6-foot putt to tie Johnny Goodman for the title. When Guldahl missed it, Armour, who was watching, sympathized with the player. The right-to-left break coupled with a tricky grain and the pressure of the moment made it a very difficult putt. Later, a member of the gallery called Guldahl "gutless" for missing it, and that insult irritated Armour, who figured the man had never felt the strain of championship golf.

Armour bet the man $375 the onlooker couldn't make the putt either. The Silver Scot talked so relentlessly about how pressure ruins everyone's putting that by the time the gentleman lined up Guldahl's putt, his jittery stab of a stroke let him down also.

A transplanted Scot, Armour was wounded in World War I and lost an eye. When not playing tournaments or later giving lessons at Winged Foot, Armour enjoyed friendly matches, "especially if the stakes were attractive." He handicapped the games fairly, but when asked about his favorite opponents, he answered, "Rich guys with fast backswings."

Pros of the period also bet during practice rounds, just as they do today. Paul Runyan, a 28-time tour winner, told a story about a proposition bet that crops up repeatedly in golf history. During a tournament in Glens Falls, New York, Leonard Dodson and journeyman pro Johnny O'Connor agreed to a $500 Nassau, but Dodson had to play on one leg. "If Leonard touches the ground with the other foot before the club hits the ball, he gets a two-stroke penalty," Runyan recalled. "Well, he lost the first three holes, then beat O'Connor all four ways. He shot 69, starting par, bogey, bogey. Next day in the tournament he's standing there on two feet and takes 77."

Bookies followed the PGA Tour from its beginning to the late 1960s. It was easy for players to supplement their income by betting on themselves or others. The bookmakers also helped people in the gallery who wanted to put some money on their favorite player.

Gene Sarazen had a story about playing in the Miami-Biltmore International Four-Ball with partner Leo Diegel, who won two PGA Championships during his World Golf Hall of Fame career. Knowing they were a better team than the bookie's 9-1 odds suggested, the two players eagerly put $100 a piece on themselves. Their confidence seemed well founded when they found themselves 2-up with four to play in the finals against Bobby Cruickshank and Johnny Farrell. "While Leo and I were thinking about how we would spend our $900, Bobby and Johnny took two of the next three holes and squared the match with the long home hole coming up." Farrell birdied 18, and Diegel's 3-footer for a halve (tie) lipped out. Playing for your own money adds extra pressure to tournament golf.

Even after winning the 1932 British Open, Sarazen didn't like his chances in that summer's U.S. Open held at Fresh Meadow Country Club in Great Neck, New York. Sarazen had been the head pro there between 1925 and 1931 and knew the course well, but his game was off. Two listless rounds of 74 and 76 left him back in the pack at the tournament's midpoint. "I was amazed to learn from Jack Doyle, the betting commissioner, that even when I stood seven strokes off the pace after the first eight holes of the third round," Sarazen recalled, "my old club members at Fresh Meadow and other old friends were still placing bets that I would win, without bothering to inquire what the odds were." Buoyed by the support, Sarazen's back nine 32 that day brought him back in contention and, ultimately, the championship trophy.

Sarazen's calling Doyle "the commissioner" is evidence of the bookmaker's status on the PGA scene during the 1930s. But as Sarazen and Diegel demonstrated in Miami, the bookmaker's odds often rankled some golfers' pride. Doyle listed Paul Runyan at even money before Runyan's first-round match with the lesser-known Levi Lynch in the 1938 PGA Championship. Those odds irritated Runyan. After beating Lynch, Runyan saw that he was a 3-1 underdog the next day against Tony Manero. Runyan kept winning and getting more peeved at Doyle along the way. He beat Ray Mangrum, despite 2.5-1 odds against him, and then, as a 3-1 underdog, ousted Henry Picard. Runyan was pleased that in the finals, he beat Snead, whom Doyle listed as a 10-1 favorite.

Tony Manero liked his chances going into the 1936 U.S. Open and felt slighted when Doyle offered 200-1 odds for Manero to win, 100-1 for second, and 50-1 for third. Paul Runyan remembered the incident: "Tony said that was an insult, and he was going to bet $20 across the board on himself, and he did. That only changed the odds to a 100-1, 50-1, and 25-1, and he said that was still an insult, so he bet another $20 across the board."

Manero surprised everyone but himself when he beat Harry "Lighthorse Harry" Cooper, so named by Damon Runyon for his fast play, by two strokes to win the Open. His first-place check was $1,000, but Runyan said Tony took $17,000 from Doyle.

Organized golf has never seen a gambling scandal, but seamy elements of society often offered the opportunity. Someone sold hundreds of thousands of lottery tickets during Bobby Jones's run for the Grand Slam in 1930 but didn't pay any prizes. Before the 1932 U.S. Open at Fresh Meadow, promoters petitioned the tournament committee to set up pari-mutuel machines either on the course or just outside. When denied, they threatened to blow up the clubhouse or throw acid on the greens. The police were everywhere during the event, with two escorting Sarazen. Nothing happened.

Racketeers sold over 63,000 lottery tickets before the 1932 PGA

Championship, with the first prize for picking the winner set at $10,000. PGA administrators found the sale to be a hoax and warned the public.

Despite the PGA leadership's anxieties, the Agua Caliente winter tournament in Tijuana, Mexico, offered pari-mutuel betting in 1935. Tournament organizers let bookies list the players and odds on a pari-mutuel tote board at the horse track next to the golf course. As well as wagering on the tournament winner, one could bet on the outcome of each round. A $2 bet on Ky Laffoon, who shot a 69 in the second round, returned $52 that day. Harold McFadden shot the low round of the tournament, a 68, and won a special 10 percent payout from the pool—$63. Wiffy Cox, another entrant, liked the idea: "It gives a player who likes his own chances an opportunity to pick up some spare change. Sure, I think the plan is swell because I won 120 bucks."

Several golfers objected and threatened to withdraw. Gene Sarazen didn't play at Caliente that year, citing the excessive betting. "I don't like the idea of pari-mutuel betting in golf," he told the press. "It is all right for horse races, but all wrong, I think, for golf." Sarazen went on to say, however, cheating would be unlikely. "You and I know that nobody playing in that tournament would make a single move that was not absolutely on the up and up, but there are always suspicious people to throw some dirt."

Sarazen made a keen distinction about betting on golf. He clearly favored a friendly wager on the links but disapproved of allowing gambling to displace golf as the main event. Golf has a way of finding its limits. The PGA excluded the Agua Caliente tournament from the tour after 1957, about the same time that concerns over excessive betting shut down many public Calcutta auctions.

—●—

The PGA Tour of the early 1930s was not the well-oiled money machine that it later became. The pros generally traveled only in the winter, because they had to work at their home clubs during warm weather to make ends meet. California hosted several events, but the $250 train fare deterred many. Florida real estate developers and resort owners sponsored tournaments during the winter, knowing newspapers in the Northeast would run stories about them.

In 1929, newspaperman Hal Sharkey volunteered to attempt to manage the tournament schedule. He also recruited sponsors and tried to get the better-known pros to enter as many tournaments as possible. He lasted less than a year, falling victim to a common conflict in professional tournament golf—namely, the players wanted more money than the sponsors were willing to pay.

The PGA hired Bob Harlow in 1930 as its first full-time tournament manager. A former newsman, Harlow had been Hagen's manager for years and used the many contacts he made while traveling with Walter to cultivate the growing tour. Although Harlow continued working for Hagen, he convinced sponsors to sequence events to facilitate traveling. He also established tournament features that fans take for granted now: published pairings and starting times, formatted standings for the newspapers, and staged interviews. Harlow, called the "father" of the PGA Tour, helped turn professional golf into a sports enterprise and made it entertaining. Fred Corcoran succeeded Harlow in 1936 and presided over a boom in pro golf that started in the late 1930s.

Walter Hagen was still a large draw at events, but his best golf was behind him. Others who won regularly included Armour, Cooper, Cruickshank, Diegel, Dudley, Farrell, Laffoon, Willie Macfarlane, Manero, Mehlhorn, Picard, Runyan, Horton Smith, and Craig Wood. Sarazen, however, drew the most attention when the fans did not have either Bobby Jones or the fading Hagen to follow.

—•—

Sarazen first drew national attention by winning the 1922 U.S. Open. Although he also won the PGA Championship that same year as well as in 1923, Sarazen's game declined slightly during the rest of the decade. In the first half of the 1930s, Sarazen became a golf superstar. In 1931, he invented the sand wedge, using the new iron to win both the 1932 U.S. and British Opens. While winning the Masters into 1935, Sarazen hit the "shot heard round the world," using a 4-wood into Augusta National's par-5 15th green for his famous double eagle. Throughout his illustrious career, Sarazen also played money golf.

The son of Italian immigrants, Eugenio Saraceni was born in 1902 in Harrison, New York, a small town on Long Island Sound just south of Rye. Like most youngsters of the age, Eugenio worked part-time to supplement the income his father earned as a carpenter. He sold the *Saturday Evening Post*, picked strawberries, and lit gas lamps, all before discovering golf at age eight. He began caddying at nearby Larchmont Country Club in 1910, and his first payday was memorable. "That 45¢ was the most money I had ever earned in a single day," he recalled. "When I handed it to my father at the dinner table, it made a great impression on him."

Hooked on golf immediately, Eugenio and his caddie friends laid out a pitch-'n-putt course on a vacant lot. They worked on their game every day, using hand-me-down clubs from the Larchmont members. Like so many boys before and after, they bet on their games, usually skins matches for pennies a hole. When Eugenio proved more skillful, the others schemed to get even. "Let's get that Saraceni," one said. "He's got our dough."

In 1913, Eugenio began caddying at the Apawamis Club near Rye, New York, but a 1917 family financial crisis forced him to help at his father's wartime job in Bridgeport, Connecticut. He was quite ill during the 1918 flu epidemic. While recuperating, he started playing at a public nine-hole course, Beardsley Park. When a Bridgeport newspaper wrote about a hole in one he made, Saraceni decided his name sounded too much like a violin player's. Welcome to the game, Gene Sarazen.

Sarazen started as a shop assistant at Bridgeport's Brooklawn Golf Club in 1918. His game improved quickly, and the head pro, George Sparling, began backing Sarazen in money games with club members. The $10 and $25 Nassaus helped Sarazen hone his skills. "I played several matches a week, money matches in which I carried the colors and also the dollars of the Sparling stable," Sarazen said of the games. "It was good under-pressure training for me and an excellent investment for Sparling."

Henry Picard, winner of 25 tournaments, including the Masters and PGA Championship, benefited from the same training regimen. Two members at Charleston Country Club, where Picard was the head pro in 1930, arranged money games each weekend to help him tune his game. "We played for quite a lot of money, more than I could afford, but I never bet more than I could pay off," Picard said. If Henry lost a match, the members would insist on playing five more holes, at $50 a hole, to give Picard a chance to get even. When the club members thought Picard's game was sufficiently polished, they lowered the bet. "We've trained you well," one said. "$1 Nassau from hereafter."

Sarazen turned pro in 1919. It was a simple process in those days, without a tour-qualifying tournament or apprenticeships in mini-tours. Instead, he paid the entry fee at a pro-amateur event at Metacomet Country Club in Providence, Rhode Island. He won $50 in prize money, and the established pros praised his game.

Short at five foot five, the dark-complected Italian became America's "melting pot" golf professional. Sporting a dress shirt, tie, and plus fours when he played, he was always a gallery favorite. Sarazen wore his trademark pants throughout his life, even at age 97, when he hit his last ceremonial tee ball at the 1999 Masters. His natty attire, plus his semiretirement in mid-life to a Connecticut dairy farm, prompted the press to bestow his well-known nickname, "the Squire." The sport mourned his passing just a month after his final appearance at the Masters.

Many professional golfers during the first quarter of the 20th century were English or Scots. Always proud of his heritage despite having changed his name, Sarazen helped ease the WASPish restrictions in golf, just as immigrants did in other professions. Before the 1922 U.S. Open, which Sarazen won, Francis Ouimet asked young Gene to join him, Chick Evans, and Jim Barnes for a practice round. Barnes objected to playing with the Italian American, and they teed off without Gene.

After winning the 1922 Open, Sarazen joined Barnes in an exhibition match. He was still cool toward Barnes after the earlier snub. "The night before the match Barnes asked me if I wanted to split the purse, and I told him no, it's winner take all," Sarazen said. "I beat him 6 and 5."

During the winter before his double triumph at the U.S. and British Opens, Sarazen began experimenting with both his swing and the club he used in bunkers. "The one department of my game that was still worrying me in 1932 was my trap play," Sarazen said. "I was throwing shots away there, scalping the ball or digging down so deep that I fluffed the shot."

Golfers of the era generally used a niblick, a 9-iron equivalent, to gouge out the ball from a bunker. Inspired by watching aircraft land and geese hit the water with their rear ends down and heads up, Sarazen added a flange to the sole of a niblick. "I was trying to make myself a club that would drive the ball *up* as I drove the club head *down*," Sarazen explained. Thus was born the sand wedge, used throughout golf since.

"Gene became the most proficient trap player in the game almost overnight," Wind wrote later. "To demonstrate to his fellow pros the wizardry he could wield with his new club, he used to invite them to place a batch of balls anywhere in a trap and bet that he could blast them all within 10 feet of the pin."

"I was willing to bet anyone any amount that I could get up and down in two from any lie in any trap," Sarazen boasted. "I lost very few of those bets."

—●—

"Hurry it up, will you, Gene? I've got a big date tonight," implored Hagen, whose penchant for a good time matched his love for golf. The two were paired in the second Masters in 1935, and Hagen fidgeted while Sarazen considered his second shot on the par-5 15th hole. Sarazen had just learned Craig Wood's birdie on 18 had put him in the lead, three shots ahead of Sarazen. He had 235 yards to the hole and knew he needed to birdie the hole to have any chance of catching Wood. Sarazen surveyed his poor lie, the pond guarding the green, and the pin's location. The distance called for a 3-wood, but he knew he needed the 4-wood's loft to overcome the bad lie.

"I took my stance with my 4-wood and rode into the shot with every ounce of strength and timing I could muster," Sarazen said of the shot. "The split second I hit the ball, I knew it would carry the pond." Running after the shot, Sarazen watched the ball land on the green and run straight for the hole. "While I was straining to see how close it had finished, the small gallery behind the green let out a terrific shout and began to jump wildly in the air." Buoyed by his monumental two, Sarazen parred in to tie Wood. He easily beat Wood the next day in a 36-hole play-off. Sarazen's triumph made him the first to win all four legs of the modern Grand Slam during his career—both the U.S. and British Opens, the PGA Championship, and the Masters.

The year after Bobby Jones won his version of the slam, he and a friend, New York businessman Clifford Roberts, bought an old nursery in Augusta, Georgia. Jones and golf course architect Alister Mackenzie then set about to build Jones's ideal golf course. In the depth of the Depression, Jones and Roberts paid $70,000 for the land and about $100,000 to build the course and convert the old farm dwelling into a clubhouse. Roberts raised some of the money from 80 wealthy businessmen—mostly New Yorkers who did business with stockbroker Roberts—who paid $350 each to join the Augusta National Golf Club, which opened in January 1933.

Jones and Roberts hosted their first tournament at the new club in 1934, calling it the Augusta National Invitational. (Jones thought the name "Masters" was too pretentious, resisting it until 1939. The press, however, used Masters from the start.) The total purse that first year was $5,000, with $1,500 going to the winner, Horton Smith. The Masters also had a Calcutta pool from the beginning. The *Augusta Chronicle* reported the auction brought a $680 bid for Jones, the highest, not only because of his past triumphs but also for his course record 65 in a practice round. Sadly, though, Jones finished ten shots back of Smith.

In the second year of the tournament, Jones again sold for the highest amount during the Calcutta, but he finished tied for 25th. Wood's play-off loss to Sarazen in 1935 earned him $800 for second place. New Yorker Alfred S. Bourne bought Wood in the Calcutta at 10-1 and then paid the player $500 out of his pool winnings. Despite another course record practice round—64 this time—Jones again was not a factor in the final round. He played in his last Masters in 1948.

Paul Runyan said Jones sold for $13,800 in the 1936 Calcutta, more than 10 times what the *Chronicle* reported. The Calcutta operators must have had two sets of books, with one for the newspapers. More likely, however, Runyan's sum probably came from a private pool. Further, the larger number fits with the bidding for Jones in the auction pool before the 1929 U.S. Amateur. He sold then for $27,000 in a pool that totaled $87,000.

Jones never broke par 72 in any Masters round. Runyan thought the pressure of the large Calcutta bets was the reason, a conclusion that fits with an assessment by Jones's biographer Sidney Matthew. He maintains Jones was very sensitive that his friends bet so heavily on him during the Grand Slam year. "[Jones] didn't want his friends to suffer because he had a bad day on the golf course," Matthew said in 2001.

The Bon Air Vanderbilt Hotel in Augusta hosted the Calcutta every Wednesday night of tournament week. Prominent newsmen were in charge. *Time* magazine editor John Martin ran the 1936 auction, with Horton Smith and Tommy Armour acting as auctioneers. The Calcutta was an important public feature of the Masters until the late 1940s, when antigambling forces chased it underground. See chapter 5 for more.

—●—

Hollywood's "Golden Era" of golf started in the 1930s, according to writers Robert Chew and David Pavoni in their book *Golf in Hollywood.* Chew and Pavoni maintain that as soon as the film industry took root in

Southern California, it formed a close and continuing relationship with the game, especially in business terms. "Playing golf in Hollywood often was, and still is, where the idea forms, the deal starts, and the next star is born," they wrote. It may not have been that complicated since the Los Angeles climate, the stars' disposable income, and golf formed a good match on their own from the first reel.

In the 1920s, the stars of the silver screen played at several Los Angeles country clubs. The most popular among the celebrities were Lakeside, Bel-Air, and Riviera instead of the staid Los Angeles Country Club. Home to the "old" money in Southern California, Los Angeles initially snubbed applicants from the movie business, including Randolph Scott. When he commiserated with entertainer Phil Harris about the club's dislike of their profession, Harris acted surprised at Scott's rejection: "You're no actor, just look at your movies."

Opened in 1925, Lakeside Golf Club sought celebrities to join the club, and its setting helped. Located in Burbank, just north of Mulholland Drive and Beverly Hills, Lakeside was adjacent to Universal Studios and Paramount's back lot. First National Studios opened in 1926 across the street from the club; the studio later sold to Warner Brothers.

Mary Pickford and Douglas Fairbanks were early members along with John Barrymore, W. C. Fields, Walter Huston, Gene Autry, Basil Rathbone, Errol Flynn, Johnny Weissmuller, and the spurned Randolph Scott. Bing Crosby, who joined in 1930, later described Lakeside: "This is no ordinary country club. Raillery, gags, ribs, frame-ups, put-ons and put-downs are incessant, and often hilarious—and no one is immune."

Another Lakeside member, Grantland Rice, was known for his ability to deliver pigeons to the club's better golfers, especially actor Guy Kibbee. "Mr. Rice works for Mr. Kibbee on a strictly commission basis, getting, it is said, 10 percent for each victim produced," sportswriter Henry McLemore said at the time. McLemore was not only a protégé of Rice's but also a Kibbee casualty.

Crosby and fellow Lakeside member Bob Hope brought celebrity golf to America, especially after their pro-am tournaments—the Crosby "Clambake" at Pebble Beach and Hope's Desert Classic—were hits on television. Both men were excellent golfers. Bing carried a 2-handicap while winning four club championships at Lakeside, and Hope played to a 4 at the height of his golfing career. Both always played for money.

Crosby was as well known for his frugality as he was for his pipe. That personality trait arose during a money game in Las Vegas. Bing backed one team in the match and arranged a $500 bet with his friend Carl Anderson, a real estate developer. When Anderson's team won, Crosby paid up. As the story of the bet circulated, the wager's size grew dramatically at each retelling, finally going up to $50,000. That sum interested the Internal Revenue Service (IRS), to which Anderson responded, "$50,000? It was only $500. Crosby wouldn't pay a dime to see a re-enactment of the Crucifixion of Christ with the original cast."

Bing Crosby died of a heart attack in 1977, just after finishing a round of golf near Madrid, Spain. He might have had a smile on his face for he had just won a $10 bet.

Hope also enjoyed money golf. In his book *Confessions of a Hooker*, Hope told of a match he and Crosby played in the Phoenix Open Pro-Am. Bing suggested Hope play Del Webb, a wealthy builder and part owner of the New York Yankees. "He's a pigeon," Bing assured Hope. "You'll beat him like a drum."

Hope and Webb agreed to a $100 Nassau the next day at the Phoenix Country Club. When Webb shot a 73, Bob took a bath. Nevertheless, the two became friends. "We played a lot of golf all over the country, mostly for big stakes," Hope explained. "Our standard game was for $25 a hole with all sorts of side bets, and we usually went double or nothing on the 18th tee. I got even with him but good one day at Lakeside. After 17 holes he owed me $875 and on the 18th, of course it was double or nothing." Hope chipped in for a birdie, taking Webb for almost $1,800.

Millionaire airline owner and moviemaker Howard Hughes belonged to Lakeside, Bel-Air, and Wilshire. During the 1930s, Hughes was trying to improve his game and playing better golfers to test himself. He always played for something, but he generally stayed away from high stakes despite his wealth. His dislike of larger wagers led other Lakeside members to needle him about his penny-ante ways. Hughes responded in the bar one day by offering a proposition: "I'll roll the dice, and you roll the dice, whoever has the higher roll wins. Here's a check for a $100,000 to cover the bet." There were no takers.

Hughes maintained a home adjacent to Wilshire's eighth green, and he used it to gain an edge during a money game. Just as his opponents prepared to putt, Hughes motioned toward the house, and out came a nude woman. Hughes won the bets as his distracted opponents struggled to putt out.

George Von Elm and Hughes played weekly for $500, with Von Elm viewing the bet as a stipend since he most always won. Hughes beat him one day, and Von Elm got a bit testy as he wrote out a check, carping that Hughes's handicap was artificially high. "Well, George, if you feel so bad, I'm going to tear this check up, and it'll be the last time we'll play golf." And so indeed, Von Elm never again saw the color of Howard Hughes's money.

—•—

Into this scene of glitter and golf strode one of the era's most interesting money golfers, Mysterious Montague.

He was a strong, good-looking man and a graceful, multisport athlete. He dated Hollywood starlets, played superb golf, and hung out with the stars of his day. All these factors plus a wonderful name and a slightly larcenous heart equaled the perfect hustler. His name was John Montague.

In 1933, his friends at Lakeside Golf Club nicknamed him "Mysterious" because he shunned publicity and refused to discuss his past. He had no discernable means of support, but the inexplicable air about Montague did not hinder his game. He thrashed everyone on the course.

Bing Crosby played regularly with Montague at Lakeside. After one round, Crosby complained he wasn't getting enough strokes from Montague. Mysterious responded with one of the greatest prop bets in golf. "I can handle you," he said to Crosby, "with a shovel, a bat, and a rake." Bing accepted the bet, with the two agreeing on $5 a hole.

In front of a crowd on the first tee, Crosby smoothed a drive down the middle of the fairway. With a swing powered by Popeye-like forearms and bulging shoulders, Montague used the baseball bat to hit his ball 300 yards into a green-side bunker. After Crosby hit a 7-iron to within 30 feet of the cup, Montague entered the bunker with his shovel. With a practiced swoop, he sent the ball and a shovelful of sand to within 12 feet of the hole. The singer's birdie putt slid four feet past, but Montague gave him the par. Mysterious lined up behind the ball as if shooting pool and then sank the putt, using the rake as a cue stick. Amazed, Crosby tossed Montague $5 and, saying he'd had enough, headed for the clubhouse.

Montague had a large bag of other trick shots, which he used to pad his

In 1933 John "Mysterious" Montague won a bet from Bing Crosby by playing with a baseball bat, rake, and shovel. After another match in the 1930s, Montague seemed pleased with his spade work on the golf course. Amateur Athletic Foundation of Los Angeles

otherwise unknown income. They included using a 2-wood to excavate a ball buried in a bunker, hitting two balls at once (one with a draw, the other a fade), and hitting blindfolded. He often took people's money by chipping a ball through a slightly opened window. He also showed off his strength, tearing telephone books in two and lifting the rear end of a car.

John Montague showed up in Southern California in 1930, quickly making friends with some of the film stars of the era: Scott, Oliver Hardy, Broderick Crawford, Fields, and the Olympic gold medal–winning swimmer Weissmuller, who played Tarzan in the movies. Richard Arlen, who had helped the Los Angeles Open with cash during thin times, took him to Palm Springs. There, Montague broke the course record four days in a row, ending with a 61. He also broke the course record at Westwood Country Club, shooting a 63, and at both courses at Fox Hills Golf Club. He beat Cruickshank, Diegel, and PGA and U.S. Open champion Olin Dutra. Von

Elm played Montague every day for a month, and Mysterious never shot above 66. Playing Pebble Beach with the course's developer, Samuel F. B. Morse, he stood on the 18th green and needed only a 2-putt to break the course record of 65. He picked his ball, claiming, "I never did care for records."

Sportswriters Rice and Joe Williams of the *New York World-Telegram* wrote often and glowingly about Montague's golfing skills. Rice declared the U.S. Amateur winner would not be the best player in the country unless Montague had entered the tournament. "Granny" Rice joined Montague at Riviera Country Club for a game with Kibbee and another actor, Frank Craven. Again on 18, Montague picked up, while needing only a four to break the course record. "It was as fine a round of golf as I've ever seen," Rice wrote afterward. This quixotic behavior, plus his mysterious past, led other writers to refer to Montague as the "Sphinx of the Links," the "Phantom of the Fairways," and the "Garbo of Golf," after Greta "I vant to be alone" Garbo.

Interest in Mysterious Montague peaked in January 1937, when freelance photographer Bob Wallace hid in the bushes at Lakeside and took clandestine photos of the golfer. Knowing of Montague's distaste for publicity, Wallace quickly replaced the film with a dummy canister. Hearing the shutter click, Montague ran over, grabbed Wallace's camera, and destroyed the empty magazine. Wallace sold the photos to *Time Magazine*, which ran them in its January 25 issue. As those pictures circulated through the news media, they caught the eye of State Police inspector John Cosart in Oneida, New York. The mystery of John Montague was about to be solved.

His real name was La Verne Moore. In 1930, he and three others had robbed a restaurant in upstate New York. Moore evaded local police and escaped to California. The New York authorities arrested Moore and took him home to face criminal charges. His Hollywood friends made his bail and testified in court on his behalf. The jury acquitted him, despite the fact he had left his golf clubs at the scene of the crime.

Following his trial, Montague rode the publicity to an exhibition match with Babe Ruth, famed woman player Babe Didrikson, and New York amateur Sylvia Annenberg. Back in California, Montague toured with Von Elm and Didrikson, signed an equipment deal with Wilson, and made instructional films. He beat U.S. and Masters champ Craig Wood in an exhibition, with Wood's backers losing a reported $11,000.

During World War II, Montague staged trick shot exhibitions to sell war bonds. Later, he and others tried to sell movie and book deals about his interesting life, but none materialized. He died in 1991.

—●—

Chips and Pitches

Fourteen-club limit. The USGA announced in 1937 golfers would be limited to 14 clubs in their bags beginning the following year. The association cited several reasons for its decision: increased mechanization of the game (a club for every shot), play delays as golfers sorted through their collection, and a desire to return individual shot-making skills to the game. Caddies loved the rule change.

A head for golf. English professional player George Ashdown gave amateur Charles Mansell a stroke a hole but still beat him 7 and 5. Ashdown also won a $250 bet on the match by successfully hitting every tee ball off a rubber tee strapped to the forehead of Miss Ena Shaw, a 22-year-old nurse. She lay on the ground on her back as Ashdown teed it up.

Johnny Goodman. In 1933, he was the last amateur to win the U.S. Open.

Lawson Little. Little won both the British and U.S. Amateurs two years in a row, 1934 and 1935. Many point at Little for prompting the USGA's 14-club limit. He carried as many as 26 clubs, including seven wedges.

Pacific Rim golf. In 1933, the Japanese ambassador to the United States, Katsuji Debuchi, paired with Adm. William H. Standley, chief of U.S. Naval Operations, in a four-ball match against two retired navy admirals. All bets on the match, which was played at the Chevy Chase Country Club near Washington, D.C., went to the U.S. Navy Relief Fund. The stakes between the United States and Japan would be much greater eight years later.

Proposition bet. Philadelphia stockbroker William R. Crissy bet his friends $2,000 in 1931 he could dine with President Herbert Hoover and play golf with Bobby Jones, John D. Rockefeller, and Britain's Prince of Wales all within a year. He did eat with Hoover, but he failed on the golfing, despite pestering Rockefeller at his club in Ormond Beach, Florida.

Window chipping. Several golfers have stories about betting on their ability to hit golf balls out windows. Mysterious Montague had one, and so did Joe Kirkwood. He bet Hagen that he could hit a ball out their hotel room window and land it next to a man sleeping across the street in a park. Done. Ky Laffoon, who won 10 times on the PGA Tour, bet a guy at Dubsdread Golf Club in Orlando he could hit a specific pane in a window. The bet was $5 a ball, with Lafoon hitting off a tile floor. He broke out the designated pane on the first chip and then hit 10 more through the same hole. Winning $55, he turned to an onlooker and said, "I been practicin' that shot for a week over here. I would have hit my entire shag bag through there if he had kept peeling off $5 bills."

Women's golf. In 1932, Great Britain hosted the inaugural Curtis Cup match between British and American women amateurs. The U.S. team won 5 ½ to 3 ½. Wilson Sporting Goods hired Helen Hicks in 1934 to promote its golf equipment and hold instructional clinics, making her the first woman professional.

5.

SNEAD, NELSON, AND HOGAN:

EVEN MONEY, 1938–59

"I HEAR A HEALTHY BET DOESN'T SCARE YOU," a man named Cy said to Sam Snead.

"It scares me," Snead replied, "but I've got the habit. Tried to quit gambling once, but it was about as much use as kicking a hog barefoot."

Cy asked for five strokes a side. "With that handicap, there's no limit to the bet," he said, "you name it."

"I thought it over," Sam later recalled. "A no-limit wager at those odds didn't sound awfully risky, but Samuel J. Snead had been burned before. 'No,' I said, testing him. 'I'll spot you three shots on the front nine and four coming back. But not five.'"

"What the hell," Cy complained.

"Suit yourself."

"Oh, O.K. If that's the only way I can get to play you."

Trinities of top golfers seem to crop up in different eras of championship golf. The "Great Triumvirate" included Harry Vardon, James Braid, and James Taylor in the early 1900s. One erudite golf writer referred to Walter Hagen, Gene Sarazen, and Tommy Armour as the "Father, Son, and Holy Ghost." The 1960s and '70s boasted the "Big Three" of Arnold Palmer, Jack Nicklaus, and Gary Player. Today, the news media want two others to join Tiger, but the other top pros—Vijay Singh, Phil Mickelson, Retief Goosen, and Ernie Els—can't seem to sort out among themselves who should join Woods.

As the 1930s drew to a close, three stars began to shine on the growing PGA Tour: Snead, Byron Nelson, and Ben Hogan. They would dominate both professional golf and the increasingly interested news media through the 1950s.

Along with Byron Nelson, Sam Snead (left) and Ben Hogan (center) dominated the PGA Tour in the 1940s and '50s. Sam was the high priest of money games until his death in 2002, and Hogan rarely played an informal round without a bet. His icy demeanor during tournaments carried over after his retirement—"I play with friends, but we don't play friendly games," he said. Comedian Jack Benny is at the far right. UNITED STATES GOLF ASSOCIATION

Snead, who won 28 tournaments between 1936 and 1942, was golf's most active bettor during the 20th century. Sam was the high priest of money golf. Nelson played a few high-stakes money matches, but he is most known for winning 11 straight golf tournaments in 1945. The dour and taciturn Hogan pursued his opponents on the golf course with the "burning frigidity of dry ice." He always had a bet during informal rounds, and he was serious about his money. "I play with friends, but we don't play friendly games," he said.

In 1936, the drums of war were beginning to beat in Europe, and in the Far East, Japan was pursuing more of its imperialistic ambitions. While the Great Depression was easing in the States, it wasn't until World War II that increased American industrial production finally ended economic hard times.

Despite the double wallop of the Depression and World War II, the 1936–46 period witnessed the birth of the PGA Tour, at least in a form recognizable today. Twenty-two tournaments took place in 1936, with all the purses totaling only $100,000. By 1946, sponsors offered 45 weeks of golf. Total prize money ran more than $600,000. Gallery size tripled in those 10 years. Tour director Fred Corcoran organized the sequence of events as a real tour, one that made orderly stops that respected climatic and geographic realities. While Horton Smith was the leading money leader in 1936 with $7,682, Ben Hogan led the tour in 1946 with $42,556.

Plenty of interesting players were on the tour during the 1940s and '50s, men whose personalities filled the gaps between Snead, Nelson, and Hogan. Dutch Harrison, the "Arkansas Traveler," had over 30 tour wins, but he was known for his needling, wagering, and hustling. Jimmy Demaret was a gallery favorite, both for his friendly demeanor and colorful, peacocky attire. Most still supplemented their winnings with on-course betting, but antigambling forces of the 1950s generally purged the tour's camp followers of bookies and Calcutta organizers. One player, Ken Venturi, stood astride the whole sweep of championship golf during the second half of the 20th century. He was the runner-up in the first U.S. Junior Amateur in 1948 and then played money matches as an amateur, backed by Eddie Lowery, Francis Ouimet's former caddie. While still an amateur, Venturi lost the 1956 Masters by soaring to a final round 80. His 1964 U.S. Open win in the stifling summer heat at Congressional Country Club provided an early drama for televised golf. Forced from competitive golf by hand problems in the late 1960s, Venturi covered golf for CBS TV for 35 years until his 2002 retirement. Throughout that time he was a money player, even playing a match with the "Fat Man," a skilled hustler named Martin Stanovich.

Despite the success of Snead, Nelson, and Hogan, the period witnessed the Calcutta's retreat from the public eye because of the game's increasing concern about outsiders' excessive gambling. This movement gained impetus from one of the few regrettable moments in golf history. It happened in 1955 at Deepdale Country Club on Long Island, New York. Handicap cheating during a club tournament drew national attention to sandbagging, one of golf's few warts.

Finally, and on a more cheerful note, most U.S. presidents played golf when in office. Most of them bet on their games. The first installment of presidential betting stories, from William Howard Taft to Dwight Eisenhower, is in this chapter.

But first, turn back the clock to 1936. Sarazen was still around and continued to charm the galleries. The fans also followed the top four money winners—Horton Smith, Ralph Guldahl, Henry Picard, and Harry Cooper. Prize money was decent and so were the crowds. Pro golf, though, needed more buzz. An engaging hillbilly from Virginia joined the tour that year and electrified the game.

—●—

"I've always believed in playing golf for a little something, even if it's just 50¢ a side," Sam Snead said. "There's nothing more boring than a walk in the park with three other guys. For me to play a casual round of golf with nothing at stake is a waste of time."

Sweet-swinging Sam Snead won most of his bets. He didn't accept any he thought he might lose. In more formal rounds, he won 81 times on the PGA Tour, including seven majors. He played championship golf for a remarkably long time, winning the Greater Greensboro Open in 1965, 28 years after his first victory as a pro. At 61 years of age, he cashed the second-place check in the 1974 Los Angeles Open. At 67, he shot his age in two rounds at the 1979 Quad Cities Open. He died in 2002 a few days short of his 90th birthday.

"The greatest golf swing I have ever seen, period," declared Rick Smith, a PGA professional who works with Phil Mickelson. Everyone thought Snead's swing came to him naturally, but Sam insisted practice produced his fluid and balanced swing. "Nobody worked harder at golf than I did." He also said, "Practice puts brains in your muscles."

In today's PGA Tour environment, where $1 million paydays are routine, Snead's lifetime earnings total of $713,155 seems but a pittance. Yet in a statistical analysis published in 1989, *Golf Illustrated* editor Al Barkow ranked Snead the number one professional player in history. Barkow's formula included several comparative metrics, especially one that weighted a player's winnings as a percentage of the available purse. This calculation permitted Barkow to place individuals from different eras in a common perspective. (Nicklaus was second; Palmer, third; and Hogan, fourth. Only 13 years old in 1989, Woods wasn't in the money.)

Snead grew up in Ashwood, Virginia, a few miles from the Homestead Resort in the Allegheny Mountains. His parents farmed in a valley Snead said was so narrow that dogs wagged their tails up and down. A talented athlete in high school, Sam got his start in golf by cleaning balls at the Cascades Inn golf course. He joined the PGA Tour in 1936.

Galleries liked Snead, both for his game and his down-home easiness. They also marveled at his length, hitting 300-yard drives in the age before "metal woods." The press hyped the hillbilly angle with some justification. Sam was a little rough around the edges at first, and many have written about his learning the game in bare feet. He once played a practice round at the Masters without shoes just to spin the publicity mill. Gene Sarazen objected, "What are you trying to play around here, Snead—Huckleberry Finn?" The Squire told Snead to be more respectful of the game, saying without golf, Sam would be shining shoes at the Homestead. Hearing that, Demaret reminded the former Eugenio Saraceni of his own humble origins.

"I'm no high-stakes gambler on the golf course," Snead said. "At times I have played for a lot of money—when the circumstances were just right— but my normal bet is a $5 Nassau." Sam said he played just as hard for $5 as he did for $5,000. "If there's a secret to my longevity in this game, besides God's blessings," he said in 1986, "it's that I never quit playing and I never stopped trying."

One of Sam's small bets turned into a $10,000 payday. He agreed to a match with a 5-handicap amateur friend in Boca Raton, Florida. The bet was a $5 Nassau, six ways ($5 on the front, $10 on the back, and $15 on the match, or six $5 bets). Sam also charged the man $100 for simply playing, sort of a lesson fee Sam generally exacted from anyone who asked him for a game. Snead won $45, including presses. After lunch, Sam and his opponent recruited two more amateurs, a 5 and an 8. Sam won $700 in the afternoon round and waived his $100 fee.

The three pilgrims wanted more, so Sam cleared his lesson book, and they played every day for a week at several southern Florida golf courses. Snead gave them their full handicaps, but he still won $10,000. He said his highest round that week was a 67, and he set four course records.

Snead's preference for modest bets didn't keep him away from a big money game if he liked the odds or his backers funded the stake. He played two matches against a skilled amateur, T. Suffern Tailer, Jr., in 1936 and 1938. Tailer's family was among the elite in financial and social circles of New York and Newport, Rhode Island. Junior played scratch or a 1, winning the Metropolitan Amateur twice and a clutch of other regional amateur tournaments. He liked to bet on his game.

Snead said a friend arranged a match with Tailer at Meadow Brook Golf Club on Long Island in May 1936. Snead was on his way north from the Greenbrier to play in his first pro tournament, the Shawnee Open in Shawnee-on-Delaware, Pennsylvania (he tied for seventh). "Who is this Sam Snead?" Tailer asked, according to Sam. "He just had his first train ride, came up from West Virginia, hayseed sticking out of his ears," Snead's friend responded. "But we'll back him for a $500 Nassau, rain or shine." Sam lost the front nine, but he won the both the back and the match.

Snead and Tailer played again two years later, also at Meadow Brook. Tailer and Walter Hochschield, a wealthy New York physician, had challenged Snead's friend Bunny Bacon to a four-ball match at $5,000 a side. Bacon could choose any pro as a partner. Bunny convinced Sam to play, offering him expenses and $300 if they lost and $600 if they won. Tailer was surprised to see Snead on the putting green before the match.

"Hello, Sam. What are you doing here?"

"I just came up to play a little."

Bacon upped the ante by making a $2,000 side bet with Hochschield. Snead said all the money made him nervous, topping both his drive and second shot on the first hole. Bacon pulled Sam aside, asking if Tailer had fixed him. "Hell, no," Sam responded. Snead pulled himself together, eagling the 17th to win the match 3 and 1. "I don't ever want to see you again," Tailer said to Snead. They must have, though, because Tailer bested Snead at the 1938 Masters by six shots and was the first amateur to break 70 in the Masters tournament.

Another of Sam's challenge matches caught the attention of the *New York Times* in 1940.

HAVANA, Dec. 22. Sam Snead, professional golf star from the United States, defeated Rufino Gonzalez, Cuba's champion pro, by a score of 137 to 142 today in a thirty-six-hole medal play match on the course of Havana Country Club to win a wager of $5,000 for his sponsor, Thomas Shevlin of New York.

The match was arranged by Shevlin and Thornwald Sanchez, Cuban sportsman, who made the bet on their respective choices in Long Island last fall.

Shevlin, whose family moved in the Vanderbilts' and Astors' social circle, was a crack amateur golfer who also played polo at Meadow Brook. Sanchez boasted Gonzalez could beat anyone. Shevlin accepted the bet without a pro in mind. He asked the president of Wilson Sporting Goods Company, L. B. Icley, for a nominee. Icley suggested Snead, who was under contract with Wilson to promote its equipment.

Snead said side bets among the gallery and around town brought the total money on the match to $100,000. All the bettors in Havana skipped the jai alai matches and cockfights, shifting their money to the golf match. Even Cuban dictator Fulgencio Batista had money on Gonzalez. Shevlin asked Sam how much of the action he wanted. "Nothing. This wasn't my idea. I've never seen this guy Gonzalez before," Snead replied. He finally agreed to a $250 side bet to increase his focus.

"When I got to the course on the day of the match, I saw all of these rough-looking hombres around the first tee," recalled Snead. "It was then explained to me that they were Batista's boys. That's all I needed to hear; I already was jumpier than a cat burglar at the policeman's ball."

Snead shot a 69 to Gonzalez's 71 for the first round. "Sensational!" Shevlin said. "Another $500 of the bet is yours, and this time it's on the house." Sam beat the Cuban by three strokes in the afternoon and then made a beeline for the airport. He was not a popular man at the moment and feared for his life. When he saw Icley, Snead said, "Next time the stakes are that high, send Demaret, will you? He likes to travel and would make a prettier corpse than me."

New York bookie Jack Doyle welcomed Snead to the tour. Sam didn't care for Doyle, however, mostly because the bookmaker often made him the favorite, as he did going into the 1937 U.S. Open. "After my defeat in the Met Open, Jack Doyle's Broadway handbook listed me—a first-time starter—as the favorite odds of 8-1," said Snead. "Tony Manero, the defending champ, was 15-1. Picard, Harry Cooper, Sarazen, [Johnny] Revolta, and other established pros were 10-1 and 12-1. The odds were ridiculous. No rookie had ever been favored in the Open. The pressure grew until I twisted all night like a worm in hot ashes and couldn't sleep." Snead overcame his jitters and posted a 283, the second lowest score ever for the Open. Unfortunately, Guldahl shot a record-breaking 281 to win.

"Sam Snead remains the all-time best practice round player," wrote Dave Hill in 1977. A member of both the PGA and Champions Tours, Hill said Snead played better in practice rounds than in tournaments. "For a $20

Nassau, that SOB will shoot anything at you—a 61, anything." There is no room here for all the Sam Snead practice round stories, but Gardner Dickinson, who won seven times on tour, tells a good one.

"In my day, we used to engage in little contests on the putting clock [practice green]," Dickinson said.

> Once in a while, I would be dumb enough to try Sam Snead. Usually I got whipped, but I got old Sambo good one year at the Citrus Open, putting for $1 a hole and double on aces. I was on a streak and had him down about $45 when Sam announced he wanted to double the bet. "Oh no," said I, "you get out of this the same way you came in, $1 a hole."
>
> "I got to go," Sam said as the starter called his name. "I'll pay you when I get in."
>
> "No sir. You can go right after you pay me."
>
> Well, he reached in his pocket and counted out all the nice green money into my hand, and that's the only time I can remember beating him on the putting clock.

Dickinson thought Snead won so many bets because of his gamesmanship. "He would always find a way to beat you."

A tour rookie found out the hard way when he kidded Snead for trying to beat the yips with his sidesaddle putting stance. "Son," Snead said, "don't fool with me. I've got a needle longer than your leg. And it's got a hook on the end of it."

Snead was strict about cheating. Most golfers who play for their own money have the same view. "Golf is the cleanest of all sports that I know about, at least on the professional level," he said. Sam found himself in a predicament, however, when he had to cheat.

Playing a made-for-TV exhibition match—"World Championship Golf"—with Mason Rudolph in 1960, Snead realized he had 15 clubs in his bag when he reached the 12th hole. Sam figured he had already lost, because the rules would have penalized him a lost hole for each one played with too many clubs. (There is a two-hole limit now.) He didn't want to embarrass the sponsor or ruin the segment, so he decided to tank the match since Rudolph would have won with Snead's penalty.

"The only problem was that Rudolph started hacking it around so bad that I couldn't give him a hole," Snead later said. Sam had to 4-putt 16 to go

1-down and then 3-jacked 18 to lose. "If Mason had hit his drive in the rock bed on 18, I would have been in a real mess," Snead said to some reporters. "I'd have had to shank a couple." Sam's comments got him into hot water with the PGA, and the sponsor withdrew its support from the show. "Leave the cheatin' for the cheaters," he said of the incident.

—•—

Byron Nelson won 18 PGA tournaments in 1945, including a record 11 straight. His scoring average for the year was 68.33, which was the gold standard until Tiger Woods nailed up a 67.79 in 2000. Nelson's was an extraordinary achievement and defined him as a player, although he also won two Masters, two PGAs, and the 1939 U.S. Open.

British pros didn't believe Nelson's scores, thinking there was a catch or something fishy with them. One unnamed critic didn't even consider U.S. professional golf to be a true test of the sport. The British maintained men played real golf by batting the ball around a natural links course in lousy weather. To make their point, two of them, Dai Rees and Dick Burton, challenged Nelson in March 1946. They proposed to play him for any amount of money on any course in Great Britain at any time. Nelson told the press he would accept only if they agreed to a home-and-home series.

In the States, Nelson fans scrambled to get part of the wager. The sponsor of the PGA Tour's richest tournament, George S. May, offered to back Nelson for $50,000. His funds pushed the total money behind Byron to $120,000. The aggressive response took the wind out of the British sails, with Burton eventually volunteering only $600 of his own roll. Both sides ultimately agreed to a less expensive 36-hole match between Burton and Nelson in the United States in May 1946. It would be the first international challenge in America since Sarazen beat British Open champ Arthur Havers in 1923. The match referee was the former wunderkind of the 1913 U.S. Open, Francis Ouimet, still a skilled amateur in 1946.

They played the first round at Charles River Country Club near Boston just 24 hours after Burton arrived by ship from England. He was the reigning British Open champion, but he had won in 1939 before the war shut down all golf in Britain. He had played only a few competitive rounds since the war's end. He couldn't even knock off the rust with a practice round at Charles River.

Nelson led by six holes after the first round. He outdrove the Englishman, and his iron play and putting were superior as well. His medal score of 71 was within three strokes of the course record he had set in 1942.

They played the second 18 as part of the first round of that week's PGA tournament. Both had entered the Goodall Round Robin at Winged Foot, so tour officials agreed to let them piggyback. Burton improved his play, but Nelson's 6-up lead allowed him to cruise to a 7 and 6 overall victory. Nelson said he won $1,500, but there is no record of Burton's share, if any. Nelson went on to take third in the Goodall, winning another $1,150. Burton finished out of the money, but he learned Nelson had a game.

Nelson was born and reared in Fort Worth, Texas, caddying as a kid at Glen Garden Country Club. At 14 years of age, he entered his first golf competition, the nine-hole Caddie Championship. He tied 13-year-old Bennie Hogan after both shot a 3-over-par 40. They played a nine-hole play-off, with Nelson winning by a stroke.

Nelson entered a small open tournament in Texarkana, Texas, in 1932. He asked an official what was required to turn pro. "Pay $5, and say you're playing for the money." He did and finished third, winning $75.

The following year, the 21-year-old Nelson became the pro at Texarkana Country Club. He often played fivesomes with the members, usually betting $1 a round with Arthur Temple, who owned the local lumberyard. Nelson's Depression era salary—60 bucks a month—was so small he used his winnings to fund dates with his future wife, Louise.

After his 1933 match with Titanic Thompson, Nelson set off on the winter PGA Tour, borrowing $660 from his future father-in-law to fund the trip. By 1935, he had won his first tournament and had become a tour regular.

Nelson won the Masters in 1937, his first major. A few years later, he and Hogan were tied after 72 holes at the 1942 Masters. They met for an 18-hole play-off the next day. "This was probably one of the most unusual play-offs in golf," Nelson said, "in that at least 25 of the pros who had played in the tournament stayed to watch us in the play-off." He and Ben were flattered by the gesture.

"Now, I didn't gamble," Nelson said later, "but Tommy Armour was a good irons player and he thought I was a good irons player, so he made a sizable bet on me." Armour may have questioned his own judgment when Nelson stood on the sixth tee three strokes down. "After the fifth hole, the man he'd bet with offered to let Tommy settle at 50¢ on the dollar. But Tommy said no: 'The game is just now starting.'" Nelson won by one stroke.

Some have downplayed Nelson's 1945 winning streak because many pros were in the armed services, but that's not quite true. Nelson failed the draft physical because of a blood condition; it was not hemophilia, but he bled easily. Snead joined the Navy, and Hogan, the Army Air Corps. Both, however, were active participants on the 1945 PGA Tour before the war ended. Sam entered 28 events, winning six and finishing in the top ten 23 times. Hogan won five tournaments and had 18 top tens.

Byron Nelson retired from full-time golf in 1946, afterward playing only a few selected tournaments and exhibitions. He said he wanted to work on the ranch he bought. "I was raised in Texas, and I wanted a ranch," he said. "I was not burned out." Cliff Roberts, Jones's partner at Augusta National, acted as his financial adviser and stockbroker. The fruits of that relationship eased Nelson's transition to cattleman. "Financially, it was the best thing that ever happened to me."

Even in retirement, Nelson had time for a little money golf. He received a call in 1949 from Ouimet's 1913 caddy, Eddie Lowery, who had become a successful automobile dealer in San Francisco. Eddie was in the middle of numerous money matches in the 1940s and '50s.

"How are you playing, Byron?" Eddie asked on the phone.

"I'm playing pretty good, Eddie."

"Are you really playing good?" Lowery asked again.

"Yes, I'm playing good, Eddie—why?"

"I've been playing out here at Santa Rosa Country Club with the Buzzini brothers, and they're picking me like a chicken. I want you to come out here and play them with me. I'll set up a few exhibitions for you, but first we'll play these guys."

Nelson and his wife traveled to Santa Rosa, north of San Francisco. He and Eddie, by then 46 years old, teed it up with the Buzzinis. Nelson said he scrambled to par the first few holes, so the brothers started pressing. Byron found his rhythm, however, and proceeded to birdie 12 holes for a 60. "Eddie got all his money back—with interest," Nelson recalled.

Nelson ventured away from the ranch in 1951, entering the Crosby Pro-Am. He won the tournament as well as the pro-am with Lowery. Eddie would figure prominently in another Nelson money game at Bing's Clambake a few years later.

Golf mourned Nelson's death in 2006.

—●—

Ernie Joe "Dutch" Harrison played on the tour for 33 years, but other players knew him best for his betting prowess. Tour players recognized Harrison and Clayton Heafner as the "unofficial" leading money winners in the late 1940s. Adding their betting income to their prize money vaulted them to the top of the heap.

In addition to the usual cons, down-home Harrison was known in the trade as an "oil artist." He buttered up his opponent as a means of playing with the man's head. "This course is built for your game, Mr. Henry—fits you perfect," or "You're such a great putter, Mr. Henry, I probably should concede that short putt, 'cause it's a lead-pipe cinch you'll make it." Introducing doubt was another angle. "That li'l ol' sand trap hiding over there won't bother you none—you cut your eye-teeth on escapin' those hazards." Former CBS TV analyst Ben Wright called the technique the "perfidious hint."

Hall of Fame professional Dutch Harrison hustled on the golf course, especially as a young man during the Depression. He was a smooth operator, always smiling while he set up bets to take an opponent's money. AMATEUR ATHLETIC FOUNDATION OF LOS ANGELES

Some of his pigeons admired Harrison's talent. One even asked Harrison to autograph the $20 bill he had just won from Harrison. "Dutch, I'm going to frame this," the man declared. Harrison took the bill back and said, "I'll write you a check, instead."

Harrison recruited a young Doug Sanders to be his ringer partner before Sanders started his successful career on the tour. Just as Titanic partnered with unknown young guns, Harrison took Sanders in 1955 to the Odessa Pro-Am, a Texas tournament that was a bettor's delight. Sanders had a notoriously short backswing that made him look like a hacker until people saw the results. Dutch gave Sanders the script: "Son, go out to the practice tee an' show nothin'. Most people won't think you can play well because of that short swing, but I want you to shank the ball an' hit a few worm-killers. When I nod at you, hit it off the toe or heel. We want those odds as high as possible."

As they walked to the first tee, Harrison impressed Sanders with the importance of starting fast. "You better come out of the chute like a greyhound. I didn't bring much green with me an' I left none at home. I'm bettin' the whole bankroll today." After Sanders birdied five of the first six holes, a confident Harrison said, "Son, Big Daddy can take over from here."

A contemporary of Harrison's, South African Arthur d'Arcy "Bobby" Locke, also liked a friendly wager. He came to the States in 1947 to play several tour events. He was a cranky sort, thick around the middle, with a full, ruddy face. Some called him "Old Muffin Face" or "Droopy Chops." He was 29 years old, but flying 100 bomber missions during the war made him look much older. He affected baggy plus fours, rolled up the sleeves of his dress shirt, and wore a white cap. He hit everything with such a sweeping, roundhouse hook he lined up way right of his target. When Lloyd Mangrum first saw him set up, he said, "Boy'd better learn how to aim his shots."

"He was the greatest putter I have ever seen," Snead declared. Locke, who coined the dictum "Drive for show, putt for dough," impressed Hogan also. "Everyone examines greens, but only he knows what he's looking for," Hogan said.

Locke finished 14th at his first tournament, the Masters, and then won the following week in North Carolina. At the next stop in Houston, Heafner bet Mangrum $500 Locke would finish ahead of Hogan that weekend. Done. Lloyd paid up and kept sending money to Heafner through the summer as Locke won seven more times before he went home. Back in America in 1948, he won twice and took five seconds.

Harrison played 13 exhibitions with Locke in 1948. At Tulsa Country Club, they arrived early in the morning after driving all night from St. Louis. After sleeping a few hours, they went to the club for lunch before playing. "Bobby, bein' quite attached to the moose milk, had a couple of 'wrist looseners' with his lunch," Dutch recalled.

"What's the course record?" Locke asked the members. "Sixty-nine," they said. Turning to Harrison, he asked what the odds should be.

"I was wonderin' about him . . . driving all night an' havin' a little toddy or two, but the others said, 'We'll give you 5 to 1, Bobby.'"

"I'll bet $200 that I shoot 64 or better," Locke announced. Harrison said Locke holed a 42-foot, downhill breaker on 18 for his 64. The cash was double their exhibition fee.

Their next stop was at Tenison Park in Dallas, a public track well known for its money golf. Locke again asked about the course record. When advised that it was 60, he demurred. "Bobby was a smooth cookie," said Dutch. "No bettin' on that score."

Locke won five British Opens, as many as Tom Watson would later. After Locke's first, in 1949, he cancelled his annual trip to the States. The PGA surprisingly banned him for life for the breach. His relations with the tour had been strained, but at least one sportswriter, Arthur Daley of the *New York Times*, suggested something else was afoot. "Is someone afraid that Locke will pick up all the marbles? No other conclusion could be drawn even though [his] personality—or lack of same—undoubtedly enters into it."

The PGA reinstated Locke in 1950, and he returned to win the Tam O'Shanter that year.

—•—

"She made her money playing the men," Frank Coffey said of Babe Didrikson Zaharias. "They would play $100 and $200 Nassaus with a lot of pressing and double or nothing on the last hole. She won about 90 percent of the time. And $200 was scary back then. My dad made $50 a week."

Coffey caddied for Babe in the early 1950s at Tampa Country Club, which she and her husband, George Zaharias, bought in 1950. Coffey said she never played with women members, choosing to compete against the men from their tees. "She would challenge anybody, anytime."

Named the greatest woman athlete of the 20th century in 2000, Mildred

Didrikson leaped into the world's sports scene in 1932 in the Los Angeles Olympics. Babe won two gold medals and a silver in the javelin, 80-meter hurdles, and high jump, respectively. The Olympics limited women to three events then. It's a shame, because earlier that summer, Babe had won the team championship at the national track and field meet by herself. She had won six gold medals and scored 30 points at the Amateur Athletic Union (AAU) championship, which served as the qualifying meet for the Olympics. The second place team, the Illinois Athletic Club, earned 22 points.

Born in 1911 in Port Arthur, Texas, of immigrant Norwegian parents, Babe grew up as the neighborhood tomboy. She got her nickname from her mother, not from hitting home runs in sandlot baseball. After high school, the Employers Casualty Company hired her as a clerk, but the owner, Melvin J. McCombs, simply wanted her to play on his semipro basketball team. Babe led the team to the AAU finals three straight years (1929–31), winning on the third try.

She played her first golf match during the final days of the Olympics. Sportswriter Grantland Rice invited her to join him and three other reporters at Brentwood Country Club. Rice and Babe teamed together for a friendly wager against Westbrook Pegler, Paul Gallico, and Braven Dyer. Didrikson hit a few good shots, but she mostly sprayed the ball about the course. At the 17th, Rice was worried. "Babe, we're all even. We've got to do something." Gallico drove the green, and both Rice and Babe were in a fairway bunker. She told Rice not to worry and then turned to Gallico. "Paul, I'll race you to the green."

"Babe kept two feet ahead of him all the way—like Rusty the electric rabbit at a dog track," Rice wrote later. "As they reached the green, Gallico collapsed, all out and all in. When it came his time to putt, Paul 4-putted. We won the hole and the match."

The AAU banned her from amateur competition for appearing in an advertisement for an automobile, although she claimed the company used her photo and name without her knowledge. Following suit, the USGA suspended her from amateur golf in 1935, just as her game was improving.

Blazing a trail for Annika Sorenstam and Michelle Wie to follow later, Babe played in the PGA Tour's 1938 Los Angeles Open. She missed the cut. She played again in 1945 but did not play on the weekend. Also in 1945, she entered the PGA Tour stops at Phoenix and Tucson, making the cut both times. She finished 33rd at Phoenix and 42nd at Tucson.

At the 1938 Los Angeles tournament, she met her future husband, a professional wrestler nicknamed the "Crying Greek from Cripple Creek," who styled himself as a ring villain. Wrestling fans also called the Denver resident "Gorgeous George" Zaharias, the "Colorado Crooner," the "Pueblo Pouter," and the "Meanest Man." After he retired, George acted as Babe's manager.

She regained her amateur status from the USGA in 1943 and, after the war, ran roughshod over the polite society of international women's golf. She won the U.S. Women's Amateur as well as a bunch of lesser tournaments in 1946. She captured the British Women's in 1947. Some of the tweedy set in Britain were scandalized by Babe's masculine brashness, while others were simply awed by her unladylike, 250-yard drives.

Zaharias bet like a man on the golf course. Playing one year in a Battle of the Babes, she had a $50 side bet with Babe Ruth on the length of their drives. She regularly outdrove the Bambino, a decent player, by 20 yards. Big Babe gave up after losing $200. She had a similar bet with Johnny Dawson, a scratch California amateur. She won the bet on all 14 driving holes.

Babe Didrikson Zaharias, shown here after winning the 1954 U.S. Women's Open, was voted the top woman athlete of the 20th century. During both her amateur and professional careers, Babe preferred to play casual rounds with men, often for $200 Nassaus. UNITED STATES GOLF ASSOCIATION

In 1951, Babe and several other LPGA golfers played an exhibition team match against several British male amateurs at Sunningdale Golf Club near London. Zaharias and Patty Berg played a foursome match against J. B. Beck and E. Bromley-Davenport. Late in the round, each team had a short putt for a halve. As Beck stood over his ball, Babe shouted, "Time out!"

"What do you mean, time out?" Berg asked. "This isn't basketball." Zaharias claimed she wanted to see if Beck was away, but she was really messing with Beck. After a measurement showed the man was away, the distracted Beck missed the putt.

The next day the women and men played each other in singles matches. Babe drew Leonard Crawley, a two-time Walker Cup player. "Crawley had this luxurious handlebar mustache," recalled Peggy Kirk Bell in a recent interview. Not yet married to Warren Bell, Kirk played in the pairing immediately behind Zaharias and Crawley. "Babe said to him that she was going to beat him and asked if he was willing to bet his mustache on the game. He had no choice but to agree to shave it off if he lost."

Babe beat him 2 and 1, and the man ran to the parking lot from the 17th green. He could not save his pride or reputation, but he did salvage his mustache.

Babe often reacted the same way after a loss. After 10-time Metropolitan winner Maureen Orcutt beat her in an exhibition match, Babe bolted from the course without paying off their $10 bet. At a later match, Orcutt asked for the sawbuck. "She made out like she never heard me," Orcutt said years later. "She didn't like to lose."

In 1947, the Associated Press named Zaharias co-woman of the year along with actresses Helen Hayes and Ingrid Bergman and opera soprano Helen Traubel. Although George's enterprises and investments generated enough income to support Babe on the amateur golf circuit, all the publicity brought her a stream of money-making opportunities. She turned pro in 1947. Sky Crest Country Club near Chicago hired her in 1950 as a teaching pro, paying her an annual salary of $20,000. She only lasted a year. One of her biographers claimed the members asked her to leave because she was "hustling them for extra money."

Babe was a founding member of the LPGA in 1949. She joined 12 other women, including Patty Berg, Alice Bauer, Helen Dettweiler, and Helen Hicks, to form the organization as a means to establish a competitive tour like the men's. (The LPGA established its Teaching & Club Professional

Membership in 1959, an order of development opposite of the PGA of America.) Wilson Sporting Goods Company donated money to help as well as to pay the salary of the LPGA's first director, Fred Corcoran, an early PGA Tour manager and Sam Snead's agent. The association scheduled 14 events during its first year, with prize money totaling $50,000. Other than the All-American Girl's Professional Baseball League (1943–54), the LPGA offered the only chance then for women professional athletes to play for pay. Babe served as the LPGA president from 1952 to 1955.

Zaharias enjoyed a friendly wager during practice rounds before LPGA tournaments, just as her male counterparts on the PGA Tour did. Patty Berg shared one Zaharias betting story. At the Titleholders tournament in the late 1940s, Peggy Kirk played a practice round with Babe, who shot an 82 to lose $2 to Peggy. Approached after the round, Zaharias said told reporters she had a 68.

"How could you say that?" Kirk asked later. "I shot 80, and you owe me $2."

"I know they didn't want to write about an 82," Babe said, "so I told them I shot 68."

"We all bet quarters and such during practice rounds," said Kirk Bell, now a renowned golf instructor and owner of Pine Needles Lodge and Golf Club in North Carolina. "It wasn't much, but betting was part of the competition. It certainly doesn't take away from the game."

Another pioneer of the LPGA, Betty Jameson was comfortable with betting on her games. Betty learned how as a young girl, betting against the boys at Oak Park in Dallas for bottles of soda pop. As a club pro in Palm Springs in 1952, she teamed with Ben Hogan in an exhibition match against two other male pros. "There were a lot of bets, which Hogan didn't like," Betty said later, "and on the 18th, where he had a 6-foot putt, I'm sure he missed it on purpose."

Before she died of cancer in 1956 at age 45, Babe won 41 professional tournaments, five of them as an amateur. During 1946 and 1947, she won 17 of the 18 amateur tournaments she entered.

—●—

Celebrated sportswriter Jim Murray mourned the 1997 passing of both Ben Hogan and his fellow PGA Tour member Jay Herbert in the *Los Angeles*

Times. He also put betting on a golf game in its rightful perspective. As Hogan ascended into heaven, Murray imagined God's greeting:

> Ben! We've been waiting for you! Now, what do you say, Ben, we have this little eighteen-hole four-ball tomorrow? St. Peter and I will stand you and Jay Herbert, who just got here the other day too. We'll play full handicap, one low ball, play it as it lies and I'll promise no miracles.
>
> "Wait a minute! . . . No disrespect, but you may need a couple of miracles, Sir. I'm really on my game and Jay is putting well. How about if we give you three shots and two miracles a side, and we'll adjust at the turn."
>
> "Fine, automatic presses, twenty dollars four ways and we'll flip for honors at the first tee."
>
> Golf without a sporting wager must be ungodly.

Hogan won 63 PGA tournaments and nine majors—four U.S. Opens, two Masters, two PGAs, and the British Open. He is one of only five men to win all four majors in a lifetime (Sarazen, Player, Nicklaus, and Woods are the others). He played the tour full time from 1937 to 1948, missing the 1943 and 1944 seasons while in the Army Air Corps. He nearly died in an automobile accident early in 1949 and missed that whole year. He won six of his nine majors during the period 1950–53. In 1953, he won five of the six tournaments he entered, including three majors: the Masters, U.S. Open, British Open, the Colonial National Invitational, and the Pan American Open. He didn't play in the PGA Championship because it was scheduled a week after the British Open. Single-minded intensity drove the quiet Hogan to professional golf's pinnacle. He was the quintessential grind on the golf course, never letting conversation, good manners, or the time of day interfere with his business. He always bet on his game during non-tournament rounds, looking after his $10 with the same determination he showed in championships. "He'll quaff a few with the boys, enjoys a joke as well as anyone," Jimmy Demaret said of Ben, "but when it comes to golf, he just can unbend."

Hogan's predatory determination led to one of his nicknames, "Hawk." His steely stare equaled that of a raptor, and he soared over the competition, snatching victory like a rabbit from the rough. Others called him "Bantam Ben" because of his slight five-foot, eight-inch, 135-pound frame. The Brits dubbed him the "Wee Ice Mon" for his aloof resolve. A reporter asked Hogan's friend Demaret what Ben said during a round the two had just completed. "'You're out,'" Demaret said.

Hogan's father killed himself when the boy was nine years old in Fort Worth. Hogan joined Nelson at Glen Garden as a caddie to earn money to help his mother. Just as every other kid in the caddie yard, he learned to bet on golf. The boys practiced on the range before the members arrived, betting nickels. In high school, Hogan and several friends frequented local public courses, playing skins for dimes and quarters and double for birdies. At 17 years old, he played money matches around Forth Worth at several courses, but he wanted more than a $5 or $10 payday.

In 1929, he turned pro at age 19, but he didn't stick on the PGA Tour until his third attempt in 1937. In between, he bumped around, trying to improve his game, and entered tournaments when he had enough money for expenses. Early on, he lived at home and worked odd jobs when not on the course playing matches for a couple bucks. In 1933, he ran the pro shop at Oakhurst Country Club in Fort Worth. Business wasn't so hot, but Hogan used the time to start a practice routine that became legendary on the tour. He also played money golf.

"Practically all of my revenue came from selling golf balls to one rich foursome, and by winning bets from them," Hogan said. "The bets those fellows made on me taught me to play under pressure, though." His game and driving accuracy improved enough for him to bet the sportsmen that his caddie could catch all of his drives on the range. He usually won. During these lean years Hogan also worked as a dealer in backroom card games.

When he did start winning on the tour—his first was in 1938—he traveled around the country by car with his wife, Valerie. Money was still short, and many pros tried to supplement their take with side bets or by putting a little something down with Jack Doyle or the other bookies. They often bet on themselves or their friends, a practice that lasted into the 1960s in the States and to the present in Great Britain. Tour player Toney Penna tells a story about his match with Hogan during a PGA Championship. That tournament was match play until 1958, when the television suits demanded the more viewer-friendly medal play format.

Penna said he was looking at the pairings board before the first round, when a bookie began to shout out the odds for the matches: "Hogan against Penna, 8-1."

"Great," Penna told the man, "I'll take $500 of that."

"Say, that's an awful lot of money," the bookie said, backing away slightly. "I don't know whether I can go for that kind of action or not. Would you take a little 5-1?"

They agreed on $500 at 5-1. When the word spread among the other players of Penna's bet, three of them, including Craig Wood, liked the odds enough to buy in on Toney's wager. They were on hand when Penna won 3 and 1. "Any time I have Penna money on the line," Toney said, "I'm hot to trot."

At Hogan's first Masters in 1938, he arrived as an unknown. His friend and defending champ Byron Nelson was working the Calcutta the night before the first round. "Ben Hogan's name came up, and no one bid on him," Nelson said. "They were about to put his name in a pot with a couple of other players when I decided to buy him, and I gave $100," Nelson continued. "The next day, Ben saw me and said, 'I hear you bought me in the Calcutta pool last night for $100.'"

"Yes, I did," Byron responded.

"Could I buy a half interest?"

Nelson agreed, but Hogan played poorly that week, so Nelson only lost $50.

During practice rounds, Hogan always bet a modest sum. He also bet to his strength—accurate ball striking. His four U.S. Opens attest to his control. Tommy Bolt described his usual wager with Hogan: "We'd play $1 for a ball in the fairway and $1 for a ball on the green closest to the hole. The putts didn't mean a thing. Well, you can imagine what this was for Hogan. He had three guys playing him 18 holes and betting him $2 per hole each."

While other players were in awe of the Hawk, he often took advantage of them and made the betting rules. PGA Tour journeyman Tommy Jacobs said Hogan often insisted on his favorite game, Points. "If you missed a fairway with a shot, you got one point tacked up," Jacobs explained. "It was two points for missing a green. One time in particular, I remember finishing with plus-24 and Ben had plus-11, and we were playing for $1 a point. I sad, 'Okay, Ben, I guess I owe you $13.'

"No, that's not the way we do it," Hogan said. "The winner pays himself, and you owe me for the total that you missed."

Young pros marveled at his control as Hogan shaped his shots to fit the hole and wind. Butch Baird, who went on to win twice on the tour, cautiously asked Hogan during a round, "Mr. Hogan, you never seem to hit a straight shot. Do you always hit it left to right or right to left?"

"Always," the Hawk answered tersely and then turned back to his ball.

Bill Collins, another PGA Tour winner, played a practice round with Hogan for a $20 bet. On the back nine, Collins mustered the courage to approach Hogan for some swing advice. "What do you think I could do to work on my game?" Collins asked. "Hogan just looks at me for a minute, then he says, 'How do we stand?' How do we stand? He wasn't gonna help me if I was beating him!"

Tommy Bolt felt Hogan only bet small amounts because no one wanted to risk real money on a game with the master. "Who in world would have gone out there and played Ben Hogan a $100 Nassau? It was unthinkable."

Hogan always had a little action when he played with friends at home. During those games, he loosened up a smidgen but not enough to change either his dour demeanor or his competitive instincts.

Dan Jenkins came to know Hogan in the 1950s in Fort Worth. Hogan invited Jenkins to play occasionally at Colonial, often with two other members. "If there were four of us," Jenkins said of the games, "we'd throw up the balls, and play a $1 Nassau. Sometimes I'd have Hogan for a partner, sometimes I wouldn't. And you didn't always win if you had him as a partner. A member and I got hot one day, made every putt, and I won $5 from Ben. I suppose I should have framed the $5 bill he gave me, but I spent it on a date."

Lanny Wadkins played casual rounds with Hogan early in Wadkins's career. The first time Wadkins won, Hogan wrote a check for $15. Wadkins kept the check as a souvenir. When Hogan's secretary called about the outstanding check, he said, "It's never gonna be cashed."

During one of his matches with Hogan, another young man joined Wadkins in the foursome. "We had a game going, and a couple of us were joking around and having a good time," Lanny said, "and Hogan looked over at me and said, 'I don't play jolly golf.' It was like, 'O.K., fine, Ben. No jolly golf.'"

Hogan couldn't win every bet, golf being what it is, nor did he always stick to modest wagers. A friend, oilman Tex Moncrief, told two stories about Hogan playing for real money. In the first, Moncrief said Hogan, in the midst of pre-round needling, challenged a third friend, M. O. Rife, to the old one-leg proposition. "M. O., I could beat you standing on one leg with a 2-iron," Hogan boasted.

"Well, I'll just bet you $1,000 you can't," M. O. said. Moncrief chimed in with another $2,000 against Hogan. Others made their own side bets.

"By the time we got around to 12, ole M. O. had him dormie," Moncrief said. "Ben never finished the 12th hole. He just took his clubs and left, conceding the match. He didn't say a dang thing. He just left."

In the 1980s at Shady Oaks, Hogan's last home course until his death, Moncrief told of a game he often played with Ben, $50 Birdies—that is, "$25 I do and $25 you don't." On the par-3 12th, playing over 200 yards that day from the tips, Moncrief recalled, "I turned to Hogan, 'Ben, you want $50 on a birdie?' Of course old Ben would just stare you down and wouldn't say a damn thing for what seemed like forever. Finally, he said, 'Sure, I'll take 50 . . . I'll take $50,000.' 'Ben, I just wanted a friendly little bet. I didn't want to get to gambling or anything.'" Moncrief made his birdie, but Ben did not. Hogan didn't speak.

On the par-3 16th, Hogan cleared his throat and then finally asked, "What about 50 here?" Game on. Tex put his tee shot within 10 or 12 feet from the stick, but Hogan dropped his three feet from the hole. Hogan won that $50. "He never said another dang word," Moncrief said.

Finally, one story suggests Hogan may have had a little hustle in him. He certainly had the poker face for it. At Shady Oaks in the 1960s, Hogan played a game called "the Swing" with a group of regulars. Similar to a game called "Wheel," one or two golfers became the Swing for a round and matched either his score or his team's score for individual bets against all the others' scores. The number of players usually made for a sizable pot. Hogan and Earl Baldridge, an 11-handicap, often took on the rest using everyone's full handicap. Considering Hogan was about a plus-4 at the time, he had to make up plenty of strokes. Despite Earl's 11 and Hogan's skill, Hogan lost more than he could stand at one point.

Hogan arrived unannounced at the club early one morning and took superintendent Henry Martin out on the course. Back in the pro shop three hours later, Hogan said to the head pro Art Hall, "I wasn't here." Then Hogan went to his office. He returned for lunch as he did everyday, declaring he and Earl would play for double the normal bet.

On the first tee, the others were surprised to see all the tee markers, including the ladies', old men's, and men's, pushed to the back right corner of the championship tee. Dr. Harvey Small asked, "What are they doing, Ben, mowing the tees?"

"That's right," Ben answered sparingly. "Hit it."

At the first green, Hogan's opponents found the hole cut on the right side, behind a bunker. Hogan had set up every hole for a fade both off the tee and into the green. Most of the others in the group only played a low draw, common among better players in windy West Texas. Hogan shot a 64; his partner, an 81. It was a get-even day for Hogan.

—●—

"Everybody cheats. It was a private club, and I needed a few dollars." This was how Bill Roberts rationalized his handicap cheating in a 1955 tournament at Deepdale Golf Club in Great Neck, New York. Everyone knows a sandbagger, but this incident unsettled the golf establishment in America. Moreover, the "Deepdale scandal" forever changed one facet of money golf in America.

A 26-year-old Laundromat worker from West Springfield, Massachusetts, Roberts registered with a 17-handicap. When his partner Richard Vitali withdrew, Roberts paid Bud Helmar $100 to play and to assume Vitali's name. Helmar claimed an 18. Both Roberts and Helmar actually played to 3. During a practice round, they caught the interest of Richard Armstrong, a New York banker and member of the nearby Sands Point Club.

At the Calcutta auction before the tournament's start, Armstrong led a syndicate in the bidding for Roberts and Helmar, ultimately paying $1,900 for the team. The betting pool, containing the bids for all the teams, totaled $45,000. Roberts and Helmar won by five strokes, shooting net 58-57. Armstrong received 40 percent of the pool, or $16,016.90. He gave Roberts $4,026 of his winnings.

Helmar, who received only his $100, also lost a match with his conscience. He soon wrote Deepdale's president to confess his sins. The news media and the USGA got wind of the incident. Deepdale became the poster child for one of the few smudges on golf's character.

The Calcutta is a betting pool scheme that migrated from horse racing to golf. At U.S. tracks in the 1860s and '70s, "pool selling" accumulated bets on individual horses and used the take to pay off the winning wagers. Pools were common at Jerome Park in the Bronx, then host of the Belmont

Stakes as well as Saratoga and the Kentucky tracks. Some suggest the term *Calcutta* is derived from horse race betting at the Royal Calcutta Turf Club in India. The Brits, however, generally called a golf pool an "auction." American gamblers even used pool selling to take bets on the 1876 U.S. presidential elections, the most contentious national election until the 2000 Bush-Gore debacle. The "pool rooms" that accommodated gambling and other socially suspect activities were not billiard rooms but off-track locations where pool sellers worked.

Calcuttas are not sweepstakes in which each entrant contributes something of value to a pot that is distributed to first, second, and third places. There are no odds or bidding in sweepstakes. During the first American golf boom in the early 1900s, almost every club regularly hosted a "ball sweepstakes." Each player anted up a new golf ball, and the payout was in kind.

Because wagering between golfers was a staple in American golf since its beginning, pool selling showed up at the golf course almost immediately. Newspapers followed the game's development, and they didn't miss the auctions' emergence. The *New York Sun* ran a piece in 1904 that explained the inner workings of pool selling during tournaments.

The frequency of pool selling increased parallel to golf's rising popularity. In 1919, both the PGA Championship and the U.S. Women's Amateur at Shawnee-on-Delaware featured auction pools. A pool was a central part of the North and South Open in Pinehurst. At the 1920 tournament, a man offered $10,000 for Walter Hagen, with odds of 1-3 against the field. A pool at the 1920 Pinehurst amateur competition sold Ouimet for $600.

At the 1921 U.S. Amateur, Bostonian R. C. Van Arsdale won $7,040 from the pool when his man Jesse Guilford won. Van Arsdale had bought Guilford's ticket for $480 from E. G. Burkham, who had second thoughts about Guilford's chances. The host club, St. Louis Country Club, sponsored the auction.

"War Is Declared on Golf Gamblers," shouted the *New York Times* in May 1920. The paper cited the USGA's predictable reaction to the rising popularity of auction pools. In a letter to all member clubs, the association's executive committee demanded they stop the practice. This order would be the association's first shot in a battle over Calcuttas that would run for years. The USGA's pressure forced pool selling underground at amateur tournaments in the States, but the huge pool that favored Bobby Jones at the 1929 U.S. Open showed the auctions were alive and well.

Public betting pools nevertheless remained a staple at pro tournaments. Participants and reporters started referring to the auctions as "Calcuttas" in the 1930s, and their popularity peaked in the 1940s and '50s. The Los Angeles Open had one as did the Crosby, the Thunderbird, and even a small pro-member tournament at Spring Lake Country Club in New Jersey. Spring Lake's pool totaled $85,000, with Lloyd Mangrum and Claude Harmon drawing top bids. The Augusta National sponsored a Calcutta in the clubhouse at the first Masters; however, organizers moved it to the Bon Air Vanderbilt Hotel in 1949.

Little-known Herman Keiser won the 1946 Masters by one stroke over Ben Hogan. Keiser, a doleful sort nicknamed the "Missouri Mortician," subsequently told the press of sinister forces bent on preventing his winning. He maintained two Augusta National members bet $50,000 each on Hogan during the auction at 4-1 odds and acted to protect their investment.

After placing $20 on himself at 20-1, Keiser shot 69-68 in the first two rounds. Before the third round, Keiser said two bookies approached him, asking, "You think you can win?" Keiser told them to get lost but not before putting down another $50 on himself. At this point, Keiser believed the club was subtly supporting the big bettors by refusing to replace his sore-footed caddie and by abruptly changing his final round starting time. Keiser's lead was down to one stroke when he 3-putted on 18 on the final day. Hogan's 3-jack on 18 gave Keiser the victory. Kaiser's $1,400 payout from the pool was icing on the $2,500 cake from the purse.

Many writers have repeated Keiser's tale, but David Owen, in his book *Making of the Masters*, refutes much of Keiser's conspiracy theory. Owen also doubted the incorruptible Clifford Roberts would permit a member to influence the tournament. No records, however, show the Calcutta bids on Hogan.

Public Calcuttas reached their zenith at the Las Vegas Tournament of Champions in the 1950s. Started in 1953 by Howard Capps, it was open only to the previous year's tournament winners. It offered a bigger purse than the U.S. Open's and was second only to that of the Tam O'Shanter. Lodging at the Desert Inn, food, and drink were gratis, and last place paid $1,000. The Calcutta was the largest in the country and was anything but a black hole. Celebrity auctioneers, such as Bob Hope and Jimmy Durante, helped with the selling. The pool totaled $380,000 by 1959, and at least $1 million changed hands in side bets outside the Calcutta.

Gene Littler won the tournament three years running (1955–57). Singer Frankie Laine—who recorded "Mule Train" and the *High Noon* theme song—bought Littler each year and bid a total of $45,000 during the period. He won $192,654 overall. Littler won $10,000 from the purse in 1957, and Laine paid him another $9,500 as the player's cut of the winnings.

Immediately after the Deepdale incident, the USGA started an aggressive campaign to rid golf of Calcutta auctions. Saying the handicap fraud had "disgraced the good name of golf," they forbid amateurs from participating in Calcuttas. The association, however, made it clear they still condoned friendly wagers and modest sweepstakes.

In 1959, USGA executive director Joe Dey grumbled about the pricey Calcutta at the Las Vegas tournament. He also said he might ban professionals who played the tournament from participating in the U.S. Open. Snead told the press Dey should mind his own business. Demaret added his feelings: "That's the silliest statement I ever heard. If they ran the pros from the U.S. Open, it would become just another amateur tournament." Demaret also said he knew of at least four top USGA executives who gambled on the golf course and "gamble good."

"Sure I've bet on myself in a golf match," Demaret admitted to a reporter. "Haven't you? I see nothing wrong in betting on myself. If I have enough confidence in my own ability, why shouldn't I bet? But if I bet against myself, I should be thrown out of golf."

"If you say I can't gamble," Mike Souchak added, "then you're telling me how to spend my money. When there's something wrong with a $2 practice round Nassau, then it's later than you think." When he won the 1959 Tournament of Champions, Souchak's backers won $136,800 from the pool, but it was the tournament's last public Calcutta. Organizers announced in September 1959 they had discontinued the auction pool, but they didn't offer a reason.

The Masters Calcutta flourished quietly for a while at Augusta's Jewish Community Center, but now all the auctions occur in private homes or clubs. The CBS TV crew discreetly held a pool for years until Neal Pilson became the head of CBS Sports in late 1986. Former CBS golf analyst Ben Wright bid on players starting in 1973, picking the winner seven times. "It was a very hush-hush affair," said Wright, whom CBS fired in 1996 for his remarks about women's golf. "It took place behind locked doors, and it was a raunchy and fairly drunken event. Bob Drum was the auctioneer." Wright said his largest payday from the CBS Masters Calcutta came in 1979, when his $50 bid for Fuzzy Zoeller won 60 percent of the pot—$26,000. Wright said the pool reached that level because the CBS people started inviting their rich friends. According to Wright, Pilson thought the big numbers unseemly and stopped the Calcutta.

In addition to the Calcuttas, "horse races" took place every evening on the second floor of the National's clubhouse. TV commentator Jack Whitaker, who covered the Masters for CBS until moving to ABC in 1981, said the bettors used tournament pairings as the horses. Each put $100 in the pot and then drew out of a hat two-man pairings for the next day. The payout went to whoever held the pair with the lowest aggregate score. Whitaker commented: "This had the effect of keeping you deeply informed and interested in all the players in the field, not just the first 10 on the leader board, and gave you a deeper knowledge of the tournament. It was wonderful discipline and great fun."

The USGA currently finds Calcuttas involving "excessive" amounts of money unacceptable forms of betting on golf. It also objects to any Calcutta that is open to non-players. The greatest threat to a Calcutta is not necessarily from the USGA but rather the IRS. Betting income is taxable.

Calcuttas still abound in golf. Those operating in the open are generally limited to charity fund-raisers. The others, however, operate quietly and in private. They are common at country club member-guest tournaments, with the auction providing a bit of spice to the weekend.

Clandestine big money auctions, throwbacks to the grand days of pool selling, also still exist. A middle-aged golfer, who asked to remain anonymous, recently described one in which he plays annually. He carries a 16-handicap and belongs to a respectable country club on the East Coast. A health care professional, he is married with kids.

> The pool runs about $800,000. Players come from all over the country. There are five per team, ranging in skill level from A to E. The handicapper scrutinizes each team, but the best deterrence against funny stuff is the network among all the Calcutta tournaments. If word gets around about a cheater, he'll never play again. Also, if a guy ain't a "player," someone who just sits around and doesn't bet, he won't be invited back.
>
> Calcutta night is organized chaos. They always start the auction

late so everyone will drink more. Cigars, noise, dark room, the whole bit. It's like the stock market trading floor—people buying and selling shares in teams—"I'll give you 1,000 for 20 percent of so-and-so." It's great fun. I always buy a share from whoever bought my team. If I didn't, I'd lose face.

We play four rounds with varying formats—Captain's Choice, better ball, or aggregate medal. Lot's of side bets. It's a great way to play golf.

Finally, Internet firms offer Calcutta software packages for sale. Google "Calcutta software golf." "Backnine Bookie" has the best name.

Golf has a way of dampening the swing toward extremes in the sport. A few over-the-top knee jerk reactions occurred after the Deepdale incident, but the game did begin to pay more attention to handicap cheating. The sport is better off for that scrutiny. Some set their hair on fire over Calcuttas and argued for strict bans. Things have settled a bit, and today's message on Calcuttas seems sensible: be discreet, keep out the nonplaying gamblers, and make golf the center of the event.

—●—

At the 1956 Masters, a lanky amateur from San Francisco led the tournament after 36 holes. Twenty-five-year-old Ken Venturi had thrown a 66 and a 69 at the old pros at Augusta National, tying the record for the first two rounds. He was four strokes clear of the field. His friend Eddie Lowery, the car salesman who seemed to know every golfer in the 1950s, bet some serious money on Venturi: $5,000 to win at 12-1, another $5,000 to place at 10-1, and $5,000 more to show at 8-1. After the first two days, both Venturi and Lowery were counting their chickens.

Venturi wasn't happy with his 75 in the third round, but the others struggled just as he did with the wind and fast greens. He was still four shots up at the end of the day. Lowery was looking at a $60,000 payday if Venturi could become the first amateur to win the Masters.

But it was not meant to be. Venturi 3-putted six greens on the final day for an 80, one stroke behind winner Jackie Burke, Jr. Despite yielding to what must have been suffocating pressure, Venturi still displayed enough game to start an illustrious professional career, which culminated with a dramatic victory at the 1964 U.S. Open. He also won 13 PGA Tour events before hand ailments prevented regular tournament appearances. He went on to work as a commentator for CBS TV from 1968 to 2002.

Venturi learned the game by caddying at San Francisco Golf Club and playing with his father at Harding Park. As a teenager, he coveted a friend's Tommy Armour putter. Doug Wadkins offered to sell it, but his $15 price was too much for Kenny. He talked Doug into a putting contest at Harding Park for 50¢ a hole in hopes of raising enough money to buy the putter. With only 50¢ in his pocket, Venturi was too young to feel the pressure. He won enough to buy the club and pocket some change. It was only one of many money games he played in his career.

After Venturi won the 1950 San Francisco City Championship, Lowery took him back to San Francisco Golf Club, not as Eddie's caddie but as his partner in $20 Nassau matches with other members. Lowery covered the bets at first, but they won enough for Venturi to accumulate his own roll. After Venturi finished college, Lowery hired him as an auto salesman. Lowery also employed another promising amateur, E. Harvie Ward, who joined Venturi on the 1953 Walker Cup team.

The Masters invited both Ward and Venturi to play in the 1954 tournament. They stopped in Miami for some warm-up rounds. Two other golfers invited them to join them for a bet of one, one, and two. "What's a couple bucks?" thought Venturi. On 16, one of the strangers said, "You got us out for $400. We'd like to press you for $200." Venturi and Ward discovered they had missed some zeroes. The young men kept their poise, however. They each won $400 and headed for Augusta feeling flush. At the Masters, Venturi tied for 16th, one stroke ahead of Ward.

Ward and Venturi played in a widely reported money match during a practice round before the 1956 Crosby. Byron Nelson called it one of the greatest four-ball matches in history. People tell several versions of the story, but this one is Venturi's.

The ubiquitous Eddie Lowery attended a party at George Coleman's Monterrey home a few days before the tournament started. Lowery was touting Venturi's skills, as well as Ward's, who had won the 1952 British and 1955 U.S. Amateurs by that point. Lowery boasted his two employees could beat anybody.

"Anybody?" asked Coleman, a wealthy oilman from Oklahoma. "Including pros?"

"Yes, including pros," responded Eddie.

"What do you want to bet on that?" Coleman asked.

"Five thousand."

Coleman recruited Hogan and Nelson, but they did not want any public fanfare. Hogan booked a practice round for the next day at Pebble Beach, but they played instead at Cypress Point to dodge the crowds. They agreed to a $100 Nassau instead of Lowery's five grand.

The two teams matched each other stroke for stroke, posting 27 birdies and one eagle between the four of them. With Hogan and Nelson 1-up on the par-4 18th, Hogan stepped on Venturi's birdie with one of his own to win the match. Nelson and Ward each shot 67 on their own ball; Venturi, 65; and the Hawk, 63.

"I'll tell you one thing," Hogan said afterward to Venturi, "I didn't want you to know it, but we wanted to beat you guys so bad. I told Byron, 'We've got our hands full with these guys.'" Hogan acknowledged he played as hard as he could and didn't want the round to end.

"If there was one more hole," Venturi said, "we would have gotten you."

In the first round of the San Francisco City tournament that Venturi won in 1950, he played a local businessman, Martin Stanovich, who enjoyed wagering on the golf course. Without Venturi's knowledge, his friends bet Stanovich $3,500 that Venturi would beat him. Venturi won 3 and 1, but Marty Stanovich would win plenty more bets in the future.

The Fat Man. "Weighing in at 230 pounds, [he] owned one of the most preposterous swings in golf," wrote one observer. "Feet planted apart, head hung low, he had a ridiculously short back swing and lunged at the ball like a man trying to kill a cockroach with a crowbar." The Fat Man was Martin Stanovich, one of golf's most improbable hustlers.

"He looked terrible hitting the ball," Lee Trevino said of Stanovich. "He used Kroyden clubs [cheap, department store sticks] with grips twice as long as normal and he'd choke way down on them. He had a God-awful swing. But it was a come-on. If you're a golf hustler, you've got to have some gimmicks. You can't look good."

During the 1950s and '60s, Stanovich, whose weight often ballooned to 300 pounds, was an equal opportunity hustler. He used his edge to win bets from pros, fellow con artists, and "nice people who just love to lose money."

Stanovich once owned a mattress and upholstery factory in San Francisco, and he learned golf at Harding Park's golf course. Stanovich moved to Chicago in the 1950s, picking up money games at the Tam O'Shanter club in the summer and migrating to the Florida hot spots in the winter. He was a three-time Chicago District Golf Association champion and played in both the French and British Amateurs. He became quite skilled, but as others before him, he declined to turn pro, claiming that he was "too old and too fat to walk with the pros." Furthermore, he pointed out, "there was more money in gambling."

A Pittsburgh businessman arranged matches in which the Fat Man beat touring pros, including Ed Furgol, the 1954 U.S. Open champion. He won money from standout amateur Frank Stranahan in 1962 and teamed with Trevino in 1965 to beat Dick Martin, Erwin Hardwicke, and others at Tenison Park. PGA Tour player Eddie Pearce won a few bucks from the Fat Man while playing at Bardmoor Country Club in St Petersburg, Florida, but Pearce lost more when the two started betting on bunker shots at the practice green. "It started at a $100 a shot and went from there," Pearce recalled. Losing $35,000 to Stanovich in an hour, Pearce marveled at the Fat Man's skill. "I was stepping on the ball, burying it, putting under the lip and he'd still knock it stiff. He'd grip it down to the steel and do things that made no sense. He drove me crazy."

"He was easily the best sand trap player I've ever seen," said Leon Crump, another legendary money player. "He wasn't trying to get up and down from the beach, he'd actually try to hole the ball. A lot of times he shot at the bunkers on purpose to keep the games going. When the money got to where he liked it, he'd just flag the damn ball."

The late Bobby Riggs, a member of the International Tennis Hall of Fame and a renowned golf hustler, told a story about the Fat Man's power of concentration and golfing skill. Stanovich, in a foursome that included Riggs, hooked his drives out of bounds on the first two holes of a match and yielded a 7 and a 6. A bookie watching the game offered Stanovich a $5,000 wager that he couldn't break 70 on the round; he accepted.

"The Fat Man then proceeded to score eight successive threes and finished with a 69," Riggs recalled. "The Fat Man was always at his best when the big chips were down."

As an amateur, Stanovich always asked for strokes from the pros. If he didn't get the right number of strokes, he walked away chanting, "See you in the fall, if I see you at all." Against unsuspecting amateurs, whatever their handicap, Stanovich gave what seemed to be a fair number of strokes. When his opponent saw the Fat Man swing, the pigeon felt he had a mortal lock. Stanovich knew better.

"The Fat Man always gave you what you thought was a fair game," Riggs said. "Trouble was, you were usually wrong. He was treacherous, and I learned a lot from him."

—●—

"Well," President Eisenhower said on the first tee at Burning Tree Country Club, "I just loaned Bolivia $2 million. I'll play for a $1 Nassau."

Bob Hope partnered with Ike that day in the 1950s at the exclusive, men-only club in Bethesda, Maryland. They played General of the Army Omar Bradley and Missouri senator Stuart Symington. Hope said he played poorly, and he and Eisenhower lost the bet. Against Ike and Bradley the next day, Hope teamed with Connecticut senator Prescott Bush, father and grandfather of presidents.

"I was back on my game and shot 75," recalled Hope. "I beat Ike for $4, and I'll never forget the sour look on his face when he pulled out his money clip and paid off. He looked me in the eye and grumbled, 'Why didn't you play this well yesterday?' He wasn't laughing, either."

Since Taft's inauguration in 1909, all but four presidents played golf while in office. Hoover fished, and Franklin Roosevelt was a solid, perhaps even gifted golfer before he was stricken with polio at age 39 in 1921. Harry Truman liked walks and poker, and Jimmy Carter played tennis and hunted killer rabbits. Almost all the men who played golf enjoyed a friendly wager on their games.

Taft was an ardent player, and at 300 pounds it took considerable enthusiasm for him to wrap a club around his ample girth. When in Washington, he played at nearby Chevy Chase Club, which was often referred to as "the seat of presidential golf" but mostly because it was one of the few clubs in the area until the 1920s. Taft had two favorite clubs: when at home in Ohio, Cincinnati Country Club, where he also served as its first president starting in 1902; and while on summer vacation Myopia Hunt Club in Beverly, Massachusetts.

Taft showed he understood the art of betting on golf during the Ouimet-Vardon-Ray duel at the 1913 U.S. Open, but biographers have passed down little information about his betting habits. In one story, however, as members watched Taft on the course during his first summer playing at Myopia, they began to bet among themselves on the president's ability to break a 100. The stakes grew to $1,000, with Taft responding by shooting a laudable 98 on his next round. "It was a rattling good score for a middle-class player," one observer noted.

Taft's two successors, Woodrow Wilson and Warren Harding, frequently played golf during their terms. Wilson played as often as six times a week, and he even used balls painted red to play in the snow. He played on the day he asked Congress to declare war in 1917 and then again the next day. Harding played a little less often, but he did so for more money.

"He and Kennedy," said Andy Mutch, USGA historian, when referring to Harding and JFK, "probably gambled more on a golf course than any other presidents." While playing two or three times a week, Harding's favorite bet was a $6 Nassau. He usually shot in the 90s. "Forget that I am the president of the United States," he told his partners. "I'm Warren Harding with some friends, and I'm going to beat the hell out of them."

Harding enjoyed side bets during his game, usually asking his Secret Service agent, Edmund Starling, to keep track of the stakes. He made bets on the low score for the round, on individual holes, and on the result of a shot while the ball was in the air, a precursor of a bet known today as an "Air Hammer." (See chapter 9 for more details.) "He made so many bets," said Starling, "sometimes he was betting against himself. I had to keep accounts, and it was a job for a Philadelphia lawyer."

Because of the money at stake, Harding was a stickler for the rules, an approach to the game most bettors share. He accepted no "gimme putts," hunted for his own ball in the woods, and never improved his lie. The only cheating he did was to ignore Prohibition. Every three or four holes at Chevy Chase, Harding took a pull from a whiskey bottle hidden in his bag. When tongues began to wag, he retreated to a private course owned by the *Washington Post's* publisher Edward McLean. There, liveried butlers served up Scotch and soda on silver trays.

Grantland Rice wrote of a 1921 match he and his pal, humorist Ring Lardner, played against Harding and his under secretary of state, Henry Fletcher. "President Harding, from the start, proved to be a sportsman who belongs among the select," Rice wrote. "Thoroughly human in every way, he has dignity without pretense and the love of a keen, hard contest that calls for a battle to the finish." Perhaps Rice's glowing praise reflected the $100 he and Lardner took from the president and his partner.

Calvin Coolidge played infrequently while in office, generally forswearing sports altogether. A reporter once asked if he had ever participated in sports, even in college. "Yes," he responded, "I did, an important part. I held the stakes."

Known for his frugality, Coolidge was also a man of few words, a trait he shared with Ben Hogan. A story about a woman seated next to Coolidge at a White House dinner highlighted his reticence. She mentioned to the president she had bet a friend she could coax more than two words out of him. Cal coolly replied, "You lose."

Eisenhower's love of golf was almost as important in popularizing the game in the United States as Arnold Palmer's charisma and style were. Ike played frequently—800 times during eight years in office—and with gusto. He installed a putting green at the White House and practiced his wedge play on the South Lawn. He often carried a golf club during the day, and the dimples his spikes left on the Oval Office floor were mute testimony to his ability to mix work with play.

He played frequently at Burning Tree and vacationed so often at Augusta National that Bobby Jones and Cliff Roberts built a cabin on the grounds so Eisenhower and his wife, Mamie, could spend their nights at the club. Shooting mostly in the 80s, Eisenhower was relatively long off the tee, but his slice tested his temper. His strength was his short game, a skill that benefited his press secretary, James Haggerty. "I don't know how much I've made on small side bets," Haggerty said, "figuring when he's 70 or 80 yards away, he's going to get down in two." Haggerty won a $5 bet during one of Ike's rounds at Tamarisk Country Club in Palm Springs, California. Sixty yards from the green, the president cut a wedge left to right around a palm tree, stopping his ball 18 inches from the hole.

Eisenhower certainly enjoyed a small wager on his game and generally respected golf's many rules. The one area where he occasionally succumbed to temptation was improving his lie, all while claiming he was just identifying his ball, each of which had "Mr. President" printed on its cover. In one instance where Ike rolled his ball about the rough, ostensibly making sure it was his, a caddie at Burning Tree chastised the leader of the free world: "Mr. President, I think you over identified that ball."

The second installment of presidential betting is in chapter 7.

U.S. president Dwight D. Eisenhower always enjoyed a $1 or $2 Nassau. His vice president, Richard M. Nixon, played some money golf, but he bent a few rules trying to improve his game. EISENHOWER LIBRARY

—●—

Journalists, authors, and golf historians who write about golf generally fall into two groups—those who understand the role of betting in golf and the others. Walter Hagen, for example, filled his memoir (as told to Margaret Seaton Heck) with dozens of stories about money golf, yet Tom Clavin skipped most of them when writing his biography *Sir Walter*. Gene Sarazen's autobiography, which he wrote with Herbert Warren Wind, *Thirty Years of Championship Golf*, recalled his many victories and the wagers he had on them.

Wind wrote *The Story of American Golf* in 1948 (with a second edition in 1956), and it's full of references to the wagering that accompanied golf when it migrated to the United States. The wonderfully illustrated *Golf in*

America (1987), however, made no mention of money golf even though George Peper, once the editor in chief of *Golf Magazine*, edited the volume. A splendid writer and golfer himself, he certainly understood the subject. Perhaps his publisher was targeting the coffee table instead of money golfers.

Wind died in 2005. His descriptions of golf and golfers were eloquent yet still readable. One can trace many of the game's euphemisms to Wind, including "Amen Corner," the name he gave to the 11th, 12th, and 13th holes at Augusta National. He also coauthored with Ben Hogan *Five Lessons: The Modern Fundamentals of Golf,* one of the most respected and widely read how-to books.

The year 1955 marked a little-known milestone in golf writing. British expatriate and literary master P. G. Wodehouse became an American citizen. "If Harvey Penick was golf's Socrates—the game's greatest teacher and philosopher—then Wodehouse was golf's Shakespeare: its master comedian and tragedian, its bard," wrote *Sports Illustrated's* Robert Sullivan in 1995. Nongolfers will remember Wodehouse for his Jeeves novels, but he wrote dozens of short stories about golf. He assembled many of them in his *Golf Omnibus,* published in 1973. All involve a match of some kind, including the associated friendly wager, proving Wodehouse understood both golf and the human race.

"Two things Wodehouse was very shrewd about were golf and relationships," said Peter Schwed, his editor. "He was an acute observer of the species, and in the golf stories the satire was right on the mark. Anyone who's ever golfed will have to laugh at the situations out on the golf course. This stuff really happens, as a golfer knows."

Most of Wodehouse's golf stories feature "The Oldest Member" as the narrator. He frequented his club's grill and veranda, ready at the drop of a sun visor to offer advice or spin a yarn. Many younger members attempted to keep their distance, knowing they couldn't escape until he finished his tale. In Wodehouse's short story, "High Stakes," a commotion on the 18th green startled The Oldest Member as he dozed in his favorite chair on the terrace. One of the junior members walked up from the green.

"What," inquired the Sage, "was all the shouting for?"

The young man sank into a chair and lighted a cigarette. "Perkins and Broster," he said, "were all square at the seventeenth, and they raised the stakes to fifty pounds. They were both on the green in seven, and Perkins had a 2-foot putt to halve the match. He missed by six inches. They play pretty high, those two."

"It is a curious thing," said The Oldest Member, "that men whose golf is a kind that makes hardened caddies wince always do. The more competent a player, the smaller the stake that contents him. It is only when you get down into the submerged tenth of the golfing world that you find the big gambling. However, I would not call the fifty pounds any thing sensational in the case of two men like Perkins and Broster. They are both well provided with the world's goods. If you would care to hear the story—"

The young man's jaw fell a couple of notches. "I had no idea it was so late," he bleated. "I ought to be—"

"—of a man who played for really high stakes—"

"I promised to—"

"—I will tell it to you," said the Sage.

"Look here," said the young man, sullenly, "it isn't one of those stories about two men who fall in love with the same girl and play a match to decide which is to marry her, is it? Because if so—"

"The stake to which I allude," said The Oldest Member, "was something far higher and bigger than a woman's love. Shall I proceed?"

"All right," said the young man, resignedly. "Snap into it."

Perhaps not as eloquent as Wind was or as widely published as Wodehouse is, sports writer Dan Jenkins has brought his own satirical view of golf to readers for years. Jenkins wrote a 1994 *Sports Illustrated* piece "The Glory Game at Goat Hills," which celebrated money golf in the 1950s. He and a bunch of irreverent friends played at Worth Hills, a Fort Worth muni they rechristened "Goat Hills." Everyone at the course seemed to have a nickname: "Cecil the Parachute" (he fell down a lot when swinging), "Magoo," "Foot the Free," "Weldon the Oath," "Moron Tom," and others. Here's how Jenkins described the play: "It was a gambling game that went on in some fashion or another, involving two to twenty players, almost every day of every year. If there were certain days when it seemed the game might help pay part of my tuition through Texas Christian University—a jumble of yellow-brick buildings across the street from the course—there were others when it seemed certain to guarantee a lifetime of indebtedness. Either way you were trapped, incessantly drawn to the Hills, like Durrell to

Alexandria." Jenkins's reference to playwright and novelist Lawrence Durrell's fondness for Egypt may be lost on the golfing set, but Jenkins's literary skills often transcend sports.

Jenkins wrote that eightsomes were common, with every golfer playing a Nassau against each of the others. "Without any presses . . . that was a sizable investment right there. But new bets came quickly because of an automatic one-down press rule, and big, get-even bets on nine and eighteen. It was certainly nice to birdie the ninth and eighteenth holes sometimes. Like maybe a hundred dollars nice."

Often bored with the usual games, Jenkins and his buddies made up others: playing the course backward, every other hole, out-of-bounds except for greens, or with one club at night. Another favorite was the Thousand-Yard Dash. Twelve players put $5 in the pot, then played one long hole that started at the farthest corner of the course, and ended with a chipped-out depression in the clubhouse porch. The final strokes on the concrete porch proved Jenkins's undoing when he 18-putted for a 23, losing to Foot the Free's 6. Foot's complete name was "Big Foot the Freeloader."

The Goat Hills crew occasionally played at nearby Ridglea. Jenkins described a prop bet that Ridglea's pro, Raymond Gafford, offered one day to Dan and his friends. Gafford climbed onto a tabletop in the pro shop and then set up to hit a ball out the door toward the first green, a par-5.

"Believe I can make five from here?" asked Gafford.

"Well, I ain't had nothin' this good lately," said Spec, a Hills regular, as he pulled out his roll. "We're gonna eat steak tonight and play golf tomorrow."

"Just get it on," Gafford said.

"On?" said Spec. "On's here in my hand."

Gafford hit a clean 4-iron off the table, through the door and onto the fairway. He was only a 3-wood and a long iron from the green; a sure five was imminent. "Oops," said Spec. "Step on the fire and call in the dogs. The hunt's over, boys."

If you don't have a stack of old *Sports Illustrateds* in the basement, you can enjoy the whole Goat Hills story in Jenkins's book *Fairways and Greens.*

—●—

Movies and novels reflect golf's relationship with betting, largely because successful golf screenwriters and authors know wagers are an integral part of the sport. A classic is James Bond's match with Auric Goldfinger in Ian Fleming's novel *Goldfinger* and the film of the same name. After some verbal sparring and negotiating, Bond and Goldfinger agreed to have a go of it on the golf course. Here's the segment:

"But I warn you I like playing for money. I can't be bothered to knock a ball round just for the fun of it." Bond felt pleased with the character he was building up for himself.

Was there a glint of triumph, quickly concealed, in Goldfinger's pale eyes? He said indifferently, "That suits me. Anything you like. Off handicap, of course. I think you said you're a nine."

"Yes."

Goldfinger said carefully, "Where, may I ask."

"Huntercombe." Bond was also a nine at Sunningdale. Huntercombe was an easier course. Nine at Huntercombe wouldn't frighten Goldfinger.

"And I also am nine. Here. Up on the board. So it's a level game. Right?"

Bond shrugged. "You'll be too good for me."

"I doubt it." However, Goldfinger was offhand, "Tell you what I'll do. That bit of money you removed from me in Miami. Remember? The big figure was ten. I like to gamble. It will be good for me to have a try. I will play you for double or quits for that.

"Oh well, all right. Easy come easy go. Level match. Ten thousand dollars it is."

—●—

CHIPS AND PITCHES

Blonde bettor. Jeanne Carmen, called "Queen of the B-Movies" for her film roles in the 1950s, worked first as a golf trick shot artist. Jack Redmond, a New York pro, hired her to model women's golf clothes. Redmond soon taught the quick-learning 18-year-old all the shots. She could hit a drive over 200 yards standing on one foot or hit the pin one out of three tries from 150 yards. After a year of $1,000 paydays performing her show, Carmen went to Las Vegas, where she teamed up with a low-level mobster named John Roselli. With Jeanne as the ringer, they hustled visiting golfers for large bets. She played the dumb blonde who was new to the game but then inexplicably played well when all the presses were on the line. She moved on to Hollywood after Roselli threw a guy off the Sands Hotel roof for not paying off a bet.

Club selection, part 1. Three-time Masters winner Jimmy Demaret was playing one day at Champions, the golf club he and Jackie Burke, Jr., built outside Houston. A member in his foursome puffed up when he reached a par-3 green in one less club than Demaret. "Tell you what," said Demaret, his competitiveness quickly kindled. "I'll bet you $100 a club I can hit that green with every club in my bag." He collected on every one but his putter.

Club selection, part 2. Ward "3-Iron" Gates, a professional gambler, made money playing with one club. He tried different clubs at chipping while recovering from a back injury and realized he could manipulate a single club for many shots. Beginning in 1940, Gates offered wagers to all comers. They could use their whole bag, while he played with just his 3-iron. He stuck a leaf behind the ball when on the tee, gaining 30 yards of extra roll since the ball had less spin. He opened the blade for bunker shots and putted with the toe.

Like every other hustler, Gates hated publicity. After articles about his gimmick appeared in the *Los Angeles Times* and *Sports Illustrated*, Gates cut back on further interviews, claiming that the publicity reduced the "opportunities" to ply his trade.

Long distance. In 1938, Olympia Fields Country Club member Smitty Ferebee bet a friend, Fred Turek, that he could play 576 holes of golf in four days. Of that total, he would play 72 holes each in eight cities across the country. The stake was half of a farm in Virginia. He traveled in a chartered plane with his physician, Dr. Rueben Trane, who paid all the expenses, estimated to be about $20,000. Ferebee played courses in Los Angeles, Phoenix, Kansas City, Milwaukee, Chicago (Olympia Fields), Philadelphia, New York City, and Westbury, Long Island. The bet also called for him to shoot below 100 for each round. Side bets between friends of Ferebee's and Turek's reached an estimated $100,000. Ferebee finished in the dark at Salisbury Golf Club, beating the deadline and winning the wager.

6.

THE "KING" AND "SUPER MEX":

ARNIE'S ARMY INVADES TELEVISION, 1960–83

"A MAN OUGHT TO DRIVE THAT GREEN," Arnold Palmer said. He was speaking of the short par-4 first hole at Cherry Hills Country Club in Denver.

"Why not," mused Dan Jenkins, who was covering the 1960 U.S. Open for *Sports Illustrated.* "It's only 346 yards through a ditch and high grass."

"If I drive that green, I might shoot a hell of a score," said Palmer. He was having lunch with Jenkins and others between the third and final rounds of the Open. He was 7 strokes behind the leader, Mike Souchak. "I might even shoot a 65 if I get started good. What'll that bring?"

"About seventh place. You're too far back," answered Jenkins.

"Well, that would be 280," said Palmer, his confidence rising. "Doesn't 280 always win the Open?"

"Yeah," said Jenkins, "when Hogan shoots it."

A few minutes later, Palmer stood on the elevated first tee, looking down the straightaway hole. He saw in front of the green the patch of rough the USGA grew to discourage players from driving the green. Determined to do what couldn't be done, Palmer threw his cigarette to the ground, hitched up his pants, and gripped his driver with his large hands. As he set up over the ball, the sinews and muscles of his forearms stood out like few others in the alpaca sweater league. He lashed at the ball with a force that almost brought him out of his shoes. The ball bounced through the grass barrier onto the green, 20 feet from the hole.

Palmer birdied the hole as well as two, three, and four. Word of his start rippled through the crowd, and the gallery surged across the course to the front nine. The press called his fans "Arnie's Army," a phrase that caught on the previous spring when he won the Masters. Palmer made the turn 5 under for the round. He kept charging, while the leaders started to fall back to him. Souchak faltered first. Then Ben Hogan found himself on the 17th tee, needing only to par the last two holes for the 280 Jenkins said would win. Sadly, the graying Hawk's once immaculate ball striking let him down, as he bogeyed 17 and tripled 18.

Arnie cooled a bit on the back nine but shot a 35 to go with his front side 30. He had his 280 and the championship, four shots ahead of Hogan. A chubby, buzz-cut, 20-year-old amateur named Jack Nicklaus finished second at 282.

In retrospect, golf historians have rated Palmer's come-from-behind win at Cherry Hills equal in drama and significance to Francis Ouimet's 1913 victory at Brookline. Moreover, Arnie's aggressive golf, coupled with his engaging charisma, pushed televised golf into the big time. He seemed to embody all the traits fans wanted in sports heroes—determined but friendly, greatness without arrogance, and energy. Arnie was not a country club swell. He called himself "a working-class guy with more grit than polish and more strength than style." He gambled on risky shots, reaping heroic rewards when he succeeded but wincing and moaning like everyman when he failed. Writer Jim Murray said Palmer mugged a golf course when he played: "He beat it like he would a man stealing his car." He pumped life into professional golf, a game almost wrung dry by Hogan's emotionless excellence. Arnold Palmer was the King.

"Just a legend, a living legend," said Tiger Woods. "If it wasn't for Arnold, golf wouldn't be as popular as it is now. If it wasn't for him and his excitement, his flair, the way he played, golf probably would not have had that type of excitement."

Arnold Palmer always bets on his game. With Sam Snead's passing, Arnie is golf's greatest acolyte of the friendly wager. He bets with the same honesty and congenial openness that made him a fan favorite, despite betting as aggressively as he plays. "I find it boring without something at stake," he said.

Born in 1929, Palmer started life at the beginning of the Depression. His father, Milfred J. "Deacon" Palmer, was a down-to-earth workingman. Deacon was the professional and greenkeeper at Latrobe Country Club in western Pennsylvania. He lived with his family in a small house on the club's grounds. Arnie took to the game as a youngster, going on to win the state high school championship and the 1950 Western Pennsylvania Amateur.

In 1953, after two years in the Coast Guard, Palmer moved to Cleveland

and began selling paint for Bill Wehnes. Despite winning two consecutive Ohio Amateurs, Palmer's goal was to be a successful businessman; he played golf to cultivate customers. Winning the 1954 U.S. Amateur didn't immediately change his mind. Meeting Winnie Walzer and pursuing a whirlwind courtship, however, made him think of turning pro. He proposed to Winnie but could not afford a ring until he went on a golf-buddy trip to New Jersey's fabled Pine Valley Golf Club.

On the drive east, Wehnes described the course's difficulty and suggested Palmer might not break 90 when playing it for the first time.

"Ninety?" Palmer asked in disbelief.

"That's right."

The challenge sparked Arnie's well-known competitiveness. Everyone agreed to a $20 Nassau with automatic presses, with Palmer and Mehnes having their own side bet. Palmer would pay Mehnes $100 for every stroke he shot over 80, with his boss paying him $100 for every stroke he shot under 70. "In retrospect, it was pretty foolish," Palmer recalled. "But you're only young and cocky and in love once."

Arnie shot 67 on the first of three rounds. "That was four Ben Franklins in my pocket," he said. "I cleaned up on all the Nassaus and that night even cleaned up in gin rummy. The next two rounds I went 69 and 68, and by the time the weekend was through I had pocketed nearly five grand, almost enough to pay off the ring."

Palmer turned pro in November 1954, when he signed with Wilson Sporting Goods to promote the company's equipment. He and Winnie married just before Christmas. They hit the road in January, living out of a trailer Palmer pulled with his old Ford. Things were rough, and they scrimped along from one tournament to the next. Palmer practiced hard, but he fretted about his putting until the "Wizard of the Flat Stick," George Low, convinced him to stick with his knock-kneed, hunched-over stance as well as his wristy stroke.

Snead met and befriended Arnie at the Masters in April. (How could these two fans of the cordial wager not like each other?) Snead invited Palmer to play in his annual tournament, an unofficial event at the Greenbrier. In the pro-am, Arnie partnered with Spencer Olin, a wealthy owner of a chemical company. Olin bought their team in the Calcutta. After Palmer's first round 69, the investment looked good. "I remember Dutch Harrison sidling over to me and telling me *he* had arranged for me to have Spencer Olin as a partner," Arnie said later.

"Don't you forget ole Dutch, Arn," Harrison said, winking at Palmer.

"Quite frankly, I didn't know whether to believe him or laugh in his face," Palmer recalled. "Dutch was a character in the same way George Low was—you never knew what sort of action he had going. All I knew was, hard pressed as Winnie and I were for funds at that moment, regardless of whether or not Dutch had somehow arranged the pairings, the last thing I wanted to do was give him a percentage of my winnings as some kind of personal gratuity!"

Palmer placed third in the pro division and won the pro-am with Olin. His $1,500 in prize money plus the $5,000 Olin gave him out of the pool winnings gave Arnie and Winnie a much-needed boost. By the end of the year, Arnie had won his first tournament, the Canadian Open, and had eight top ten finishes. Between 1957 and 1967, Palmer won 47 times on the tour, a streak equal to that of Snead, Hogan, or Byron Nelson. He ultimately won 62 PGA Tour events and another 10 on the Champions Tour. He also won seven majors—four Masters, one U.S. Open, two British Opens—as well as the hearts of many Americans.

In addition to bringing golf into American living rooms, Palmer helped revive the British Open in 1960. His entry recast the tournament in the PGA Tour players' eyes as a Grand Slam event equal to the Masters, the U.S. Open, and the PGA Championship. He qualified for the field through a 36-hole tournament. Four strokes back going into the Open's final round, Arnie staged another charge at the leaders. He fell one stroke shy, losing to Kel Nagle. He returned in 1961 to win the first of his two consecutive Opens.

As a tune-up for the 1960 British Open, Snead and Palmer entered the Canada Cup. It was an annual matchup of two-man teams representing the golfing countries of the world. Held in Dublin two weeks before the Open, British bookies listed the two Americans as the favorite, 2-1. Typical of both Snead and Palmer, they arranged a practice round before the tournament with a little side bet to make it interesting. They took on two British Ryder Cup members, Bernard Hunt and Harry Weetman, in a four-ball match for a "substantial number of quid." A gallery of 2,000 followed the action. Palmer birdied 17 and 18, boosting the team to a 2-up win. They shot a better-ball 61, and the crowd and the press loved it. Palmer's hard-charging finishes, even in an informal money game, captivated the Brits.

Clearly Arnold Palmer is a competitive man, whether he is trying to win the Claret Jug at St Andrews or $10 from a friend. His competitive fires stoked the explosion of prize money on the PGA Tour, and then later he invigorated the Senior/Champions Tour. Through most of his career, however, another player met him head on—Jack Nicklaus. The two battled each other in many tournaments. Even in informal games, each still wants to beat the other. They always play money golf, even if they have been trading the same $20 bill since the 1960s.

"Over the years, Arnold's the only guy I've played against for more than $10," Nicklaus said. "We usually play for $20." When asked who was up lifetime, he pointed at Arnie.

"But it doesn't matter," Palmer responded, "because Jack never pays me."

"I'd rather owe it to you and then beat you out of it."

It doesn't take another superstar to get Palmer's juices flowing. The late

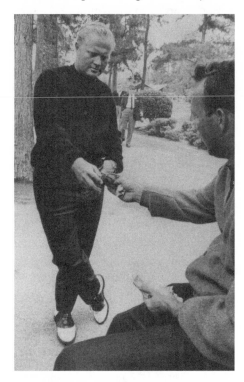

Arnold Palmer and Jack Nicklaus have bet on their informal matches since the early 1960s. In this photo, perhaps taken in Houston in 1967, Palmer appears to be handing Nicklaus a $50 bill. Each maintains he would rather have the other owe the money than actually pay off the bet. A debt yields more needling leverage. HISTORIC GOLF PHOTOS, THE RON WATTS COLLECTION author George Plimpton told a story about Palmer's competitiveness, an incident witnessed by Frank Gifford, the former NFL football player and TV announcer.

Palmer and Winnie were dining at the New York restaurant P. J. Clarke's with Gifford and his wife. A man at an adjacent table rudely tried to goad Palmer into a golf match. "I mean he was telling Palmer that he didn't think that there was much difference between a crack amateur and a pro, and he was willing to prove it," Gifford said. He offered to play Palmer for a $500 Nassau the next day, as long as Palmer gave him a stroke a side. Arnie politely declined, saying that he was leaving in the morning for Egypt. The man turned to his friends and declared that Palmer had backed down from the challenge.

At that point, Palmer turned to the chump, tapped him on the shoulder, and said, "All right. I'll tell you what I'll do. I'll postpone my trip to Cairo. We'll tee off at Winged Foot at nine o'clock tomorrow morning. O.K.? Except I'm not giving you one stroke a side; I'm giving you *two* strokes. And we are not playing a $500 Nassau. We'll play a $5,000 Nassau." The astonished heckler gulped and did not speak again.

Gifford thought Palmer would have stayed and raised the bet not to intimidate the man but to make the delay worth his while.

As any golfer might imagine, playing a round of golf with the King is the treat of a lifetime. The other pros see a match with Arnie as fun, but to an amateur, it's an extraordinary event and one to savor, even if the price is a lost bet. Joel Hirsch, a Chicago insurance and real estate executive, has played a number of practice rounds with Palmer. Hirsch has won two British Senior Amateur Championships, was the low amateur at the 1998 U.S. Senior Open, and collected dozens of other titles. (He credits much of his success to putting lessons from George Low.) His record got him into enough tournaments that he ran into Arnie regularly.

"At the 1993 U.S. Senior Open at Cherry Hills, I approached Arnie on the practice tee," Hirsch said in a recent interview. "I said, 'Mr. Palmer, I'm an amateur from Chicago. May I play a practice round with you next month at the British Senior Open?' He gave me a quizzical look for what seemed an eternity, and then said, 'How about Tuesday at noon?' I was absolutely thrilled."

Later that day, Hirsch walked up to Gary Player in the locker room. "I thought I might be on a hot streak after Palmer, so I took a chance and asked him for a practice round too at the British Senior. He agreed, luckily for Wednesday. I worried about being too forward, but I wasn't about to pass up the opportunity to play with two men who I held in such high esteem. I thought I had died and gone to heaven."

At the 1997 Senior Open at Olympia Fields near Chicago, Hirsch had an expensive round with Palmer. "We played what Arnold calls a "$100 walk-in." It was $100 on the match, plus automatic 2-down presses. It cost me about $600 in the end. I'm usually just a $5 or $10 Nassau guy, but 600 bucks was a fair price to play with one of my childhood heroes."

At the following year's Senior Open, Hirsch and fellow amateur Gordon Brewer, who won the 1994 and 1996 U.S. Senior Amateurs, took on Palmer and Nicklaus. "It was a dream come true. Plus, I only lost $30 that day on a $10 Nassau."

Hirsch finally got some of his money back from Arnie at the 1999 Senior Open at Des Moines, Iowa. "I won $600 from him, but he said that he didn't have his wallet. I guess he was expecting to collect, not pay. The next day, he came straight over to me and peeled off six, crisp $100 bills. He's a true gentleman."

"Overall, I lost over $1,000 to him in the 1990s," Hirsch said. "I don't regret a cent. He was a gracious loser and a gracious winner."

Despite playing fewer tournaments now, Palmer still plays almost every day he is at home. The Bay Hill shootout is just the kind of golf he will play until he's too old to swing. "And I'm still winning most of the skins on the games I play at Latrobe in the summer or Bay Hill in the winter," he said in 2000. "If I can take a skin off a 33-year-old guy who hits it for miles, you bet I enjoy that."

He played in his last British Open in 1995 and his final Masters in 2004. He memorialized his final Open appearance at St Andrews with, what else, a little money golf during a practice round. His foursome was as special as the occasion—Nicklaus, Raymond Floyd, and Tom Watson.

"I arranged it," Watson proudly told the news media. He and Palmer teamed against Nicklaus and Floyd for £20 a side. The four had won 37 majors and 10 British Opens combined. They didn't act like old champions in rocking chairs, though. Hundreds of spectators followed the group, and some said the players constantly needled each other. When Palmer bunkered his tee shot on the par-3 11th, Nicklaus and Floyd dared him to go for the pin instead of the smart play, hitting it out sideways. Arnie got it out on the fourth try. "He was buried in there," Jack said. "We were really giving it to him."

Floyd was over a putt on 13 when an R&A official behind the green walked through Raymond's line. "Guys, we're gambling now," the suddenly serious Floyd said to the man. "We're having a little game here."

Watson and Palmer won four and three and then posed for photos on the Swilcan Bridge at 18. Afterward, Floyd gave his £10 to Watson. Nicklaus reached for his money clip, laughing. "I hate to do this," he said, handing his tenner to Palmer. "It's about as embarrassing as it gets."

—●—

The game of golf has produced many characters over the years, unique people who are the source of wonderful stories. One in the top ten is George Low, the man who helped Palmer and Hirsch with their putting.

A middling member of the PGA Tour in the 1940s and '50s, Low didn't come to prominence through the excellence of his ball striking. He cashed a winner's check only once, but that tournament had an asterisk. Amateur Freddie Haas won the 1945 Memphis Invitational, ending Nelson's winning streak at 11. Low was second, Nelson tied for fourth. "Haas won the tournament, but I won the front money," Low said. "I was the first pro to beat Nelson. Look it up."

George Low stories arose from two skills unmatched in the game's history—putting and living the good life of a golf pro without any visible means of support.

Low learned putting as a teenager in Scotland on Carnoustie's practice green. His father, George Low, Sr., was one of the many Carnoustie professionals who moved to America during its first golf boom. He finished tied for second in the 1899 U.S. Open and was the pro at Baltusrol for 25 years. Legend has it George Sr. coined one of the game's truisms, "Golf is a humblin' game." Junior was born in New Jersey, but the family moved to Scotland upon his father's retirement in 1927. The son returned to the States to take up professional golf.

He soon became widely known for his putting skill and his ability to describe the art. Always for a fee, he shared his gospel with wayward souls struggling in a putting slump. Ask any PGA Tour veteran older than age 60 about Low, and they will remember someone profiting from his advice.

Low was so adept at scrounging a meal, a place to sleep, or a borrowed Cadillac that everyone called him "America's Guest." He drifted between the weekly tour stops, a constant presence on the clubhouse veranda and the putting green. He didn't play or sell equipment; he just seemed to hang out. Jenkins called Low the "stand around champion." He was actually working, looking for his next freebie. He was the artful cadger. "I like to hang around guys with a lot of dough because occasionally a leaf falls off," he said. "When you're around guys with no dough, you can't get a leaf." Low claimed the only time he ever picked up a tab was to hand it to someone else. George called anyone who didn't pay the bill an "empty wagon."

He also looked for his next pigeon to pluck on the putting green. Mere mortals couldn't get a fair bet with him unless he used a driver, a wedge, or one of the pins from the practice green cups. He even won bets using his shoe. "Three cases of beer to two you can't get it down from here," Bo Wininger said to Low, pointing at George's foot. Wininger, a tour regular during the 1950s, dropped a ball 75 feet from the cup. George took the bet and then kicked the ball to tap-in distance.

Jimmy Demaret said Low was driving from the West Coast to Florida one year in a Cadillac he borrowed from the wealthy amateur Frank Stranahan. He stopped at a tournament on the way to raise some funds. He got into a putting match for $1,500, considerably more than what he had in his pocket. "I'll bet you my car," Low said, waving at Frank's Caddy. His opponent agreed and proceeded to win the bet. Low gave him the keys and went off to sponge another ride. Demaret said the cops and Stranahan's lawyer later fixed everything.

Low once had a game with Britain's Duke of Windsor—the former King Edward VIII before his abdication—at Seminole in Palm Beach. Also in the game was R. R. "Railroad" Young, a Wall Street wizard who controlled both the Chesapeake & Ohio and New York Central railroads. During the match, Low gave putting tips to Windsor, who, in return, tried to hand George $100 after the match.

"No, no," Young protested. "George can't take that."

"You run the railroad," Low said to Young, slipping the $100 into his pocket. "I'll run the Duke."

—●—

The uncomfortable issue of purse splitting arose in American professional golf in 1962. The news media got wind of a long-standing practice among some players of divvying up prize money. The reports raised the possibility of impropriety, largely because it smelled as if the fix was on. Had the devil found its way into golf?

Sports Illustrated ran a story in September 1962 titled "The Big Golf Secret." In a mild exposé, the magazine explained how two touring pros in a tournament play-off often agreed to split evenly the combined total of first and second money. If the public was upset, the PGA wasn't. "For a number of years," said PGA president Lou Strong, "we have known that at certain times the money has been split between players in a play-off after the regular tournament. We've never had any complaints. We have no official policy, and no regulation against it. Nor can we see any problem."

Many of the golfers *Sports Illustrated* interviewed saw little harm in the practice. Most cited the sudden-death play-off format adopted for TV golf as the main reason. "A guy who's worked hard for 72 holes to gain a tie shouldn't have to throw it away on one hole," Palmer said. "I've always played for the title, which is very important."

"I'll be the first to admit that I've split in some play-offs," Gary Player said. "I'm in favor of it, especially in sudden-death play-offs. I tell you, when it comes to a split, I'm never ashamed to ask for one or accept one."

Nelson said about 60 percent of the players split play-off purses when he played and saw nothing unethical about it. "If anyone asked you to split with them before the play-off round, the sporting thing to do was agree. If you didn't, you were apt to lose friends." Nelson told the magazine Clayton Heafner approached him about splitting after the two tied at the 1942 Tam O'Shanter. "You're going to beat me anyhow," Heafner said, "so why don't you be a good guy and cut the money up?" Nelson said he couldn't refuse.

Jack Nicklaus disagreed, "I've never split, and I don't really approve of splitting." During the U.S. Open at Oakmont the previous June, Palmer and Nicklaus tied and played 18 on Monday to decide the championship. Arnold offered to split, but Jack declined, saying it would not be fair to either of them. Palmer said later he was just trying to help a young pro win some extra money.

Sports Illustrated barely mentioned another facet of prize sharing—players agreeing to pool their winnings before the tournament's start. The convention dates to the PGA Tour's beginnings, when paltry purses forced many pros to resort to the practice. During Gene Sarazen's 1922 swing through the winter circuit, a group of pros (including Cyril Walker, who would win the U.S. Open two years later) invited him to join their "syndicate." They all agreed to share any prize money equally with the others. (Only the top 15 or 20 finishers won any money in those days, with a 15th-place check amounting to about $15.) Sarazen felt good about the arrangement after finishing out of the money in his first tournament in San Antonio. He began to question his decision when he finished second in Shreveport. After Gene won the Southern Open in New Orleans and $1,000, he had to pay the others $800. He quickly left the syndicate and played solo from then on.

Walter Hagen did the same when he started, but soon he struck off on his own. "I never liked syndicate golf," Hagen said later, "and after several brief experiences, I never played it again. I went into the tournament as a lone wolf, and the fierce competition I met made a better and much more consistent player out of me." Hagen refused Jim Barnes's offer to split in their 1920 challenge match. However, in his 1922 winner-take-all game with Sarazen, they agreed beforehand the winner would get 55 percent of the purse. In another example of this early custom, Demaret and Jack Grout, later Jack Nicklaus's coach at Scioto Country Club, agreed to pool their winnings in 1935.

George May's 1946 "World Championship" at Tam O'Shanter was a $10,000 winner-take-all event with only four participants: Nelson, Snead, Lloyd Mangrum, and Herman Barron. They agreed to divide the purse evenly. In the 1950s, Al Besselink routinely approached others with a deal to split winnings. He got 10 percent of Dick Mayer's $50,000 first prize at the Tam O'Shanter in 1957. Had Bessie won, he was prepared to do the same for Dick. Similarly, at the 1959 Palm Springs tournament, journeyman players Joe Campbell and Buddy Sullivan agreed to split the $50,000 winner's check if either won. Campbell did win and Sullivan was delighted.

The event that sparked the *Sports Illustrated* piece was the 1962 "World Series" of golf played at Firestone Country Club in Akron, Ohio, a few weeks before. The only entrants in the unofficial event were "the Big Three": Nicklaus, Palmer, and Player. A wire service report stated the players talked of splitting the $75,000 purse. They ultimately demurred, wanting to keep things "legal." Palmer later confirmed they had no agreement, and in 1994, Nicklaus gave the news media his recollection. He said the tournament organizers told the three players each would get the same amount of money, no matter who won. "I won it, and after the event, I thought it was wrong. So did Arnie and Gary. The next year Arnie was on the policy board, and he got it changed so there was no more purse splitting."

Purse splitting didn't go away forever. In 1994, it reared its head again, this time on the Champions Tour. Commissioner Deane Beman fined 51 tour members at least $2,000 each for splitting prize money. The matter involved "Shoot-Outs" Merrill Lynch sponsored during the 1992 and 1993 seasons. They were nine-hole events staged before the start of the regular tournaments. The weekly versions offered a purse of $12,000 to $20,000, but the season-ending Shoot-Out Championship was worth $400,000.

The players felt the events were purely for entertainment, "putt-and-giggles" events staged for the gallery. "We didn't think we were doing anything wrong," said Jim Dent, who admitted being part of the deal. "After all, they weren't tour events." Larry Ziegler, who wouldn't say if he was involved, echoed Dent. "It was just an exhibition to entertain fans. Guys were talking when another was putting. And they were walking in putting lines and doing all sorts of things to distract. These things are never done during regular events."

In neither 1962 nor 1994 did anyone suggest purse splitting was akin to fixing a golf tournament. No one made comparisons to basketball point shaving or influencing a baseball game. Whenever people collude about money in sport, it's easy for observers to assume something fishy is about. However, considering golf's 600-year history, 1962 was but a few blinks from the Depression when the pros went along to get along. Further, the Shoot-Out players in 1994, who were almost the same generation who split play-off money 30 years earlier, knew the difference between competition and sideshows. Deceiving the paying public is indefensible, but the tour dealt with the problems and moved ahead.

Regarding the pros agreeing to share earnings, none of the golfers who have spoken or written about syndicates accused the participants of cheating or foul play. Golf weathered these bumps in the road without lasting effects. The sport seems to heal itself, calling straying players back to the central tenets of honor and self-enforced rules.

—●—

"A fellow really doesn't think of the money," replied Nicklaus in 1967 after a reporter had asked if large purses made him nervous.

Suppose I have to sink a 3-foot putt to win a friendly $5 Nassau bet. It might be a tougher putt for me than sinking the same miserable little putt for a $50,000 first prize.

The five bucks comes out of my pocket, and it therefore becomes a conscious act. But the 50 grand is just paper. It's something I don't have in my possession and it's something I still haven't had—and may never get. It's a fine distinction, but it's there nonetheless.

Coming from the greatest player of all time, his analysis puts betting on golf in its right setting. He has said throughout his career he is not a big bettor; however, he understands the role of a friendly wager in golf. He used the $5 comparison because that's about what he bets in during informal rounds. Lanny Wadkins or Phil Mickelson might have used a $500 Nassau to make their point but not Jack.

In contrast to Palmer's aggressive play and betting, Nicklaus wagers as he plays, conservatively. "I've won most of my tournaments playing what I call a patient game, waiting for those other guys to gamble," he said in 1984. "When I look back on the gambling shots of my career, I count the successes on one hand and the failures in the hundreds."

There seems to be a rough parallel between a player's style or strategy on the golf course and his approach to wagering. Hagen and Bobby Locke pushed hard. Hogan's bets were businesslike and disciplined. Snead was as Tiger is today—always betting on golf but picking high-risk shots judiciously. Mickelson's betting interests were in complete consonance with his style of play until the 2005 season, when he began showing some restraint on risky shots.

A couple of examples illuminate Jack's modest approach to betting on golf. The spectacular Spyglass Hill Golf Course opened in Monterrey, California, in 1966. The following year, in addition to Pebble Beach and Cypress Point, the Bing Crosby Clambake used Spyglass for the early rounds. Before the tournament, Bing told Nicklaus that he thought Jack couldn't break par his first time at Spyglass. Nicklaus bet Bing $5 that he could. He and Arnie gave it a whirl the next day. Palmer shot a 2-over 74 and Nicklaus a 2-under 70. Five bucks was indeed sufficient to get Jack's attention.

Calvin Peete, a 12-time winner on the PGA Tour, competed with Nicklaus through much of the 1970s and '80s. Peete arrived on the tour with a large Afro and diamond chips in his front teeth. Peete admired Nicklaus and cited a round with him during the 1982 U.S. Open as the best lesson he ever had on course management.

A self-confessed street gambler before he discovered golf, Peete carried his interest in a friendly wager onto the course. A reporter asked him in 1985 who he liked having a bet with in practice rounds. He named three known devotees of money golf: Wadkins, Fuzzy Zoeller, and Lee Trevino. Why not Nicklaus? the reporter asked. "I would say Nicklaus, but he's not a good player to gamble with," Peete said.

Jack didn't grow up in the caddy yard; instead, he learned the game with his pharmacist father. By the age of 13, he had a plus-3 handicap. Despite a brief bout with polio, he grew up to be a burly, multisport athlete in high school. He won the 1959 and 1961 U.S. Amateurs as well as the 1961 NCAA individual title while at Ohio State University. He broke into the big time as an amateur against Palmer in the 1960 U.S. Open. Nicklaus said the 1960 Open was the only time he bet on a golf tournament's outcome. He talked about it in a 1994 joint interview with Palmer George Peper conducted for *Golf Magazine*.

> The week of the tournament, my Dad came up and said, "Jack, as the national amateur champion, they have you at 35-1 odds to win the Open. Would you like to make a bet on that?"
>
> "You're damn right I would—I'll have 20 bucks of that."
>
> "Do you want place or show?"
>
> "Hell no, I'm wanna win." Nicklaus said he thought about the bet during the final round. "I was about to get married, and I needed the money. Arnie, you were the only one who kept me from winning that $700."
>
> "My apologies," Palmer said with a wink.

Nicklaus turned pro in 1961 and proceeded to win 73 PGA tournaments, including 18 majors, and 10 more tournaments on the Champions Tour.

Plenty of stories cite Jack's bets during practice rounds, but one stands out. At the 1982 U.S. Open at Pebble Beach, Watson chipped in on the par-3 17th on the last day to win the tournament. Nicklaus graciously complimented Watson but said later Tom might need 1,000 balls to do it again. Watson's responded, "Let's go out and do it. I might make a little more money."

At the Masters the following spring, Nicklaus, Watson, Player, and Tom Weiskopf played a practice round filled with the usual needling and boasts. They arrived at the 18th green all square and all the bets on the line. Watson's ball was off the green, about the same distance from the cup as he had been the year before at the Open. "I told Tom, 'If you chip this in, I'm going to bury this putter in your head,'" Jack said after the match. Lightning struck twice. "He chipped in for all the cash," chuckled Nicklaus.

—•—

Another superb player followed Nicklaus out of Ohio State, Tom Weiskopf. In 1973, he won seven tournaments, including the British Open at Troon. A man who always seemed to stand in Jack's shadow, Weiskopf quit the PGA Tour at age 40 after winning 16 times. He has played irregularly on the Champions Tour, winning four times.

He left college as a junior, setting off on a money golf odyssey that lasted two years and essentially completed his higher education in pressure golf. Tom talked of those times with a *Washington Post* reporter during the 1981 Kemper Open near Washington, D.C.

"Used to play for the Mafia," he said. "Used to get 20 percent of whatever was bet. I also got $50 for every birdie I made and $100 for every eagle." Weiskopf met a gambler in Columbus who backed him in matches throughout Ohio, Pennsylvania, Indiana, and Michigan. "I'd always go into these towns and play a practice round the day before the match. Seemed like just about everywhere I went I shot the course record. I got beat once in a while, too, but it was great incentive, where I really learned to play 'cause the better I got the more money I earned."

"At the end of two years I had $15,000 in cash in a brown paper bag," Tom recalled. "How 'bout that? In my room. Kept it in my closet." Weiskopf was reluctant to put the money in a bank, assuming there would be questions. "What would I say about my job, how I got all that cash? That I hustle?"

Weiskopf said he quit because of a jam he got into during a match. He was up on all his bets at 18, and his opponent pressed again. After Weiskopf put his drive in the fairway, the man hooked his into the trees. As they walked toward their balls, the man approached Weiskopf, "I gotta win this hole."

"All you got to do is beat me," answered Tom.

"You don't realize," he said, with tears in his eyes, "my business is on the line if I lose this."

"Hey, you're a big fellow. You ought to know what in the hell you're betting. It's not my fault you're in the trees." Despite his remarks, Weiskopf said he felt sorry for the guy. He pleaded again with Weiskopf after their second shots, "Can't you help me?"

After that exchange, one of the good fellas grabbed Tom's arm and demanded, "What'd he ask you?"

"Nothing," Weiskopf said. But the gangster gave Tom a look that carried a clear message—don't throw this match. "That's when I knew I'm in the wrong business," said Weiskopf.

Weiskopf was in the green-side rough in two. His distraught opponent, after two more shots, was in the bunker laying four. He bladed his sand shot, hit the flagstick, and watched the ball drop into the hole. With his stroke, he had a four. "He's down on his knees crying for joy," Weiskopf said.

"You better get that ball up and down," the Big Guy warned Tom.

"I'd never felt pressure like that before in my life," Weiskopf said. "I pitched up there to about four or five feet. I looked the putt over and over, thinking if I miss, they'll figure I did it on purpose. I knocked it in, and we tied the hole. That's the last time I ever got in a situation like that."

—●—

"A Gambler's Dream: At Ten to One, How Could Besselink Refuse?" The *San Diego Union* ran this headline to introduce its story about PGA Tour player Al Besselink's bet during the first round of the San Diego Open. The incident did not occur during the cash-strapped 1930s or the bet-happy '50s. It was in 1965.

"Bessie" boasted he could shoot 66 or lower in the tournament's first round. Since Besselink was a distant 60th on the money list the previous year, the bookies must have thought they had a sure thing. One offered him 10-1 odds he couldn't post that low a score. Al called him, pulling 10 $100 bills from his pocket.

"I sweated around that course," he said later. "My caddie was dying. He knew about the bet and knew he would get a bonus if I won it." On 18, his ball was 20 feet from the hole, but Bessie only needed a 2-putt for a 66. When his lag went in the hole, Bessie started counting his $10,000.

Considering 32 other pros broke 70 that day—Gene Littler shot a 62—Besselink knew something the bookie didn't.

The PGA was not impressed. Unlike the nonproblem about play-off purse splitting three years earlier, tour officials acted swiftly against Besselink. They put him on probation for a year, a slap on the wrist that might have been even less had it not been for the NFL's betting scandal of 1963–64. The NFL gave indefinite suspensions to Green Bay's Paul Hornung and Detroit's Alex Karras for betting $50 and $100 on NFL games. (The league reinstated them after one year.) Golf has a long and healthy relationship with betting, but the growing TV audience and its sensitive sponsors made the PGA think more about the game's public face. An unrepentant Besselink, however, kept playing money golf.

"If professional golfers were cars," golf writer Curt Sampson imagined, "Al Besselink would be a two-tone, '59 Cadillac convertible with towering tail-fins and crushed velvet seats. A pair of fuzzy dice would hang from the rearview mirror and would be stuck on seven." Bessie was one of the PGA Tour's true characters in the days before swing coaches and personal jets. And he bet on golf starting from his days as a caddie. "If I couldn't bet, that would be terrible," he told Sampson.

A New Jersey high school dropout, Besselink nonetheless captained the 1942 University of Miami golf team. During the conference tournament, Bessie bet the team's expense money—$500—on himself to win the individual title, which he did in extra holes. Tall and tanned, he had the curly blond hair the gals liked. He soon turned pro and started hanging around south Florida golf courses, looking for some money golf. "We used to go over to Normandy Shores on Miami Beach and sit around all morning trying to make a game," Besselink said of the time. "There'd be all kinds of games, $50 games, $100 games, $500 games, $1,000 games, you name it. You sit around long enough, you'd find what you'd want."

Besselink denied that he hustled, knowing the difference between lying to get a game and simply playing for money. "I never had to cheat anybody. My best game was playing hustlers, playing the guys who cheated and tried to take advantage of everybody. I wanted to play either them or multimillionaires. I never tried to beat anybody who didn't have any money."

"We won all our money gambling," he said later. "You didn't make shit with the golf. I was spending $100 grand a year, living like King Farouk [of Egypt]. What did I make in prize money—$5,000, $10,000 a year?"

Besselink and Las Vegas golf were made for each other. He won the inaugural Tournament of Champions at the Desert Inn. After sinking a clutch 6-footer on the last hole to win, he accepted the $10,000 first prize in silver dollars. Bessie made a little extra in the Calcutta by betting $500 on himself at 25-1 odds. The bet made him flush enough he could donate half his official winnings to the Walter Winchell–Damon Runyon Cancer Fund, the tournament's main charity. He later became the director of golf at the Dunes casino, a position that allowed him to pursue all his hobbies regularly.

If Besselink found himself out of contention during a tournament, he said he tried to post a high score on Saturday so he would have an early tee time on Sunday. He then would find a bookie and set up a wager on himself. "There would be no wind, no pressure on trying to win, and smooth greens with no spike marks. I'd bet my score against the 10 leaders. I'd shoot 68 and beat nine of 'em and make more money than the winner."

Tour winner Dave Hill made similar bets in the 1960s. "People want to bet on the leader, but they don't realize the leader is not going out there to try to shoot a 64 or 65," Hill wrote in his book, *Teed Off.* "The player who's back in the pack, on the other hand, is anxious to move up and make a good check. He's going to take a few chances he wouldn't ordinarily take, and he's liable to shoot lights out."

—●—

When Tiger Woods won his first Masters in 1997, he publicly acknowledged his good fortune in professional golf was in part because of the game's African-American pioneers. "People like Lee Elder, Charlie Sifford, and Ted Rhodes made it possible for this to happen," he said. "Without them, I might not have had a chance to play golf. I might not have had the chance to be here."

Woods is one-quarter black and half Thai. He refers to himself as a "Cablinasian," or part *ca*ucasian, *bl*ack, American *In*dian, and *Asian.* Woods has acknowledged the struggle African Americans faced in the search for equality not just in everyday life but also in golf. The 100 years between African-American John Shippen's fifth-place finish in the 1896 U.S. Open at Shinnecock and Tiger's arrival on the tour is a struggle marked by discrimination and frustration.

The USGA and its regional affiliates did not officially exclude African-

American amateurs from tournaments. The practical barriers were significant, though. The golfer had to belong to a club, establish a handicap, and play regularly enough to build a game good enough to compete. African-American golfers eventually broke through those obstacles, but before the civil rights movement, their fairways were full of hazards.

To reach a wider sector of society, the USGA established the men's Public Links Championship in 1922. That cut through the club membership requirement but did nothing to help African-American golfers learn the game. (The women's Public Links didn't start until 1977.)

Despite these hurdles, pockets of African-American golfers formed, mostly middle-class folks or professionals who gradually found golf courses that accepted them. Some enterprising and devoted golfers built courses that catered to African Americans. Others founded associations to advance their game and to fight for acceptance. The Windy City Golf Club in Chicago started in about 1915, while others started similar groups in Washington, D.C.; New York; and Philadelphia. In 1925, these regional entities coalesced into a national organization, the U.S. Colored Golf Association (USCGA), which later changed its name to the United Golf Association (UGA).

The USCGA/UGA sponsored its first championship in 1925 at Shady Rest Golf & Country Club in New Jersey. Shippen won the 72-hole event and $25. In 1926 the tournament, called the "National" or the "Negro Open," moved to Mapledale in Stow, Massachusetts. Soon it included an amateur division.

Advances in amateur African-American golf were as slow in coming as the overall civil rights evolution in America. The UGA provided increasingly frequent amateur competitions for aspiring golfers. Progress was limited, however, until advances in school desegregation and voting rights spilled over into golf. Two highlights marked the early stages of equality. Ann Gregory was the first African-American woman to play in the U.S. Women's Amateur in 1956, and Bill Wright won the 1959 Amateur Public Links Championship at Wellshire Golf Club in Denver. He became the first African American to win a USGA championship.

For African Americans who wanted to make money playing golf, the path was just as slow and arduous. They had no route to the PGA. At its inception in 1916, the PGA bylaws did not specifically exclude African Americans, but the obstacles to their membership were as real as those inhibiting their entry into USGA competitions. The association formalized the implicit ban when it amended its constitution in 1934, flat out limiting its membership to caucasians. That ruling left the UGA as the only game in town for African Americans.

The UGA was a loose confederation of African-American golf courses, associations, and individual members. It offered a series of events in the same vein as the Negro Leagues, which gave black baseball players a chance to play ball. It helped schedule tournaments, but its ability to raise purses and sponsors was scant. Most tournaments were two-day events on the weekend, since few golf courses wanted to sacrifice regular play. The prize money was also limited, with about $50 for first and perhaps $200 total. Only the lucky could afford touring expenses. The men traveled six to a car and slept two to a bed, when they could find a hotel that would accept them. The pickings were so slim the players called it the "neck bone circuit."

Two African-American golfers, Bill Spiller and Rhodes, with assistance from African-American boxer Joe Louis, took on leadership roles in the struggle to convince the PGA to accept African Americans. Spiller, a college graduate from Texas, moved to Los Angeles in 1938. While working as a redcap at the train station, Spiller took up golf in 1942. He attempted to qualify in the 1944 Los Angeles Open but failed. By 1946, he had won all of the UGA tournaments in southern California and then turned pro in 1947.

Louis held the heavyweight crown from 1937 to 1949. He became a fairly skilled player in those years, and he frequently entered UGA amateur events. He always played for a little something and sometimes for serious money. Spiller won $7,000 from Joe in an all-day match. He used the proceeds to buy a house near the Western Avenue golf course in Los Angeles, the center of African-American golf for years. The current name of the course is Chester Washington Golf Course.

Many regarded Louis as a pigeon, or even a meal ticket, because of Joe's insistence on playing the hustlers and pros instead of other amateurs. "He was a wonderful man," recalled one veteran of Western Avenue, "who would give you the shirt off his back—and most of the time he did." Louis's son, Joe Louis Barrow, Jr., said his father was as intrigued with betting on golf as he was with playing the sport. Barrow, now president of First Tee, a golf and youth development organization, estimated the champ lost close to $500,000 while playing golf.

Rhodes grew up in Nashville and learned the game while caddying. From the late 1940s to 1960, he won 150 tournaments, mostly on the UGA

Tour. Sifford called the sweet-swinging Rhodes the "black Jack Nicklaus." Rhodes met Louis in 1945. The champ hired him as his personal golf pro and playing partner and even bought him a new Buick. Rhodes didn't drive at first, so his friends did the honor. Louis paid Ray Mangrum, Lloyd's brother, to give Rhodes lessons and backed him in money matches.

On one occasion, Louis also helped Rhodes by losing a lopsided bet. Rhodes asked Louis for a $200 loan for the rent. Louis guessed Rhodes needed another $200 for food, so he proposed they play 18 for $400. Louis was happy to lose that bet.

In 1948, Spiller and Rhodes sued the PGA after the organization denied them entry in a tournament for which they had qualified. They later agreed to drop the suit when the PGA promised to cease its discriminatory policies, but not much changed. The PGA simply asked sponsors to change their tournaments from "opens" to "invitationals."

Spiller, Rhodes, and Louis forced another confrontation in 1952. The two pros and amateur Eural Clark qualified for the San Diego Open, and the sponsors invited Louis to play as an amateur. Again, the PGA balked. Louis, a World War II veteran, publicly likened PGA president Horton Smith to Adolf Hitler. The PGA relented on Louis but not the others. The champ told the press he would continue his fight "to eliminate racial prejudice from golf, the last sport in which it now exists." (The Dodgers had called up Jackie Robinson the previous year.)

Smith discussed the matter with members of the PGA tournament committee after the third round of the San Diego event. They agreed to permit African-American golfers to play in the next two tournaments, Phoenix and Tucson. In the longer term, the PGA granted qualifying African Americans "approved entry" status, allowing them to play if sponsors invited them.

"Bill Spiller had the original impact," said Jackie Burke, Jr., a member of the tournament committee. "He could play and he deserved a chance."

Spiller got his final jab on the PGA's chin in 1959. Caddying at Hillcrest Country Club in Los Angeles to make ends meet, Spiller complained to member Harry Braverman about the PGA's exclusion of African Americans. Braverman took the matter to California attorney general Stanley Mosk. Along with other state attorneys general, Mosk threatened to bar the PGA from their states' courses. In November 1961, the PGA removed the "caucasian only" clause from its bylaws.

Sifford was the next African American to take on the PGA. He was also the first to see tangible rewards, becoming the first African-American member of the PGA Tour. He carefully acknowledged the sacrifices Spiller and Rhodes made in paving the way for him.

Sifford caddied as a kid in Charlotte, North Carolina, and started playing after moving to Philadelphia as a young man. He gravitated to one of the few courses available to African Americans in the 1940s, Cobbs Creek, where local African Americans regularly played money games. The cocky Sifford soon felt he was ready to take on one of the regulars, Howard Wheeler, the cross-handed veteran of the UGA Tour.

"I heard about Wheeler's prowess on the course," Charlie said in his book *Just Let Me Play,* which he cowrote with James Gallo. "But I took one look at his swing, and with the wisdom of the adolescent, said to myself, 'Hell, he ain't nothing.'" With only $20 in his wallet, Sifford was in for a plucking.

"You Howard Wheeler?" Sifford asked as he approached the man on the range.

"Uh huh."

"I'm Charlie Sifford, and I'm gonna whip your ass on that golf course."

Wheeler proceeded to take Sifford apart, one cross-handed swing at a time. "My first 10 dollars went into his pocket after the fifth hole, and he cleaned me out by the tenth." (A UGA player in the 1970s, George Wallace—not the governor—also played cross handed. He said his grip gave him a lock on bets. Charles Owens won twice on the Champions Tour in 1986 playing cross handed.)

Sifford moved to Los Angeles in 1947 when he was 25 years old. The African-American singer Billy Eckstine hired Sifford to be his golf pro and chauffeur, just as Louis had taken in Rhodes. Sifford played often at Western Avenue, which was the West Coast capital of black golf hustling and a "gambler's paradise" according to those who teed it up there. Sifford earned the nickname "Little Horse" for standing up under the pressure of high-stakes golf. Spiller, Rhodes, Pete Brown, and many others called Western Avenue home while they were trying to make it to the big dance.

Sifford won five consecutive UGA Nationals from 1952 to 1956 and another in 1960. He also played in "white" tournaments when sponsors let him in. He won the Long Beach Open in 1957 against a good field that included Billy Casper and Al Besselink. He shot a 64 on the last day and then won in a play-off against Eric Monti. The PGA didn't consider the tournament an "official" event because the men played only 54 holes. Three years later, at age 37, Sifford caught the wave of change in the PGA at just the right moment. The PGA granted Sifford the status of "approved tournament player." That got him on the tour in 1960, but he didn't become the first African-American full PGA member until 1964.

Golf recognized Charlie Sifford in 2004. PGA Tour commissioner Tim Finchem called him with the news: "Charlie, we can't pay you back for the trouble you went through or the obstacles you faced, but we are going to put you in the World Golf Hall of Fame."

Lee Elder became the first African American to play in the Masters in 1974. His invitation marked African Americans' full acceptance in American professional golf. In 1972, Clifford Roberts changed the criteria for invitations to include any PGA Tour event winner during the previous 12 months. Under their previous standards, the Masters had overlooked Sifford as well as Brown, who had won the 1964 Waco Turner tournament. Elder earned his ticket to Magnolia Lane by winning the 1973 Monsanto Open in Pensacola, Florida.

Elder moved to Los Angeles after his father died in World War II. He started caddying and soon learned the art of golf hustling at Western Avenue. Soon he played full-blown money golf around the country.

Carrying a little Sunday bag with seven or eight clubs, Elder disguised his talents at first, patiently setting up a mark by losing a few bucks as bait. "If your bankroll was in good shape, you might drop $500 to a guy who couldn't break 80," Elder said of his youthful persuasions. "But you knew you could always get him back. You were shooting for the big fish he plays with. You can't go right into a $10,000 or $20,000 match. You've got to feel him out." He found matches easily. "Everybody wants to beat a hustler."

"Sometimes you played for stakes and you didn't have the money in your pocket to pay if you lost," Elder said of the hard times. "You'd be in trouble then, no doubt, but you had to take that chance to live. Self-preservation is the first law of nature."

"Pressure is sinking a putt when you have a $50 bet going and you only have $10 in your pocket," Elder said, echoing other money golfers. "Pressure is when you're playing for your next meal or your car payment, or something like that. That is the kind of pressure so many of us played under all the time, so that when we got a chance to play in big tournaments, so many of us were successful."

He met Titanic Thompson while on the road. They teamed for many money matches until the army drafted the 24-year-old Elder in 1958. Two years later, he was out and began a seven-year apprenticeship for PGA tournaments. He spent all of his time on the UGA trail, playing either for purses or the next guy's roll.

"I would go to golf tournaments and have no entry fee, and have to talk my way in," he recalled. "I got to know the girl handling the entry fees for the events and I became her favorite. She'd let me in all the time because she knew that I would win some money and pay the fee afterwards."

"We did a fair amount of gambling on the UGA Tour," Elder said. Many of the regulars showed up early for a tournament looking for a game. "Every town we played, there were a lot of players who wanted to gamble. Knowing you could hustle a few extra dollars made it a lot easier on expenses. We'd give a couple shots and still win enough to pay the motel bill and travel expenses."

As Elder became more well known he had to heavily handicap himself. The most frequently told story about Elder features a prop bet he made at an old Detroit track named "Pipe O Peace Golf Course." It was a municipal course and is now named Joe Louis "The Champ" Golf Course.

"This guy was about a 10-handicapper and he was crazy about golf," Lee said. "It was one of those hot summer days, not a cloud in the sky. Must have been 100 degrees." The man offered to play Elder straight up—no strokes—but only if Elder wore a full rain suit. The bet, $500 for nine holes, was one Elder could not pass up.

"So they dress me in this rain suit," Elder explained. "Zip it up to my collar. Taped at the sleeves and legs so I couldn't get air. I thought I was going to suffocate. He did, too." Elder won the match on seven.

"I'm not ashamed of it," Elder said. "I had to depend upon my hustling ability to make a living in golf. I didn't make any match that was a 50-50 chance; it had to be 80-20."

Jim Thorpe is a member of the next generation of African-American golfers who followed Elder and Sifford. A three-time winner on the PGA Tour, Thorpe grew into a consistent money winner on the Champions circuit. Prior to joining the regular tour in 1976, Thorpe tried to support himself by arranging money games and by playing on what he called the "chitlin' tour."

He started at Baltimore's Clifton Park Golf Course, where he played for

$25 a match, shooting whatever it took to win. "Hell, if I had to shoot 36, I shot 36," Thorpe said. "If I had to shoot 40, I shot 40. I won the matches before I teed off."

After marrying his second wife, Carol, who worked for the federal government, they lived in suburban Washington, D.C. "Carol would give me $700 to pay the rent, but I went to the golf course with it," Thorpe said in a 2002 interview with *Golf Digest*. "I'd get one of those Detroit bankrolls—about 100 $1 bills and put 50s on top of it, and everybody at the golf course would come at you, man. I was loaded for bear."

Thorpe said he migrated to the action at Washington's East Potomac Park. "There was a lot of money there. A guy named Waldo used to wear pants three sizes too big with $20,000 in each pocket. It was easy pickings," Thorpe said of the matches there, "because I was the best player there. I'd shoot 30-29 and make like $14,000."

Thorpe did not limit himself to one course; instead, he traveled the country in search of money golf. His biggest payday was a 1977 match at Detroit's Radrick Farms. Thorpe had just joined the tour and struggled to find the financial backing he needed to cover expenses, so he played money matches to build his bankroll. He took his Detroit opponent for $55,000, surpassing the first-place money of $40,000 at that year's Masters.

"Of course I lost sometimes," said Thorpe of those years. "I was playing this guy at Coffin Golf Club in Indianapolis. I was playing him for five grand, which was a lot of money. I shoot 33 on the front, he shoots 32. On the back nine we play for another $5,000. I shoot 33, he shoots 32. I said, 'You know what, my friend? You're the best.'"

Thorpe played a betting game called "the Wheel" at East Potomac. As Hogan did at Shady Oaks, a two-man team played better ball against everyone else. It allowed a large number of bettors to play each other, and the stakes could get high. "There'd always be all kinds of money bet on these matches," Thorpe told *Golf Digest*. "We'd play for $1,000, sometimes as much as $5,000. There were a couple guys we called Saginaw Pete and Potato Pie. They'd bet on anything. About every half-hour, they'd bet on the time of day. They all bet, and some of them couldn't play a lick."

"There were no 'life or death' putts on tour," Thorpe said. "It's life or death when you play against those guys at East Potomac. If you don't have that money in your pocket, you'd better win. I've had putts where there was more money riding [on one shot] than I had in the world."

For years, East Potomac Park was a center of money golf in Washington, D.C. There are still cash games there, but the management takes a dim view of betting on the main putting green. Michael K. Bohn

Washington area golf instructor Henry Seymour played money games at East Potomac Park during the late 1960s and early '70s. "There were 20 to 30 guys who played about every day," Seymour recalled. "Lots of action, as much as you wanted."

Seymour told a story about George the Greek, one of the East Potomac regulars, who asked for "steps" instead of strokes during a game. "He usually got to tee off 17 steps in front of the tee," Seymour said. "But his were not normal paces. He got a running head start, then took giant, running steps. In track meets in those days, it was called the 'hop, skip, and jump,' now the Triple Jump."

"There was another George," Seymour said. "We called him Big George. He never played, just bet. He came up to me one day while I was chipping on the practice green. He bet me $200 that I couldn't get up and down twelve times in a row. I did, and when he paid up, he just shrugged off the $200. 'I'll make more tomorrow,' he told me, 'when I bet on you out on the course.' He won four grand betting on me the next day."

Seymour took on "Red Eye Charlie," then a drug dealer but now deceased. Playing for $2,000, Seymour, who had given Red Eye four strokes, needed a birdie on 18 to win the match. After Seymour chipped in, Red Eye erupted, "You lucky bastard! I'm not paying you a frigging penny." Despite the bluster, Red Eye paid up, and Seymour ran to the parking lot.

"I was about to get in my car, and there was Red Eye with a gun pointed right at my head," recalled Seymour. "I said, 'Here, let's forget this. Take your money back. This is ridiculous, me winding up dead and you in jail.' He stared at me, thought about it, then took $1,000 back."

Seymour now spends most of his time giving golf lessons at a suburban driving range. East Potomac players, however, still bet enough to catch the pro shop's attention. The staff installed a sign that bans money games on the main putting green. Andy Viglucci, lead PGA teaching professional at the course, pointed out a group of regulars. "They play money games every day," he said. "Their profile is lower than the old days, and I darn sure don't see any guns."

—●—

Tour events generated increasing television revenues, which led to a confrontation in 1968 between the players and the PGA. By the start of the year, revenue growth exceeded the increase in purses, with the extra either supporting general, non-tour PGA expenses or going to charity. The public perceived the touring pros as rich guys getting paid to play golf; rather, the pros were independent, non-franchised performers. Unlike other U.S. professional sports at the time, the golf pros did not have a contract with a team. They didn't make any money if they failed to make the cut, so they were sensitive about who controlled the cash. They also grumbled about the PGA's concentration on the club pros at the touring players' expense as well as about the high number of club pros at the PGA Championship in 1967. In the 1960s, the ratio between the two groups of members was about 5-1 in favor of the club pros.

In August 1968, a large number of players announced they planned to break away from the PGA and form their own tour. Gardner Dickinson, the head of the PGA tournament committee, led the rebellion that ultimately included all of the established stars. They called themselves the American Professional Golfers (APG).

The splinter group aggressively courted sponsors, and by November it announced a lineup of 19 tournaments for 1969 with a total purse of $2.3 million. The PGA wilted and offered a compromise, a semiautonomous "Tournament Player's Division." A 10-man policy board, comprised of three outsiders, three from the PGA, and four touring players or their representatives, would oversee the division's operations. The board hired longtime USGA executive secretary, Joe Dey, to become the division's commissioner. His successor, Deane Beman, reincorporated the division and renamed it the PGA Tour, an entity entirely separate from the PGA.

The PGA continues to run the PGA Championship and the Ryder Cup matches. Save for the Masters and the USGA tournaments, the tour sanctions all other professional events in the United States.

—●—

"Let's play a couple holes," a portly insurance salesman said to Lee Buck Trevino. It was 1961 in Dallas, and Trevino was working at Hardy's Driving Range, which also had a nine-hole pitch-'n-putt course. Little did the businessman know the 21-year-old would join the PGA Tour six years later and become one of its superstars

"No," Trevino replied. "Hell, you can't beat me."

"But you know I'm good," countered the salesman, referring to the dozens of times the two had played the par-3 course.

"Hey, I've got a new deal for you. You might have a chance to win," said Trevino, sensing his source of extra income was about to evaporate in the Texas sun. Picking up a large, empty Dr Pepper soft drink bottle, Trevino declared, "I'm going to play you with this bottle."

The two men agreed to play the first and ninth holes, with Trevino getting a half stroke on each hole. He stepped onto the first tee, grabbed the 32-ounce glass bottle by the neck with his right hand, tossed a golf ball into the air with his left, and hit it onto the green using the bottle as a bat. His opponent gaped incredulously at what he just saw but steadied himself enough to hit his ball onto the green using a regular golf club. Trevino putted by swinging the bottle between his legs.

Both parred the two holes, with Trevino winning each.

Unknown to the pigeon, the young Mexican American had practiced long and hard on hitting a golf ball with that bottle. "I wore a glove on my

As a young pro, before joining the PGA Tour, Lee Trevino practiced playing golf with a large Dr Pepper bottle. He became skilled enough to win money from unsuspecting pigeons. Once the story got around, Dr Pepper signed Trevino to an endorsement contract, and the Lee played exhibitions in the late 1960s with a bottle. In this photograph, he finished his follow-through with the bottle over his left shoulder. DR PEPPER MUSEUM AND FREE ENTERPRISE INSTITUTE

right hand and wrapped adhesive tape around the neck of the bottle so I wouldn't cut my hand if it broke. I got better and better with it, so I went to the pitch-'n-putt to try it out there."

Hours of practice, to say nothing of great hand-eye coordination, gave Trevino a skill that his opponents could not match. Successful golf hustling depends on an edge, or, in this case, a quirky dexterity honed to perfection. Trevino rarely hustled at golf, preferring straight-up money games, but the Dr Pepper bottle caper was important to his career.

"After I won the U.S. Open in 1968, there had been so much publicity about me and that old bottle that Dr Pepper signed me to a four-year contract at $50,000 a year. I did television commercials, held clinics, and represented the company at special gatherings." Trevino stopped the soda bottle exhibitions when kids cut their hands trying to practice the gimmick.

"But people never forgot. They still ask me about that Dr Pepper bottle. And somewhere that fat little insurance salesman may still be wondering how I did it."

Trevino joined the PGA Tour in 1967. Besides the 1968 U.S. Open, he won 27 other tour events, including five majors. After joining the Champions Tour in 1989, Trevino won another 29 times. He is a member of the World Golf Hall of Fame.

Galleries loved Trevino from the get go. He was a common man among the cookie-cutter, tall, blond guys. His only concession to the pro golfer model was covering a tattoo on his forearm with a Band-Aid. He always chatted up the gallery, his pairing partner, or a fence post if he was alone. Some opponents told him to shut up on the first tee. Asked in 2004 why he talked so much, Trevino blamed it on his money golf days.

"I think it came from more or less playing quarter skins, $1 skins, stuff on the golf course," he said. "We were great needlers. You could get guys so angry. They were 12-handicappers and, you were scratch, and they'd play you for $10 just to keep your mouth shut, and then you'd needle them some more, and that's how you got all your bets. That's actually where it came from."

Playing partners didn't always enjoy Lee's gabbing. Nicklaus turned to him one day on the first tee and said, "Lee, I just want to play golf today; I don't want to talk."

"That's all right, Jack, you don't have to talk," Trevino said. "You just have to listen."

Trevino grew up in Dallas, reared by his mother and a grave-digging grandfather. He discovered golf as a kid and caddied at the DAC Country Club across the street from his home. He quit school at age 14 and joined the Marine Corps at age 17. Four years later, Trevino returned to Hardy's and decided he wanted to become a golf pro. He joined the North Texas PGA section and began playing in any tournament he could enter. Soon he was supplementing his winnings by playing money golf around the Dallas–Fort Worth area—Lakewood, DAC, Glen Garden, and especially Tenison Park. It was only 10 minutes from Hardy's, and young Lee found all the action he needed there.

Tenison Park was one of many public golf courses throughout the country where money golfers congregated like iron filings around a magnet. Jenkins's Goat Hills story (see chapter 5) as well as Rick Reilly's tour of Ponkapoag Golf Club near Boston (see chapter 7) captured the feeling. The money golf games were also akin to the floating crap games Damon Runyon wrote about in *Guys and Dolls*. The betting was continuous.

The oldest public course in Dallas, Tenison is a few miles east of downtown. It has 36 holes, hundreds of pecan trees and, in the 1960s, boasted only one bunker. Trevino called it the hardest "easy" course he ever played. The USGA found the track enough of a challenge to hold the 1968

Amateur Public Links Championship there. Over the years, Titanic, Floyd, and Elder made money at Tenison. Most of the players there were not famous pros, just anonymous sorts who sported nicknames—"Ace," "Fat Mickey," and "the Fly."

"After I won the U.S. Open in 1968, a story went around that I learned to play golf at Tenison as a little boy," Trevino said in 1982. "The truth is that I never set foot there until the summer of 1961 when I was 21. But once I did, I knew it was my kind of place. It was always exciting." Other stories had Trevino playing at Tenison for big bucks, but he denied those accounts too. "Sure there were some very big games, but I didn't have the money to get in them. The biggest bet I ever made in those days was 5 bucks, but that's big enough if you don't have a penny in your pocket."

In addition to straight-up money matches, the regulars at Tenison tried to liven their days with odd-ball betting games. Trevino called one the "Tunnel" game. Everyone threw $25 in the pot and then played cross-country from a far corner on the course back to the clubhouse through a concrete tunnel under railroad tracks. "If a guy didn't put his ball in the right position, he might make a 12 or 13 getting through it."

In Honest John, each player paid all the others $10 for each stroke he took over his predicted score. A bad day meant a hole in your pocket. Another game was Trees. A player paid $10 for every tree he hit. Cutback involved playing the first five holes of the east course and then moving over to the back nine for 15 through 18. "You'd see a gang coming down number five—maybe a half dozen of the biggest gamblers in Dallas with 15 or 20 people following them in carts," Trevino said. "Next thing you knew, they'd jump over in front of you on 15. No one would dare say anything to them. No telling how much artillery they had under their jackets and in their socks and golf bags."

Hustlers were not the only people picking pockets at Tenison. Trevino tells a story about two guys with shotguns stepping out of the bushes in a deserted part of the course. They made all of the players empty their pockets. One of the victims was down $1,000 at that point, so instead of giving up his cash to the robbers, he paid off his competitor. "Here," he said, "we're even."

Trevino said the only time he played at Tenison for real money was after he joined the tour. He had a game with the pro Erwin Hardwicke; a local golfer named Dick Martin; and one of the assistant pros. They played a

Nassau with Lee betting $75 to the others' $25 a piece. "I lost as much as $1,000 on 18 holes, but what the hell, I had the money. It was fun doing it, with all those people following us. And we were lucky. We never got robbed."

Dick Martin was a legend at Tenison. Trevino called him "probably the best player I ever saw until Jack Nicklaus." A slight five-foot-five man, Martin was a superb player who used his skill to set up prop bets and to separate an opponent from his money. One, called "Chip Again" or "Chip Back," allowed a high handicapper to knock Martin's ball off each green. In another, Martin let his opponents putt for birdie on every hole. Martin, though, got to place the ball wherever he wanted on the putting surface. His knowledge of Tenison's greens gave Martin the edge in those bets. He also made money on the Bobby Jones game, which involved allowing his opponent to hit his second shot from the point where Martin's tee shot landed.

Former PGA Tour player Doug Sanders said Martin wanted money riding on every hole he played. "I won't play for fun," he told Sanders. Sanders revealed Martin's love of the action backfired occasionally, which led to Martin's pronouncement, "When there ain't no suckers in the room, you're it."

Martin did not bet large sums on his matches, only enough to make a decent living and invest in Dallas real estate. When someone asked him why he didn't turn pro, he responded, "Because I can't afford it."

He played in tournaments all over the Southwest during his career, from local to regional events as well as head-to-head matches with the era's best pros. One story had Martin all square with Tommy Bolt on the final green. Bolt was faced with an 8-footer for birdie, just inside Martin's ball and on the same line. He watched carefully as Martin's 10-footer curved into the hole. Bolt played the same break, but his stayed high. "I hooked mine," said Martin, admitting he worked his putt right to left to deceive Bolt.

The heavy side action between observers eventually led to the demise of big money games at Tenison. "It got so bad that [nonplaying] bettors were using cars to follow the players around the course," said Hardwicke. "I put a stop to that, and I started charging green fees for anyone who wanted to watch." In 2003 Bob Smith, the director of golf at Tenison Park, said the course had not been a hustler's haven in years.

The most frequently told betting story about Trevino featured a match he and Floyd played in El Paso in 1966. Trevino had left Hardy's Driving Range because owner Hardy Greenwood would not sponsor Trevino into the PGA. Lee and his wife moved to El Paso, where he joined the staff at Horizon Hills Country Club (now named Emerald Springs).

Floyd turned pro in 1961 and won two tournaments by 1965, the St. Petersburg and St. Paul Opens, in what might have been a religious experience. He lived in Dallas at the time and enjoyed a friendly wager. "I prefer practicing alone than playing for nothing," he once said. Because he was so good, the only way he could get a bet with the amateurs was to play two balls off the tee, then take his worst shot, and play two again and again until he holed out. Another bet had Floyd playing his best ball of the two, and the money rode on his pre-round prediction on his score for the round, usually 62 or 63.

Another regular at Tenison in 1966 was Titanic Thompson, who at 76 years old, still shot his age. Because few players would give the man strokes, his score did not win many bets. Thompson's friend Ace Darnell suggested that Ti start backing younger golfers instead of playing matches himself. "Hell, Ti," Darnell said, "what you ought to do is let some of the hotshot young golfers that can go out and shoot a damn course in nothing make your money for you, and just ride around in a cart and enjoy yourself." Darnell thought they should back Floyd against a young hotshot in El Paso named Lee Trevino.

Accompanied by another Tenison Park regular, Fat Mickey, Ace traveled from Dallas to El Paso to set up the match. Several wealthy cotton farmers who played at Horizon agreed to back Trevino and arranged the bets with the Dallas visitors.

A couple of days later, Floyd, who had never met Trevino, arrived at the course in a white Cadillac. Trevino met him in the parking lot with a cart, then carried Floyd's bag into the clubhouse, and shined Raymond's shoes.

"Well, who am I supposed to play?" Floyd asked the friendly attendant.

"Me," Lee replied.

"You? What do you do?"

"Well," Trevino said, "I'm a combination everything. I'm the cart man, shoe man, clubhouse man, and pro."

Trevino won the first round, using his considerable knowledge of the course to his advantage. He shot 65 to beat Floyd by two shots. Thompson and Darnell lost $9,000 each. After carousing that night about Juarez, Mexico, El Paso's neighboring city, and perhaps suffering what Bing Crosby used to call the "whips and jingles" after a long night, Floyd teed it up for round two. Trevino beat him again, shooting another 65 to Floyd's 66. The Dallas boys lost another $9,000.

On the third and final day, Floyd went out in 31. Trevino shot 30 on the back nine but lost by two. Thompson and Darnell recouped some of their losses after pressing on the back nine, and Floyd declared he'd had enough. "Adios. I've got easier games than this on the tour."

—●—

"I guess I first got my reputation as a pressure player when I was about 13 in North Carolina, playing for $100 Nassaus with older men and beating them," Floyd said of his younger days. He is not bashful about his fondness for betting on golf. Journalists always ask him about it in interviews, and he readily tells his best stories. Many writers use him as a metaphor for golfers in stressful situations. Some even edge toward hyperbole: "The money he won and lost on golfing wagers would have financed a Latin American revolution."

Most of the PGA Tour players who turned pro around 1960 or before learned golf and how to bet on it in the caddie yards. Sarazen, Snead, Hogan, and Trevino are examples of that culture. There is another category of players, those who learned from their fathers or other adults. Raymond's dad, L. B. Floyd, was an Army master sergeant who spent much of his career managing the enlisted men's golf course at Fort Bragg near Fayetteville. Raymond studied the game there as well as at a driving range his father owned off base. At six years old, Raymond could play either left or right handed. "I don't mean to brag on the boy," L. B. said in 1992, "but Raymond can still turn the club upside down and hit it 250 yards off the tee left handed." Floyd used those skills to hustle the Army guys for money.

The elder Floyd said Raymond never needed money as a teenager, an odd situation. Turns out he was earning enough by betting on his own game. "He would go out on weekends and just clean these men for big money," L. B. said.

"When I grew up, golf was a gambling game. That was just the nature of it," Floyd recalled. "And as for me, that was the fascination of it. Had it not been for gambling, I don't believe I would have enjoyed the games as much or stayed on top of it. I started playing for quarters, and for a long time I guess I never played a game of golf that I didn't have a bet on." He went on to say without a wager, a four seemed the same as a six on a hole. "The higher the stakes, the more intense your interest becomes."

Phil Rodgers, who joined the tour in 1962 and became a five-time winner, also learned how to bet on golf as a kid when he caddied for LoBall Johnny Wilson. A San Diego bookie, Wilson taught Rodgers how to win golf bets. "Gambling at golf is all about using psychology and human nature to your advantage, and by age 13 these things were instinctive to me," Rodgers explained. "I played in a lot of big gambling games. That's probably one of the things that influenced my ability to score. I didn't go out and laugh and giggle. I became a very tough player, and I was still a junior."

Rodgers was clearly ahead of his peers in the art of money golf. That skill gave him a problem when he was 15 years old, though. During a practice round before a junior tournament, Phil won another kid's traveling money—$39. The youngster's mother complained to the state golf association, which suspended Rodgers from tournament play.

"I was devastated," Phil said. "I didn't know I'd done anything wrong." USGA executive secretary Dey heard about the matter and came to Rodgers's rescue. Dey helped Phil write a successful appeal on USGA stationery that pointed out the custom of betting between golfers. "When you have the support of Joe Dey, who was a respected and moral guy, it's like having your Sunday school teacher testify on your behalf," Rodgers said. "I felt bad about taking that kid's $39. But not bad enough to give it back."

Rodgers's tour career was relatively short, and to some, he never lived up to his potential. "I've never seen a player with more innate ability," said veteran Paul Runyan, who gave lessons to the teenager. As a youngster, Rodgers had learned how to make a sand wedge sing and later used his skills to become a short-game guru. He has tutored many players, including Nicklaus in 1979, the first year after 1961 that Jack didn't win a tournament. Phil also used his favorite club to take some of Runyan's money.

The two agreed to a four-hole match in the early 1960s at La Jolla Country Club in San Diego. Each would use only one club—Rodgers, his sand iron, and Runyan, a 5-wood. Rodgers put a 5-iron shaft on the wedge. He won the match on the final hole with a 30-foot putt in front of a huge, side-betting crowd. Runyan demanded a one-hole press, but Rodgers declined, afraid his luck would not last any longer.

David Duval is another example of a youngster influenced by adults on the golf course. His father, Bob, was the pro at Timuquana Country Club in

Jacksonville, Florida, when David was growing up. (Bob later played on the Champions Tour when David was staring his career on the PGA Tour.) David learned how to bet on golf as a teenager while playing at his dad's course. He soon began collecting bets from men in their 40s, who were excellent golfers in their own right. David kept his winnings in a cigar box at home, reportedly totaling at least $1,000 at one point. "Damn it, Pro," the men said to Bob, "we'd rather have you out there than that little shit son of yours."

As a teenager, Gardner Dickinson discovered what every golf bettor ultimately understands, his limit. Some learn $10 is about right, while others need larger sums to get their interest.

Dickinson played often in high school with his buddy Wendell Barnes. They played a money match about three times a week. Soon Dickinson's father, Gardner, Sr., began following the kids and making side bets on Junior against another adult who backed Wendell. "We got to playing for quite a bit of money," Dickinson said later. "The matches were pretty intense because Wendell and I got a piece of it if we won.

The pressure reached a point where the two teenagers weren't friendly anymore. The fun was gone. After Dickinson made a 4-foot putt for an $800 payday for his dad, Gardner told him, "If you want to play any more gambling games, you'll have to get another boy. I've lost the best friend I've got, and it's not worth it."

The young men who now join the PGA Tour generally learned to deal with pressure through junior golf, college, and the mini-tours. Few caddied, mostly because of the job's demise but also because they wouldn't have had time to play in American Junior Golf Association (AJGA) tournaments. The AJGA is now the training ground for future tour players. There are 160 AJGA alumni on the U.S. pro tours. In 2006, 5,000 juniors played in 75 tournaments. The competition is intense in both the boys' and girls' divisions. Colleges won't offer even a walk-on spot, much less a scholarship, to a recruit who doesn't have a good record in national and regional junior tournaments. Many of the kids don't even play for their high school team because of the AJGA circuit's demands.

Despite all of this, kids still learn about betting on their game. At a 2006 AJGA tournament, *Sports Illustrated* polled 36 boys and 36 girls, ages 13 through 18, with questions including "Do you make wagers on the course?" 52 percent said yes.

Lee Trevino does his part in introducing junior players to money golf. During the 2006 Wal-Mart First Tee Open at Pebble Beach, an annual pro-junior event, Trevino played with Amber Hardeman. In the second round Lee told the on-course TV commentator he had a $1, closest-to-the-hole bet with 15-year-old Amber from Murphy, North Carolina. A commercial break kept viewers from finding out who won.

Doug Ford, an old-schooler, still maintains playing for money is important. "Being able to play under pressure is what makes a player," he said recently. "I would always tell a kid coming up: 'If you want to build your game, go gamble with your last dollar.'"

———•———

In 1972, Trevino beat Nicklaus by one shot in the British Open, denying Nicklaus's bid for a Grand Slam. "I don't remember what I won in the golf tournament," said Trevino, who picked up a $13,750 first prize, "but we won a lot more gambling. First round, I shot 71. My odds went up, so I bet again. I bet with six couples, friends of mine. When I won, the bookmaker showed up at the party with a suitcase full of pounds to pay me. It was about 32 degrees outside, but he was perspiring. Heavily." Lee won £5,500.

Golfers have bet on them themselves in tournaments for a long time. Some still do today. Amateurs may be limited to the club Calcutta, unless they're playing in a big event in Nevada or abroad. Besselink's excellent San Diego adventure in 1965 ended the custom on the American PGA Tour, save for the Las Vegas Invitational. The British Open, however, is a different story altogether.

Responding to a *Sports Illustrated* poll of 50 PGA Tour players in 2005, 40 of them said they had bet on themselves at the British Open. Six indicated they had bet on another player. In any other sport in the United States, such an admission would be a disastrous calamity. The besmirched sport would have to commit ritual suicide at home plate to cleanse and make itself whole again. Golfers can bet, though, because of the sport's traditions.

Watson, a five-time winner of the Open, said he has bet on himself because it's part of the fun when playing in Britain. "I don't have any problem with it." When he arrived in the United Kingdom for the Open during the years when he was playing well, Watson usually approached a Scottish oracle named Richie, who always bet on Tom. "What odds you got?" he asked Richie.

"Five-1 or 6-1," he answered.

"You're crazy to keep on betting me at those odds."

"Yea, mon, you're right," said Richie, "but I keep on winnin'."

In 1989, when the 49-year-old Watson was a bit past his prime, he was disappointed when the bookies had him at 66-1 before the Open at Troon. He went to the betting window with his practice rounds' winnings and put the lot on himself. "I'm not the same player I was in the [early] 1980s," Watson said, "but there's some of that left."

When Ian Baker-Finch won the 1991 Open, he passed up betting on himself, even though his friends took advantage of the 50-1 odds on him. "I got all sorts of faxes, telexes, even a case of champagne, from guys who won money on me."

"I bet him £100 each way," said Nick Price, describing his wager on Baker-Finch. "I think I won £4,500 on a £200 bet. It paid for my whole trip over here," recalled Price. Nick also fancied Ernie Els during the final round of the 2002 Open. Els hit a spectacular pitch onto the green from a difficult lie on the 72nd hole to win the tournament by one stroke. "A beautiful shot," Price recalled. "I bet a friend £50 he'd get it up and down, so I won, too."

Curtis Strange sums up the feeling among the older pros: "I've always said we gamble on ourselves every day, when we play as professional golfers. We're going for a million bucks in a major. What's another couple pounds going to mean?"

Professional caddies have the same outlook. "Caddying is a gambling lifestyle anyway," said Malcom Mason, a veteran European PGA Tour caddie. "You come out every week, and you don't know if you're going to win money or lose money. It's the type of people we are: we like a bet." Among the caddies, the rule about betting on their man is if you do, keep it a secret. One caddie, however, is more realistic. "There's no point in betting on your man to win the tournament," he argued, "because if he does, you'll make plenty of cash anyway."

Some of the younger, more image-conscious players take a different stance, at least around a reporter. Woods and Mickelson always bet when they play informal rounds, but when speaking publicly, they take care to avoid the poisonous perceptions in the public's mind about athletes betting on themselves with a bookie. "I've never laid a bet on myself," Woods asserts. "I won't do that." Mickelson repeated that line: "I don't do that in golf. It's not an area I want to go in."

Ironically, a player named Rose took advantage of Tiger during the first round of the 2002 British Open. British pro Justin Rose was paired with Woods and Shigeki Maruyama. Rose bet on himself to post a better score than Woods would that day. "I made a couple quid on the 18 holes today," Rose declared after the round. "I think I got 5-2 odds."

The LPGA generally accepts their players betting on themselves in venues where it is legal. "It's all very open," said Laura Davies in 2001, "but I realize that here [in the United States] it's looked at much differently. There's nothing sinister about it." A popular online betting shop, sportsbook.com, sponsored Davies for several years starting in 2001. The LPGA didn't object.

"I don't have control over Laura," said Commissioner Ty Votaw in 2001. "She's an independent contractor. All I can do is counsel her. Our tour has accepted money from gambling establishments. My position is if we've done it, how can we ban it?" Concerning the PGA Tour's sensitivity to gambling, Votaw pointed out, "The PGA Tour has a few more regulations than we do." Votaw went on to say other sports "have suffered insidious effects from gambling, but not women's golf. If there's a problem, I might take a different attitude."

In the minor leagues of professional golf, light years away from the $1 million checks on the tour, betting during tournaments hasn't changed much since Besselink's heyday. In 2003, journeyman pro Mike McNerney teed it up at a 36-hole Maverick Tour event in Florida. Although he won the tournament, McNerney supplemented the meager $1,400 first prize with side bets to help with expenses.

A longtime veteran of the bottom of golf's food chain, McNerney has never advanced to the PGA Tour. He used to play on the old southern Florida mini tour, where the tour operator set odds on the players and took bets. "I frequently bet on myself to win," he said. "You could pick up an extra $800 to $1,500, depending on the purse. It makes you a better player. It's part of being educated about pressure."

The Prairie Golf Tour operated between 1996 and 2000. It was a 14-tournament circuit played in the Midwest. John Turek ran the weekly show, and holding the bets was one of his many jobs. In California, the Golden State Tour is larger, but it did not have any sponsors in the late 1990s. The entry fees made up the purse, so each tournament was not much more than a sweepstakes. "It's organized gambling," said John Flannery, one of the players at the time.

The Hillcrest Invitational is one of the regular stops on the Dakotas Tour, hosted by Hillcrest Golf and Country Club in Yankton, South Dakota. In 2005, the total purse for the 72-hole event was $75,000, with $20,000 going to the winner. That take is not bad for a mini tour. The tournament also boasts a pro-am with a Calcutta, proving old-fashioned golf betting still takes place in America's heartland. The pool totaled $26,000 before the start, and another auction after the second round attracted $16,000.

—●—

After Babe Didrikson Zaharias died in 1956, the U.S. women's game didn't attract much attention. Mickey Wright and Kathy Whitworth dominated the LPGA Tour during the 1960s and early '70s. They were great players but didn't have the pizzazz to draw fans and sponsors to the tour. While U.S. sports broadcasters chased after Palmer, Nicklaus, and Trevino, no one seemed interested in the women's game.

That situation changed almost overnight with the remarkable debut of 21-year-old Nancy Lopez, a Mexican American from New Mexico. Blessed with a winning smile and healthy, girl-next-door looks, Lopez helped soften the stereotype of the athletic yet business-like LPGA players. Moreover, she had a helluva game. She hit the LPGA Tour like a lightning bolt in her rookie year of 1978. She won nine tournaments, five of them in a row. She also picked up honors for Rookie of the Year, Player of the Year, and the Vare Trophy for the lowest scoring average.

The news media loved Nancy for her openness and charm. She quickly became the Arnie Palmer of the LPGA and generated needed publicity for the women's tour. She was quite a change from Whitworth, who kept to herself and didn't say much to reporters and TV commentators. "Had someone else been winning besides myself, who had more charisma, we might have grown faster in that earlier era," Whitworth admitted.

The 1970s witnessed the LPGA's first dramatic growth spurt since its creation in 1949. At the start of the decade, the tour sponsored 21 tournaments with a total purse of $435,000. By 1979, it ran 38 events and offered $4.5 million in prize money. While Lopez gave the tour a big push, LPGA president Carol Mann also contributed by revitalizing tour management. In

1975, she hired Ray Volpe as LPGA commissioner, and he brought needed marketing experience to the LPGA.

Many of the women professionals of this era bet among themselves during informal games. Few talked about their wagers, which were modest and similar to the $2 bets Peggy Kirk Bell enjoyed 30 years earlier. "I'm not a heavy bettor," Lopez admitted later. "I bet for Cokes and stuff. I choke when I play for $5."

Jane Blalock won 27 times on the LPGA Tour. She liked to make small bets during tournament rounds, perhaps to spark better play. In 1978, she shot a first-round 67 at the Lady Keystone Open in Hershey, Pennsylvania, and broke the women's course record. Standing on the 16th tee during the round, her caddie, Lee Hetrick, bet her a dinner that night she couldn't birdie the last three holes. She did and said after their game, "I'm going to look through the Yellow Pages and pick out a place that looks expensive." Blalock finished second that week, and coincidentally, Lopez finished tied for 13th, breaking her five-tournament winning streak.

Blalock and Pat Meyers made small bets between them when paired together in tournaments. In the first and second rounds of the 1985 Uniden Invitational in Costa Mesa, California, they bet each other a beer for birdies and bogeys. By Saturday evening, Blalock was 1-up on the beer tab and ready to collect.

LPGA Hall of Fame member Mickey Wright didn't approve of friendly wagers on the golf course. Asked in 1985 how a long absence from tournament competition affected a player's game, she answered, "There's no way to simulate competition. Some people say you can do it with a $5 Nassau bet, but when I'm playing golf, I don't gamble. To me, that's like spitting in church. Golf is too holy to me to gamble on it."

Mickey didn't know it at the time, but she was the subject of a bet between Gardner Dickinson and Marlene Bauer Hagge, a contemporary of Wright's on the LPGA Tour. Over drinks one evening in the 1960s during the old Haig & Haig Mixed Team Invitational, Hagge told Dickinson about Wright's length off the tee. She boasted Mickey could play on the men's tour and even be the leading money winner. Gardner, a slight man who weighed 125 pounds when he joined the tour, disagreed, saying Wright didn't have the length to compete with the PGA pros. When he said he could hit a ball farther with his 4-wood than Mickey could with a driver, Marlene bet $10,000 that he couldn't. The following morning Dow Finsterwald, who was Hagge's partner in the tournament, talked her out of the wager.

"The next day I saw Mickey hitting balls on the range," Dickinson said years later. "I waited until she had worked through her shorter clubs and began hitting her driver. I motioned my caddie out beyond hers and hit my 4-wood past her longest drive."

—●—

To prove the theory that aggressive golfers are also aggressive bettors, look straight at Lanny Wadkins. The golfing news media dubbed him "Mr. Tuesday" and the PGA Tour's "prince of practice rounds." He shot a 63 at the 1971 U.S. Open, a 62 at the 1973 PGA Championship, and a 61 at the 1984 PGA, all on Tuesdays. He won a bunch of bets on those rounds, as he does whenever he plays informal rounds. Wadkins likes money golf. "It keeps you on your toes," he explained. "It just makes you more competitive. When you win, it's not the money that matters most. Nobody's trying to make a living off another player. It's the bragging rights."

Wadkins, who grew up in Richmond, Virginia, was a teenage phenom, winning the Virginia State Junior twice. He later won the Southern, Western, and U.S. Amateurs and was an All-American at Wake Forest University. He was playing money golf in college against his teammate Jim Simons, who also went on to play on the PGA Tour. Wadkins said he never lost to Simons. "If I made $6 off Simons, I could eat at McDonald's for lunch and the chicken place for dinner."

He turned pro in 1971. He was part of a lustrous Q-School class that included Watson, John Mahaffey, Larry Nelson, David Graham, Bruce Fleisher, Steve Melnyk, and Gary McCord.

Wadkins played an aggressive game on the PGA Tour. Jim Murray said in another life Lanny would have been a riverboat gambler, one who always said "Hit me" instead of "I'll play these." In 1985, Nicklaus talked about Lanny's propensity for shooting at flags: "He thinks the course owes him something." Watson agreed, "When Lanny's on his game, it's like having a cobra in the basket with the lid off." Wadkins admits to his hard-charging style: "The way I play is the only way I can play. Besides, it's more fun to have a go at it."

Wadkins's betting during practice rounds helped energize his career. In 1973, his second year on tour, he won two times, had 13 top tens, and ended up fifth on the money list. He credited his success to weekly money matches he and Bert Yancey played against Palmer and Weiskopf. Lanny said the stakes were mostly for pride. "The most money that ever changed hands was maybe $500 to $800. But if you beat Arnold, he wanted to keep playing. Then you went to dinner and gave each other grief. Great times."

At the Heritage tournament in Hilton Head, South Carolina, Tom and Arnie lost "a few dollars" on the round. Palmer called for an "emergency nine."

"Arnold wanted a chance to get his money back," Wadkins said later. "But when Bert and I won that nine, too, Arnold said, 'We're going another nine.' We played the last two holes in the dark, but we beat 'em again."

Ben Wright, the former CBS TV commentator, spoke of the Wadkins-Palmer games during a recent interview. "Lanny Wadkins absolutely milked Arnold Palmer on practice days. It was a license to steal. Lanny used to tell me that if he were short of money, he would needle Arnie into a game. He would call him "Old Man" and tease him."

"You have to have a shot of testosterone in the morning before you play with some of those guys," Peter Jacobsen said of Wadkins and the other aggressive bettors. "Lanny would make six birdies on the front nine on Tuesday at the Oakmont Open, and you can't even hit the green. He'd say, 'Well you're already down nine-eight-seven-six-five, three, and one on the front, so you owe me $1,800.'"

Lanny won 21 times on the PGA Tour, including the 1977 PGA Championship. He has won once on the Champions Tour and was the lead golf analyst for CBS Sports in 2002–2006.

—●—

CHIPS AND PITCHES

A real player. "You wanna see somebody play hard for $2," said Lee Trevino, "it's that Gary Player. It's just his pride." Jack Nicklaus knows firsthand how intense Player is about his golf bets. Nicklaus watched him continue playing during a practice round's thunderstorm break before the 1975 U.S. Open at Medinah. Nicklaus, huddled under an umbrella in a low spot, watched Player trying to get up and down on the 17th green. "Don't you know the course is closed?" asked Jack.

"No, haven't heard anything," Player said. "Besides, I got a $160 press going here."

Fiction as truth. In Dan Jenkins's 1971 novel, *Dead Solid Perfect*, Kenny Lee Puckett is a rookie on the PGA Tour. The scene is on the range the

Tuesday before the Los Angeles Open starts. Donny Smithern, another pro, approaches Puckett.

"Got a game? I got Zark and Ruffin at one o'clock."

I thought about that. Rex Zark and Eddie Ruffin. Good players. Tournament winners. Names.

"What kind of game do you guys play," Puckett asked.

"I'll be the bookkeeper," Donny said. "You just make some birdies."

He asked what my name was. We shook hands. Then he said we'd play Zark and Ruffin a $50 Nassau. Automatic 1-down presses. I said that was pretty strong for me. He said he'd take my half. I said, naw, I didn't travel that way.

"Then I suggest you play your ass off."

Money and mouth. Doug Sanders rarely turned away from a wager, even on the practice tee. According to Chi Chi Rodriguez, who was an eyewitness, a spectator heckled Sanders at a 1964 tournament. "Sanders, you don't hit it as straight as people say you do," the fan yelled from the gallery behind the tee. Sanders turned, pulled out his money clip, and said, ""I'll hit one ball with this driver and bet you a $1,000 my caddie doesn't have to move more than two steps to catch it." The fan agreed. After making the man show his money, Sanders hit the ball 255 yards to his caddie on one hop. Sanders pocketed the money and resumed practicing.

Movie greatness. The best golf movie ever made, *Caddyshack*, appeared in theaters in 1980. Bushwood Country Club, Judge Smails, Lacy Underall, Ty Webb, Al Czervik, and Carl Spackler—all these names are forever etched in the minds of golfers of a certain age. Most have the lines memorized: "Hey, Smails, 1,000 bucks you miss that putt!" "Noonan!"

Trade secrets. Fred "Lil' Pro" Carter played regularly at Chester Washington Golf Course in Los Angeles. A sanctuary for African-American golfers in the 1940s and '50s, the course was a gambler's paradise. "I once made a killing playing from a paper cup," Carter recalled. "I'd hit all my shots out of a cup except putts. I could never get a bad lie because the ball was sitting up. My opponents thought they were robbing me, but I was robbing them." (The cup takes the spin off the shot, allowing the ball to fly farther with less hook or slice spin.)

7.

HIGH-STAKES GOLF:

MONEY GAMES, 1984–97

ARNOLD PALMER'S ENERGETIC INTRODUCTION OF televised golf to the public in the 1960s firmly seated touring professionals as the game's stars around the world. While successful players in Australia, Asia, and Europe have reaped financial and personal rewards, the competitive center of show time golf has been America's PGA Tour since the mid-1980s.

The tour's leading money winner averaged $493,000 between 1980 and 1986, a princely sum by any standard. Yet in 1987, Curtis Strange won $925,941 and then broke the $1 million threshold in 1988 with winnings of $1,147,644. In real estate, location is important, but for most golf professionals today, it's money, money, and money. Only the rarest of players measure their success by titles and majors won.

Byron Nelson and Sam Snead used wagering to supplement their income from club jobs and tournaments. Players need not do so now, considering the ever-upward spiral of professional tournament purses. Tiger's $10 million earnings in 2006 is a bunch of dollars to Curtis Strange's doughnut. While betting between the tour players during practice rounds continues, it is not for financial gain. They do it because it's fun and helps focus their concentration.

Some players, however, still play for large sums of their own money. Most seem to congregate in Las Vegas, where they can enjoy the, um, full spread of wagering. If the names Bill Walters and Dewey Tomko don't ring a bell, then Michael Jordan's will. Some of these players have passed on professional golf because they didn't want to take a pay cut.

Nonplayers also still bet on golf tournaments. Tiger Woods's arrival on the tour in 1996 drastically changed the landscape of organized betting on golf. He became the hot topic among bookmakers, whether they are the pros in Vegas and the United Kingdom or the guy in the locker room at your club. Tiger has even drawn bettors away from the NFL and the NCAA basketball tournament. Odds on him to win any tournament he enters are unreasonably low, but those who bet on him are undeterred, including the PGA Tour boss. "I learned a long time ago not to bet against Tiger Woods," said Tim Finchem, PGA Tour commissioner.

Golf's other major developments in the 1980s and '90s were the technological advances in the equipment. There have been several club and ball revolutions over the long sweep of golf history. The latest equipment improvement is golf's largest oxymoron, metal woods. Both pros and hackers accepted the new clubs by the late 1980s. A parallel development, square grooves on irons, coupled with the debut of high-performance golf balls formed a rising technology tide that lifted all boats in the game, especially on the professional tours. Some stars have lamented the changes, though. "The new equipment is reducing the element of shot making and consolidating the talent," said Tom Watson. Jack Nicklaus added, "It's harder for the cream to rise to the top. The equipment is putting everyone at one level."

—●—

"Michael, are you prepared to play for $1.25 million?"

"Let's play for it."

According to former San Diego businessman Richard Esquinas, he and basketball star Michael Jordan made this golf wager in September 1991. The two had been betting on their games for the previous two years. Early in 1991, instead of paying off the bets after each round, the two agreed to keep a running tab on who was ahead. The run-up to the $1 million wager started a few days earlier. At The Farms, a private club near San Diego, they agreed to a two-way bet of $160,000 for 18 holes—$80,000 on the outcome scored as match play and another $80,000 on stroke play. They joined two other men for the game. Hank Egan, the University of San Diego's basketball coach at the time, teamed with Jordan, and Jim Brandenburg, then San Diego State's basketball coach, joined Esquinas. Egan and Brandenburg thought the two teams were playing for $2 three ways.

When Jordan lost to Esquinas in their match within a match, he owed Esquinas a total of $313,000 for the year. After the coaches left the course, Esquinas said Jordan asked for double or nothing. "Come on, E-Man, we've got time."

"I kicked his butt," Esquinas wrote later in his self-published book, *Michael and Me: Our Gambling Addiction . . . My Cry for Help!* "I shot a 37 with two birdies, a bogey, and a double bogey. M. J. shot a 42 or 43. The number, his debt to me, was $626,000."

Jordan wanted to get even, pushing for another round the next day. The two played at Aviara Golf Club north of San Diego for $626,000 two ways. Esquinas closed Jordan out in the match play on 17 and won the medal bet on the last hole. After adding some side bets for birdies, Jordan owed Esquinas $1,252,000.

Esquinas said he offered to negotiate the amount down to $500,000, but he wanted $50,000 on the spot. Jordan was in a hurry to leave for Chicago.

"I'll be in touch," Jordan said. "Really, E-Man, I'll make it right."

When Esquinas published his book in June 1993, his allegations of Jordan's golf losses added more fuel to an already hot fire. First, there was a matter of a dead man. In early 1992 in bail bondsman Eddie Dow's North Carolina home, police found his body and checks from Jordan totaling $108,000. Dow's brother said the money represented gambling debts Jordan paid for losses in golf and cards. Dow's attorney told the news media Jordan and Dow usually bet $1,000 a hole and played high-stakes poker. After reviewing the case, the NBA declined to discipline Jordan, who acknowledged poor judgment.

Also surfacing in 1992 was Michael's $57,000 payment to James "Slim" Bouler. Jordan was on the wrong end of a few $1,000 Nassaus with Bouler during a three-day golf weekend in October 1991. His check turned up during Bouler's trial for drug dealing and money laundering. Again, the NBA chastised Jordan.

During the May 1993 Eastern Conference finals between the Bulls and New York Knicks, Jordan and his father took a field trip between games to Atlantic City and played some blackjack. He had just weathered the Bouler storm when the Esquinas allegations hit the news. The NBA again swung into their familiar Jordan investigation mode.

Public reaction to Jordan's golf betting habits varied. Those who could add and subtract understood that $1.25 million, compared to Jordan's enormous earning power, was not that big a number. His betting on his golf game didn't surprise professional players. "I think it's too bad," Fred Couples said at the time. "If Greg Norman and I go one-on-one [playing basketball] for $100,000, who cares? This is this guy's hobby. If he plays golf for money, I don't see that it matters."

Jordan reacted predictably to Esquinas's claims, considering his need to ease the shock on his sponsors. He issued a written statement admitting he had bet on his matches with Esquinas. "Because I did not keep records, I cannot verify how much I won or lost. I can assure you that the level of our wagers was substantially less than the preposterous amounts that have been reported." In an interview with his friend Ahmad Rashad of NBC TV, he said, "Yes, for what I bet, it was a little more than I wanted to lose. I didn't bet to lose, but I lost it."

Esquinas said later Jordan paid some of the debt and won some back in 1992, leaving a new balance of $902,000. Esquinas also said he accepted Jordan's proposal to pay only $300,000 and told the news media Jordan's representatives had sent a partial payment of $200,000.

Many of Jordan's supporters considered Esquinas a sleazeball who used his book as leverage to get Jordan to pay off the whole bet. "This book is not about settlement or getting money," Esquinas rebutted. "I'm beyond anger. I felt anger, I felt frustration. I'm beyond that. This book is my catharsis." *Baloney* is the scientific term others use to describe Esquinas's statement.

During the third and final NBA investigation into Jordan's gambling, Esquinas told officials New York Giants linebacker Lawrence Taylor owed Jordan $150,000 from golf betting. The news media jumped on that story like Taylor sacking Joe Theisman. "Believe me, I'll gamble some on golf," Taylor admitted, but he pooh-poohed the reported figure. "But when you're talking numbers like that, I don't make the kind of money Michael does. It's just a stupid number."

Esquinas also told the NBA he heard Jordan on the phone discussing the spread on a basketball game. This allegation, which *Sports Illustrated* said "smells like another Rose," did not prompt a direct response during the NBA investigation. It did lead, however, to a conspiracy theory that has floated around since the revelations of Jordan's gambling habits.

Jordan announced what turned out to be his first retirement from basketball on Wednesday, October 6, 1993. He cited a variety of reasons: burnout, his father's murder earlier in the year, fulfilled goals, and such. Two days later, the NBA told the news media it had completed its investigation of Jordan's gambling and found he had violated no league rules. Reporters quickly asked NBA commissioner David Stern if he had made a deal with Jordan—namely, allowing Jordan to retire for a year or two in exchange for dropping this hot potato. Stern denied any connection between the investigation and Jordan's unexpected departure. "The investigation was nearly complete," Stern said. "We had a meeting scheduled [with Jordan], but we deferred it because of this." Jordan's subsequent baseball adventure may have resulted from an enforced time-out from basketball.

—•—

"You owe me six," Dewey Tomko said to his friend Billy Mac.

"Six?" Billy Mac asked, caught slightly off guard.

"Six."

Knowing Tomko was honest about their golf bets, Billy Mac reached in his pocket and fished out six rolls of $100 bills, each containing 100 Ben Franklins for $60,000 total. He gave them to Tomko as if he were buying a newspaper. "Same bet today?" Billy Mac asked.

"You got it."

Sports Illustrated writer Rick Reilly profiled Tomko in his book *Who's Your Caddy?* Reilly's angle in the book was recounting his caddying stints for famous golfers: John Daly, Donald Trump, Tomko, and others. When researching Tomko, Reilly tagged along during a match Dewey and his friends played at Shadow Creek, an exclusive Las Vegas golf course built and owned by hotelier Steve Wynn. Reilly called Tomko the world's biggest golf gambler.

Joining Tomko that day was Hilbert "Hilly" Shirey, Dewey's longtime pal and betting partner (they split wins and losses). Also in the sixsome was an East Coast bookie named Phil, Billy Mac, and Dave, a California businessman whom Reilly said was out of his betting comfort zone. The sixth was Ty, an employee at Shadow Creek and an aspiring money player.

On the first tee, Tomko and Phil agreed to a $20,000 Nassau with 2-down automatics. Dewey also had a similar bet with Hilly, Billy Mac, and Ty, but only for $5,000, and a pocket change wager of $1,000 with Dave. Tomko gave everyone strokes as well as a "spot" to Billy Mac, which allowed him to start from the women's tee. Although Tomko agreed to let Reilly caddy, he told Rick to stay in the cart and out of his way.

Tomko shot 41 on the front nine, losing a total of $27,000. He tried to up the bets on the back, but no one was interested. Another 41 on the back won $26,000 on nine bets, but he lost a total of $21,000 for the round. Hilly pocketed $68,000, none of which came from Tomko, so half went to Dewey per their standing agreement. Hilly also covered half of Tomko's loss. Counting his bets with Dave and Ty, Tomko netted $8,500 for the day. Dave told Reilly his $20 Nassaus at his home club would never seem the same. Betting that kind of money, however, has its drawbacks. "If you start thinkin' of what you could lose," Dave said, "you wanna go slit your throat."

Tomko grew up in western Pennsylvania and caddied as a teenager. He learned to play cards at the golf course. "The older kids didn't bother caddying," he said in a 2006 interview. "They stayed in the caddyshack and played blackjack. I'd lose all the money I'd just made caddying."

After college, Tomko became a kindergarten teacher in Haines City, Florida. He started playing poker on school nights at the Moose Lodge in nearby Winter Haven. He stayed out so late he would lie down on the floor every day with the kids for a nap. Making only $6,400 a year, Dewey found himself winning and losing similar amounts every night. He also started playing money golf. Through golf and playing at increasingly larger poker games around Florida, he built himself a $98,000 bankroll.

Feeling flush, Tomko arranged to play golf with poker legend Doyle Brunson in Nashville in the early 1970s. He left for Tennessee after playing cards for two straight days. "I intended to fly in, get some sleep, then play the next day," Tomko recalled. "But Doyle met me at the airport and said, 'Dewey, you can sleep later.' He beat me out of the whole 98 grand, sent me home without any sleep, and I had to teach school the next day!"

Tomko soon quit teaching and began playing poker full time. He played in his first World Series of Poker in 1976 and steadily through the 1980s. He reportedly won over $2.5 million on the high-stakes poker circuit between 1983 and 1988. He ultimately adapted to the pressure, but after his first trip to "Bean Valley," slang for losing $100,000 in one day, he couldn't sleep for two days. He burned out on cards by the early 1990s, but he kept betting on the golf course.

According to Reilly, Tomko improved his golf game to the point he began separating tour pros—Davis Love III, Paul Azinger, David Frost, and others—from their money. They allowed Dewey to play from the middle tees and skip the par-5s. "They're too good on the fives, so we don't play 'em," Tomko said. "Then I figure I'm even [odds] to beat 'em from the 150s in, 'cause I can putt lights out. And I can get to the 150-yard marker a lot easier than they can. They got to hook it around trees and lakes and shit, and I don't."

Tomko described a money game he and Frost played with their better ball against seven other golfers. Frost shot a 62 and when Dewey won $100,000, he gave $10,000 to Frost. "He couldn't believe it. He had no idea we were playing for that much. That's why I didn't tell him. He might not have been able to breathe."

Just as other high-stakes golfers, Tomko and his crew modify the rules of golf to fit their betting habits. Following are his variations and comments about them from Reilly's book.

- No gimmes or free drops.
- No out-of-bounds. "If you can find it, hit it."
- No lean-overs. Don't even tie your shoes. Lose the hole if it looks like you are touching your ball.
- OK to tap down spike marks.
- No 14-club limit. [Tomko carried 38 the day Reilly was with him, including tiny left- and right-handed clubs for tight spots in the rough.]
- Switch balls at will. Top Flight's for distance off the tee, nice Titleists for putting.
- Grease is good. Vaseline on the face of your driver will add 50 yards and cure a slice [it reduces spin].
- No leaving early. A bet's a bet.
- No handicaps. "Handicaps are for guys to cheat with. Cuz if you cheat, you'll never get a game again."
- No strokes.

As he did with Billy Mac at Shadow Creek, Tomko gives spots instead of strokes. Tomko told Reilly of a bet he made with Stu Ungar, a three-time World Series of Poker winner. With $100,000 on the line, he allowed Ungar to start from the 150-yard marker and tee it up anytime. Ungar showed up with his bag loaded with tees of different lengths, one just right for the rough and another to even out a side hill lie. After hitting into a pond, Ungar pulled out a 3-foot tee, using it to give himself a dry shot. Ungar won. "Some lessons you learn cost more than others," Tomko lamented.

Tomko's gang only plays for cash. "If you don't got cash," said Hilly Shirey, "then I don't want to be paid." They also don't play regular golfers or businessmen. "I won't play Square Johns," Dewey said. "You beat 'em, and they say, 'You hustled me,' or 'You conned me,' or 'You set me up.' I don't need it. I don't play pigeons, neither. Everybody thinks we're out here conning people. We ain't! We're playing each other."

This policy doesn't mean Tomko is above using a gimmick or two against "proper" opponents. He tries to play men who have just gotten off a plane to take advantage of their stiffness. Before some matches in central Florida, he offers the other player a free lesson with teaching guru David Leadbetter, a seemingly gracious proposal. As many of us know, playing well is hard to do immediately after a lesson; the mind is too full. "Then I'd take them out and bust their ass for 36 holes," Tomko said, rubbing his hands together.

Tomko, Brunson, and casino owner Jack Binion bought Southern Dunes, a golf course and housing community near Haines City in 1992. Tomko ran it until recently when the group sold it, but he owns a casino in Costa Rica.

Now older than 60, Tomko admits he's eased back on high-stakes betting. "I've sorta lost that killer instinct. You know what I mean? I used to bet a $100,000 on a football game; we'd play golf or poker for a $100,000 or more a day. I couldn't do that now."

—●—

"I've probably won more money than Jack Nicklaus," Bill Walters declared. "Of course, I didn't keep all of it. Or much of it."

Walters is a golf course developer in Las Vegas who owns four courses and operates them through his company, Walters Golf. He once played scratch, but his game was still good enough for the 59-year-old to make the cut at the 2006 AT&T Pebble Beach National Pro-Am. (He and his pro, Fredrik Jacobson, tied for ninth.)

During the 1970s and '80s, young Bill Walters played high-stakes poker and golf, mostly in Las Vegas. In 1975, he met another gambler whose name Walters declined to share. For three months, the two circled like wary boxers, playing matches for lunch money while they tried to find the right wager without showing their real game. "Neither one of us ever broke 90," Walters said of the preliminaries. They finally settled on a $100,000 Nassau. They both shot in the 70s, with Walters winning $550,000. Asked by a reporter how his opponent paid up, Walters said, "In a bag."

"A bag? You get $550,000 in a bag?"

"Easy," Walters said. "Hundreds."

"What did you do with $550,000 in a bag?"

"I spent it," said Walters, "in two days."

Walters took up golf when he was 20 years old in Louisville, losing a $100 Nassau to his brother in his first round. Considering Billy had been playing pool in his uncle's pool parlor since he was four years old, betting on golf was a natural progression for him.

He moved to Las Vegas in 1982, winning Amarillo Slim's Super Bowl of Poker in 1986. About the same time, Walters rocked the sports betting universe with large-scale betting predicated on computer analyses of football and basketball games. He and his partners literally changed the prevailing winds in sports betting. In 1998, a spokesman for a company that tracks these things said, "Bill Walters is considered one of the largest bettors in the world." He has had several brushes with the law, but the most serious resulted in his 1992 acquittal of betting conspiracy charges. In 1999, the Las Vegas newspaper *Review-Journal* named him one of the 10 most influential nonparticipant figures in sports.

"I've probably won more money gambling than anyone you know," Walters said in a recent interview. He said he gets the action because he "gives a lot of gamble," as opposed to "nut peddlers," or those unwilling to risk their cash. "In the gambling world, if a guy has a reputation as a nut peddler, a lot of people won't gamble with him." Since Walters boasted of playing a $100,000 Nassau on five different occasions, he wasn't selling nuts. The most Walters ever won in one day was $3.8 million playing roulette.

Walters said he won more than $1 million from an opponent during a multi-round stretch of money golf. He offered a well-known actor, again no name mentioned, a bet the other man couldn't refuse. Bill offered him 10 strokes a side in the match play and 24 in the medal bet.

"The first day, we played a $10,000 Nassau, and I was down after 14 holes and then he fell apart," Walters told writer Jack Sheehan. The guy had received too much instruction in the preceding days and weeks, and he hadn't played enough big money golf to maintain clear thinking when he had to execute important shots. Walters said the man's "circuitry was overloaded" with too much information. "He busted out in three weeks, but to his credit he paid off every dime he owed me."

He quit poker in the early 1990s and said he no longer plays high-stakes golf, even on his own courses. "I play for fun these days. If my members want to wager, I keep it to a $10 Nassau."

—•—

Wealthy golfers don't always wager large amounts. Perhaps they have enough action during the business day, or by the time they have achieved such status, they've seen plenty of juice.

Microsoft head Bill Gates and investor Warren Buffett are the two richest men in the world, according to *Forbes Magazine*. Gates and Buffett often play golf together, but the stakes on their matches belie their great wealth. Their usual wager is $1 for nine holes, and whoever shoots the first par wins the pot. If neither has a par by nine, the lowest score wins the bet.

Ben Wright swears the following tale about Jack Stephens, chairman of Augusta National during the 1990s, is true. Stephens, who died in 2005, was a self-made billionaire whose family's financial company has been the fourth-largest investment bank in the United States. He was highly influential in both New York and in his home state of Arkansas.

The club had just accepted a new member, a flamboyant sort, with tons of money. As a courtesy to the new man, Stephens offered him a game and suggested a $2 Nassau. The newcomer scoffed at those stakes, boasting of his $100-a-hole bets back home in Texas.

"I'm sorry," Stephens replied, "at this club I don't play for more than $2." Throughout the game, Wright said the new member pestered Stephens to raise the bet, but the chairman politely rebuffed each request. "As they repaired to lunch after the round," Wright said,

> the fellow suggested a poker game, also for high stakes, even a hand of bridge. By this time Stephens was pissed and had enough.
>
> "I gather you have plenty of money," Stephens said to the annoying man.
>
> "I have a sizable amount."
>
> "How much is your net worth, right now?" Stephens asked.
>
> "Oh, give or take a few dollars, about $40 million."
>
> "OK," Stephens said, reaching for a deck of cards, "I'll cut you for $40 million."

Wright said the fellow almost retched with embarrassment and immediately left the room. Ben thought the story put betting on golf in the right perspective. It's not always the amount of money that counts. It's just the pleasure of a gentlemanly wager among friends.

Stephens's successor, Hootie Johnson, also bet modestly on the course. Johnson preferred a $2 or $5 Nassau, but he was as poised negotiating strokes as he was in confronting activist Martha Burk about women members at the Augusta National.

—●—

Great wealth or large stakes are not prerequisites for betting on golf, nor is a famous name. Your name can be Tater Pie, Cement Head, or Fairway Louie, and you can still play a $2 Nassau at Jackson Park in Chicago, Palmer Park in Detroit, or Chester Washington in Los Angeles, all public courses with reputations for hosting money games. The "foot soldier" of golf, as Rick Reilly described the habitué of municipal golf courses, is the "guy who's up at four in the morning to pay $12 to wait three hours to play a six-hour round to lose six bucks in bets." Golf betting is an equal opportunity sport, open to all who have money in their pockets. Reilly's favorite venue is Ponkapoag Golf Club in Canton, Massachusetts, just south of Boston, and known locally as "Ponky." Donald Ross, the creator of Pinehurst #2, Seminole, and Inverness, designed the first of two 18s at Ponkapoag in 1933.

However, "golf isn't the sport of choice at Ponky," as Reilly wrote in a 1988 article in *Sports Illustrated*. "The sport of choice is betting. Golf is just a convenient vehicle for it. At Ponky, they bet on whether the pro on TV will sink his next putt. They bet with their partners, and they bet against their partners. They bet on whether they can chip into the garbage can or off the ball washer."

The golfing life for Ponky regulars—Brooklyn, Ziggy, Socks, Can Man, and others—contrasts sharply with the scene at The Country Club, up the road in Brookline, where Francis Ouimet won the 1913 U.S. Open. The Ponky hackers, or "chops," however, carried the same color money as the country club people and were eager to see it change hands. "Man," exclaimed a chop named Bluto, "wouldn't you love to get a 3-handicap from The Country Club out here for a little $50 Nassau?"

"I get a game with somebody from The Country Club," added Jimmy, "I start refinishing my basement."

Most of the bets at Ponky were $5 Nassaus, with automatic presses and "get-evens" on nine and 18. Many of the side bets were the same Greenies, Sandies, and Barkies known to golfers around the country. Strangers, however, avoided two prop bets—one by Pappy "the Edgeman" (so nicknamed for always wanting the edge in a bet) and the other by Little Eddie. Pappy liked to win money by offering to putt with his wedge, while Eddie offered to stack two balls, one on top of the other; hit both; and catch the top ball in his pocket. Card games and nighttime putting contests were part of the Ponky program as well.

There were a few hustles at Ponky. Reilly told about a match Pappy and Jimmy Sullivan, a 12-time club champ, arranged with two men from Franklin

Park in nearby Roxbury. Seeing one of the visitors walked with a limp and played cross handed, Pappy got greedy and offered a $50 Nassau. Down a couple holes by the time they got to nine, the locals realized they were being hustled by Charlie Owens, who later played on the Champions Tour. With a fused knee because of a war injury, Owens had always played cross handed, a quirk unknown to the Ponky regulars.

To these guys, the locale was almost as important as the money golf. Pete Peters, whom Reilly described as a "died-in-the-polyester Ponkian," swore he wouldn't trade his days at Ponky for a membership at The Country Club. "I wouldn't hesitate a second. I'd stay here where I can get some action, have a lot of laughs, relax, and be with my friends.

Reilly used his experiences at Ponky as the basis of his 1996 novel, *Missing Links*. He changed the courses' names from Ponkapoag to Ponkaquogue and The Country Club to the Mayflower, and the names of the usual suspects. The novel's plot revolves around "The Bet."

Raymond Lee Hart, the book's narrator and leader of the Ponky chops, proposes they all kick in $1,000 flat tender, with the pot going to the first who plays 18 at the exclusive and completely fenced Mayflower Country Club. The winner has to present a signed scorecard and two witnesses within a one-month time limit. Three of the regulars sign up: Stick, Two-Down, and Dannie. Hart is Stick, and Two-Down is so named because he always says, "Boys, the bets don't start until I'm 2-down." Daniela Higgins, a red-headed, green-eyed pro shop assistant, is the third and most attractive chop to agree to the bet. Thud, Crowbar, Chunkin' Charlie, Hoover, and the others pass.

Each hatches a different scheme to weasel past the Mayflower gates. It's mostly Keystone Kops on the green, and the us-versus-them shtick smacks of Rodney Dangerfield and Judge Smails at Bushwood. But it's a good story, and anyone who has ever put a ball in the rack at a public track will enjoy reading the book.

Reilly wrote a sequel in 2006, *Shanks for Nothing*, in which Stick and the other chops try to keep the Mayflower members from buying Ponky for their own use. The novel's main event is, of course, a money game.

—●—

"The Match." That was what four LPGA players called their annual $50 Nassau on the Wednesday before every U.S. Women's Open from the late 1980s through the 1990s. Laura Davies, Patty Sheehan, Jane Geddes, and Amy Benz got together for a spirited game complete with presses and side trash for closest to the pin, eagles, birdies, and such.

With 10 majors between them, Davies and Sheehan might have been favored to win most of those games, but Geddes and Benz proved to be money players. "We were 1-down on 17," Sheehan said of their 1990 match. "Laura was the only one on the green. She 3-putts and Benz sinks a 20-footer for par." Patty remembers she lost $485 in that match and that Amy shot a 65.

"Every year I just bring my money," said Sheehan, who thinks she lost thousands over the years. Patty's normal practice round wagers are far more modest, sometimes just for desserts after dinner. "It's the only time I do this," she said. "That's why I get so excited."

In their 1996 game at Pine Needles, Liselotte Neumann subbed for Benz. Davies birdied 17 to close out the regular Nassau, and Sheehan rejoiced over a rare win. She and Laura didn't come away the total winners, because they still had a couple leftover presses worth $600 that Neumann and Geddes won on 18. They all went to the merchandise tent, where the losers bought clothes for the winners.

Davies had plenty of cash on hand since two days before the 1996 match she had won the JC Penney/LPGA Skins Game and collected $340,000. She had also won the McDonald's LPGA Championship two weeks previously. Laura was at the peak of her game in the States in the mid-1990s, winning nine times between 1994 and 1996. She was also first in the Order of Merit in 1996 on the Ladies European Tour.

Laura plays a robust golf game, especially in those days, bringing the same excitement and length off the tee that John Daly introduced in the pre-Woods era on the PGA Tour. She plays hard both on and off the golf course, especially in her expensive and fast cars; she bought a Ferrari with her Skins Game winnings. She also loves to gamble, again both on and off the course, and she has warmed many chairs at blackjack tables around the world. Laura is the LPGA's answer to Arnold Palmer and Lanny Wadkins when it comes to aggressive play and betting.

Laura caught the wagering bug as a kid growing up in Surrey, England. She played many games as a youngster, including golf, and some with her fiercely competitive brother Tony. "We had bets on everything we did," she recalled. "I wouldn't have a putt without a bet on it. Even at Trivial Pursuit we would play for a fiver or there was no point."

Laura soon began excelling at golf, winning several large tournaments and playing in the 1984 Curtis Cup. As an amateur, she also worked as a bookie's assistant, a combination of activities that would have been almost lethal in the United States. She turned pro at age 21 and quickly began winning on the European women's tour. She won the 1987 U.S. Women's Open and played her first LPGA event in 1988.

"Lots of people gamble to try to win money," she said in the mid-1990s. "I gamble for fun, and I know I will lose. Gambling and golf go hand in hand. Nine out 10 golfers gamble, even if it's only a $10 Nassau. I'm not a compulsive gambler; I'm a compulsive golfer who plays at gambling."

She bets on other golfers routinely. She said her best payoff was a 16-1 wager on Jose Maria Olazabal to win the 1994 Masters. That bet paid almost $14,000.

"Most of the women on the LPGA Tour bet when they play practice rounds," said Charlie Mechem, the former LPGA Tour commissioner (1991–96) and commissioner emeritus. "They don't bet much, perhaps a couple bucks. They consider it part of the fun and an interesting twist to the competition. The small amounts are probably carryovers from the not-too-distant past when they didn't earn much money." When asked if aggressive betting is perhaps foreign to many women, sort of a Mars-Venus issue, Mechem generally agreed.

Laura Davies (right) is the most aggressive bettor in women's professional golf. Annika Sorenstam, shown here with Davies at the 2005 Solheim Cup, enjoys a friendly wager when playing the likes of Tiger Woods and Michael Jordan. Associated Press/Wide World Photos

———●———

Phil Mickelson's well-known affinity for playing and betting aggressively has made him the logical heir to the money golf throne previously claimed by Walter Hagen, Dutch Harrison, Arnold Palmer, Al Besselink, and Lanny Wadkins. Although he recently retreated from his go-for-broke style, Mickelson has always publicly acknowledged the pleasure he takes from attempting high-risk, high-reward shots. He has also admitted a $10 Nassau is insufficient to keep his interest. Phil is a throwback money player, one whom the Honourable Company of Edinburgh Golfers would have welcomed in their Dinner Matches.

Public attention to Mickelson's playing style peaked at the Bay Hill tournament in March 2002. In the hunt on Sunday afternoon, Mickelson hit his drive into the tall grass on the right side, with a group of trees blocking his line of sight to the green. Instead of pitching sideways from "Bambi's couch" back to the fairway and perhaps grinding out a par, he tried to bend his approach around the trees to the green. When it splashed in the greenside pond, Phil had gambled his way out of contention. Afterward, reporters second-guessed Mickelson's decision, with NBC's Johnny Miller calling the shot "crazy."

"I think I have had good results with my style of play," Mickelson said to the news media later. "I have won more tournaments than anybody playing the game right now other than Tiger." But since Phil was still the best player at that time to have never won a major, his claim didn't change many minds. He went on to say in 2002 playing conservatively is boring. "I just know for me to play my best, I need to be creative. I need to attack. If I just hit fairways with irons, and play to the middle of the green, it's no fun. I don't play well when I am not having fun."

Clearly Phil likes the rush at the redline. He once broke his leg and ankle while bombing a ski slope and rolled his BMW while attempting to pass another car. He is a licensed pilot but doesn't just fly to get from here to there. "I do like aerobatics," he said.

"I guess you could say that I'm aggressive at things that I feel confident doing," Mickelson said in 1995, three years after joining the tour. "I've always been that way, whether it was in sports at school as a kid or on the golf course. I enjoy being aggressive."

"Keep charging, man," Arnold Palmer wrote Mickelson after the Bay Hill incident, predictable advice from the King. "That's the way to play, the

Phil Mickelson bets on his golf game as aggressively as he plays in tournaments. Although he claimed that he had tried a slightly less risky style after winning his first Masters in 2004, Phil the Thrill gambled and lost on the last hole of the 2006 U.S. Open.
ASSOCIATED PRESS/WIDE WORLD PHOTOS

way to win tournaments," Arnie continued. "Keep going for it and the majors will come." Another aggressive payer, Greg Norman, echoed Palmer, "I hope Phil doesn't change."

The style of play from "Phil the Thrill" generated enough inconsistency in his tournament play that bookies in Great Britain offered a new bet in 2003 for anyone wagering on Mickelson. "Taking the Mick" paid off whenever Mickelson followed a birdie with a bogey.

After winning the Masters in 2004, Phil announced he had become "conservatively aggressive"; "I'm picking my spots. Off the tee, I've throttled back." As an example of his new approach, he cited the second round at Augusta when he elected to pitch out from the trees on 18 and then hit a wedge to the green for a par. He also conceded his change of tactics after he won the 2006 Masters. Mickelson sadly reverted to his old form, however, a few months later at the U.S. Open. He hit a risky driver on the last hole, compounded his error with a chancy second shot, and bogeyed the hole to lose the championship.

Jerry Tarde, chairman and editor in chief of *Golf Digest*, attested to Phil's shift in a 2005 column. He recalled playing with Phil at Pine Valley in 1990 when Mickelson was in college at Arizona State. Tarde bet Mickelson $50 that Phil couldn't make it through nine holes without a double bogey. Pine Valley is plenty tough, but that year Phil had won the U.S. Amateur and one of his three NCAA individual championships.

"After he lost, I'd let him double the bet," Tarde explained. "He kept losing. It took him to the sixth nine-hole match to win his money back." During the summer of 2005, the two played again at Pine Valley. "We're playing that double-bogey game, right?" Mickelson asked. Tarde agreed, but he opted for a single $100 bet for the whole 18.

Tarde said Phil played for pars, hitting controlled drives and approaches, but had to scramble on eight to avoid a double. On 18, his drive found a pot bunker. Faced with 170 yards over water to a slippery green, Phil played a safe shot to the fairway. A wedge and two putts gave him a bogey. Tarde looked on with a smirk and called Phil's conservative decision "candy-ass golf." Mickelson took Tarde's $100 and then went on to Baltusrol, where he won the PGA for his second major.

Mickelson joined the PGA Tour in 1992, a year after he won a tour event as an amateur, the 1991 Northern Telecom Open in Tucson. He quickly became one of the foremost exponents of the friendly wager during practice rounds. His threshold is higher than most, though. "Playing for $10 or $15, it's easy to get a little distracted," he said. "You get something going for $100 or more. It definitely keeps your attention." Phil makes it clear, however, he doesn't view his Tuesday matches as gambling. "If you're in Las Vegas and playing in the casino, that's gambling. I consider golf wagering a form of competition. We're all competitors. When you enter a tournament, you pay an entry fee [of $100]. This is the same thing."

He also likes spontaneous golf bets, perhaps the equivalent of a loop-de-loop during a boring cross-country flight in his aircraft. "Bet I get down in two," he might say from the rough, "or $20 says I can skip it across the pond onto the green."

As an example, once during a practice round at the 2000 Mercedes Championships at Kapalua resort, Maui, Phil thought about taking a short-cut to the green on the 398-yard sixth. He turned to golf writer Cameron Morfit and said, "Ten bucks, 10-1 odds, that I hit this green." When he missed, Mickelson told his caddie, Jim MacKay, "Bones, pay the man." (Jim got his nickname years ago when he was as slim as a forged 1-iron.)

According to *Golf World* writer John Strege, Mickelson made a bet with CBS television commentator Gary McCord in the midst of a tournament round. McCord, covering the 16th green, suggested to Phil off camera that Mickelson couldn't make an 18-footer for par. Mickelson took that challenge for $20. When he made the putt, McCord threw the money down from the camera tower behind the green.

Strege captured in 2000 the full flavor of Mickelson's inclination for impulsive bets. The story is about a game called "Hammer" between Phil and Paul Azinger a few days before the 1993 Tour Championship at San Francisco's Olympic Club. A Hammer is similar to a press, but it doubles the bet for a specific hole on the results of a single stroke. If a player faces a bad lie or a tough shot, his opponent will hammer him to ratchet up the stakes.

Both players were in the fairway on 18, and Phil was up $400. Both were woofing at the other, talking trash, and sticking the needle. Mickelson's approach checked up 10 feet below the hole, but Zinger was short of the green and in the rough. "Well, obviously I'm going to hammer you," Phil said.

"I'm not going to take it," Paul responded, not willing to accept another $200 bet.

"That's just what I thought you'd do," chided Mickelson.

Just as Azinger was ready to chip, he backed off. Looking at Mickelson, he said, "You're on." He set up again and then holed the chip. The talk started flowing the other way. "If you thought the celebration at the Ryder Cup was bad, you should have seen this celebration," Mickelson recalled. "It was two minutes before I finally putted." Azinger wasn't through, however.

"You know what's coming now, don't you? I'm hammering you," Azinger said. Lefty missed his putt and lost all bragging rights until the next Tuesday.

Mickelson's spontaneity follows him off the course. Late in the day during the 1996 Sprint International at Castle Pines Golf Club in Colorado, he ended a long putting practice by dropping three balls on the green 40 feet from the cup.

"I've got a proposition for you," Mickelson said to Bones. "Three putts, $20. I need to make just one to collect."

"OK," agreed MacKay.

"Loser pays cash money?"

"This is a one-time offer. You're on."

When Phil sank the first attempt, Bones paid up. "I'll buy you a milkshake," said Mickelson as the two headed for the locker room.

Another post-round Mickelson wager, one typical of his betting style, caused a minor stir in 2001. At the World Golf Championships–NEC Invitational, Jim Furyk's approach shot landed in a green-side bunker on the first play-off hole with Tiger Woods. Furyk's third shot didn't clear the bunker's lip, and the ball rolled back down to his feet. As he pondered his next attempt, several other golfers watched the drama on the locker room's TV. Mickelson offered 25-1 odds Furyk would hole his next shot to save par. Stewart Cink and David Toms passed, but Mike Weir accepted for $20. Furyk indeed holed his second bunker shot, but he ultimately lost the play-off to Woods. Carrying only $100, Weir promised to pay Mickelson $500 at the next tournament. The news media picked up the story, one that was routine to golf insiders but one whose "gambling" angle titillated others.

PGA Tour officials went through the motions of "reprimanding" Mickelson and Wier for the "technical violation" of regulations that prohibit wagering during a tournament. Tour commissioner Finchem ignores these friendly bets because they are harmless and integral to the game. Some reporters, however, likened the wager to Pete Rose's betting. "I make a $20 bet in what should have been the privacy of a locker room," Phil said of the nosey news media, "and it's headlines that I violated PGA Tour rules. But then the PGA Tour calls the next day to say, no, the press made a big deal out of nothing."

Mickelson's bet on Furyk was news for another reason, Phil's highly visible betting on NFL football and the World Series. By the time of the NEC tournament in August, word had gotten around Phil won $500,000 betting on the Baltimore Ravens to win Super Bowl XXXV in January 2001. Interest again picked up later that fall when the news media reported Phil won $760,000 at 38-1 when the Arizona Diamondbacks won the World Series. "Mickelson's gambling problem" quickly became the tag line.

The facts gradually pushed aside the more lurid versions of the wagers. Phil and 27 family members and friends, including his mother-in-law, pooled their money to make a $20,000 preseason bet in Las Vegas on the Ravens in August 2000. The syndicate bet at 22-1. Phil's cut of the winnings was $50,000. "I cashed the ticket a few weeks ago," he said in April 2001. "We flew up on a private jet and pulled an all-nighter with my wife, parents, and my in-laws. I put the money in a large sack, all in large bills, and buckled it into its own seat for the ride home." It's not exactly a tale of seamy, underworld gambling here, folks. He just had more zeroes on his bets than most people.

He scoffed at the Diamondbacks' odds. They played the Yankees, but no team in the World Series during the modern play-off scheme is that long a shot. Phil said he won $60,000 on that bet. "The Diamondbacks were a heart play," he told the media. Mickelson lived in Scottsdale then and went for the home team.

"Crazy," Mickelson said in 2001 of the hubbub about his betting. "I picked NFL games on the radio this season, just for kicks, but that just fed the frenzy. No more. I love sports, but if I do bet a game, that's nobody's business anymore, either." Mickelson told the news media in 2005 that he had quit serious gambling after the difficult birth of his son, Evan, in 2003. His wife, Amy, had almost died during delivery.

Finally, as an example of both Phil's sense of humor and wagering style around golf, he bet Justin Leonard $100 that Leonard couldn't go through a press conference without talking during the 2005 Presidents Cup. Justin did well until Mickelson sandbagged him. Reporters asked how team members felt about the match compared to the Cup two years before. Mickelson said, "Justin was talking about that last night on the bus, about the difference. Go ahead. Why don't you tell him what you were saying last night?"

All Leonard could say to the reporters was, "I just lost $100."

Moe Norman is a member of the Canadian Golf Hall of Fame and the winner of two Canadian Amateurs and two Canadian PGA Championships during a 45-year career that started in 1949. He held more than 30 course records, shot three competitive 59s, and won 54 tournaments before he died in 2004. He also suffered from autism, an affliction unknown to his family and his opponents when he started playing golf. He spoke rapidly, often saying the same thing twice; was a whiz with numbers; and remembered the yardage of every course he played. It wasn't until the release of the movie *Rain Man*, a story about an autistic savant played by Dustin Hoffman, that Norman's friends understood his illness.

An unkempt appearance and homemade golf swing made him a square peg in professional golf's round hole. He played briefly on the PGA Tour, but his affliction immediately obscured his talents. Further, he was short and overweight, and his hair stuck out in all directions. One tour player accosted Norman about his dress and demeanor, and Moe, humiliated, left the tour.

His odd swing, which Natural Golf's Jack Kuykendall used to pitch his teaching system in the 1990s, was a thing to behold. Gripping the club in his palms, he stiffly spread his legs wide, grounded his club a foot behind the ball, and used a backswing that reached only shoulder level. He turned on the same plane, back and through. Norman was a hitting machine in his prime playing years, and many thought he was the most accurate ball striker in golf. "I'm the machine, poetry in motion, the only man on earth who can hit the ball straight every time," he boasted during one of his Natural Golf appearances.

One story about Moe involves a 1969 exhibition match he played with Sam Snead and Porky Oliver in Toronto. On one hole, the smart play was to hit a 4-wood or long iron off the tee because a creek cut the fairway at 240 yards. Moe pulled out his driver.

"This is a lay-up hole, Moe," Snead said. "You can't clear the creek with a driver."

"Not trying to," Norman replied. "I'm playing for the bridge." True to his word, Moe's tee shot bounced in the fairway and then rolled across the bridge toward the green.

Norman used his appearance and unconventional swing to supplement his tournament winnings. Fleeing Canadian winters, he hustled through the U.S. South, pursuing what he called "bootleg golf." Wearing a dirty turtleneck sweater, no matter what the temperature, and pants that were too short, he didn't fit the hustler's image. He had a huge edge.

"There's lots of guys in Florida who want to bet," Moe recalled of those days. "Lots of time I show up in a locker room with my old blue jeans and shout, 'Anyone for $10 a hole?' They look at me and think, 'Who is this big-mouth little guy?'"

"Moe made his living down here by hustling," Toronto golf writer Jack Marks said of Norman's Florida forays during the 1960s. "He'd figure out who the best players were at the different clubs and ask them for a game." In 1964 at Bayshore Golf Course, a Miami muni, Moe approached Jeff Alpert, a member of the University of Miami's golf team. "I was in the locker room," Alpert said later, "and this guy comes in and says, 'You want to play a little golf game, want to play a little golf game?' He looked disheveled, like he had just waked up."

Alpert agreed to a match and invited Marty Stanovich, the Fat Man, to join them. "I was probably two or three down early on," recalled Alpert, "but I thought he's gonna make a bogey or double sooner or later. I thought maybe he's just lucky. But that swing. Every hole, he stuck it in there two or three feet from the hole.

"It wasn't even close," Alpert continued. "He made 11 birdies and seven pars and shot a 61. Nobody shoots 61!" Norman took $70 from Alpert and $300 from Stanovich. Norman beat Alpert again the next day but without Marty. "The Fat Man packed it in," said Alpert. "He'd had enough of Moe."

—●—

Moe Norman probably never hit a mulligan in his life, but in the 1990s one high-profile golfer's game seemed to revolve around an extra shot, Bill Clinton.

The president's propensity to give it another go certainly fit with his retakes in explaining his relationships with women, such as Monica Lewinski and Gennifer Flowers. "Nothing in all of sport seems a better metaphor for Clinton's own career of missteps and regrets," a reporter wrote in 1994 in the *Washington Post*. "If only the public had granted him mulligans with his Vietnam draft record, his appointment of Lani Guinier [failed Supreme Court nominee], or his health care plan."

Clinton undercut any claim he made about his handicap with his well-publicized mulligan habit. Even the Irish had heard of the presidential "do over." He told *Golf Digest* in 2000 about his visit to Ballybunion.

They asked me what my handicap was, and at the time, I was playing pretty good, and I said I don't know, maybe 12 to 13. They said, "How many links courses have you played?" I said, "Two." They said, "Good. We're taking twenty to one odds you can't break 100." So I was 10-over for 15 holes and 13-over for the last three. I was playing with Christy O'Connor. Howling wind. I made seven on [16], then I made 10 on [17]. I kept going back and forth, back and forth. Otherwise, I played well. So I won. I was 23-over—95.

Clinton played Britain's Prince Andrew while on vacation on Martha's Vineyard in 1999. Asked later about handicapping, Andrew said they played "flat, no strokes." During their first round, Andrew declined Clinton's offer of a mulligan after the prince's stray tee shot.

Before the second day's match, played with two businessmen, Clinton explained his wager with Andrew to the news media.

"You know what the bet is, don't you?" Clinton asked the reporters. "If he beats me, we have to give him back the island. It belonged to the Duke of York in the 17th century, and if I lose today we have to give it back."

A thunderstorm ended the match on the 15th hole, and the group declined to identify the leader at that point. Andrew, however, pulled out a wad of U.S. greenbacks, declaring, "I have still got a little money in my pocket."

It is not a coincidence that of the three presidents who occasionally ignored the rules of golf, two —Nixon and Clinton—got into trouble while in office. Lyndon Baines Johnson (LBJ) played little during his White House years, but his love of mulligans might connect with many who criticized him for not revealing the real prospects for winning the Vietnam War. Golf can provide a window into men's souls.

The origin of the term *mulligan* is hazy, but the most oft-quoted story involves a Canadian named David Mulligan. He managed the Biltmore Hotel in New York and played at Winged Foot. He was a slow starter and frequently mangled his first attempt on number one tee. Another theory ties the term to saloons where the bartender put out a bottle of whiskey called a "mulligan" for sips on the house. A freebie at the bar might have lent its name to the freebie on the course.

Kennedy was the best player among the presidents, carrying what amounted to a handicap of between 7 and 10. He rarely played 18 holes at once, largely because he felt Ike's frequent golf outings led to a public perception that his predecessor was not tending to the people's business. While his campaign aides pledged JFK wouldn't play during working hours, the young president did sneak out for a quick nine when he could, but he allowed few photographs of himself holding a club. One wag suggested he played golf as surreptitiously as he met his extramarital paramours.

Raised in a family whose motto was "Finish First," Kennedy learned about stakes golf from his father, Joe Kennedy. Although Pop played for $10,000 or $20,000 a side in Palm Beach, John favored a smaller sum of often $10 a hole. That was the wager when Kennedy played with Chris Dunphy, the chairman of Seminole Country Club in Florida. Bob Hope, who also was in the foursome, later told the story:

> On the first hole, Kennedy had a 3-foot putt for par. "You're certainly going to give me this, aren't you?" Kennedy asked.
>
> "Make a pass at it," Dunphy said. "I want to see your stroke. A putt like this builds character. Besides, it will give you a little feel for the greens."
>
> "I work in the Oval Office all day for citizens like you," JFK responded, "and now you're not going to give me this putt?"
>
> Dunphy looked at the sky.
>
> "OK," Kennedy said, "but let's keep moving. I've got an appointment after we finish with the director of the Internal Revenue Service."
>
> "That putt's good," Dunphy said, his jest loosing air like a bad tire. "Pick it up."

Kennedy had a fluid golf swing, especially before his back problems and other ailments robbed him of his athletic rhythm. But according to his press secretary, Pierre Salinger, the smoothest part of his game was his gamesmanship. JFK got into his opponents' heads regardless if they were friends or family. He chattered nonstop about hazards and out-of-bounds markers, commented on someone's swing weakness, and confused his opponent on the first tee with an array of bets.

"Through a complex system of betting, which only he understood fully, JFK won most of his matches before the first ball was even hit," Salinger wrote in his book, *With Kennedy*. "There were bets not only on who won the hole, but for the longest drive, first on the green, closest to the pin, and first in the hole. In addition, there were automatic press bets whenever one team fell two holes behind, and bonus points for birdies and tee shots holding the green on par-3s." Salinger said Kennedy's bets gave his opponents little time to concentrate on their game. "The president was a master psychologist," Salinger said, evoking memories of Titanic Thompson.

JFK's successor refused to accept a poor shot. Johnson's standard of excellence did not necessarily mean he bore down with steely resolve on the next hole; instead, he'd throw down another ball and hit again. "He just hit

President John F. Kennedy was the best player among U.S. presidential golfers and offered the most side bets during a game. He is playing here with his press secretary, Pierre Salinger, during the summer of 1963.
JOHN F. KENNEDY LIBRARY

until he liked one," said James Jones, LBJ's chief of staff in 1968. "He'd hit extra balls as if that was part of the game."

Johnson took up the game early in his career in Washington, seeking relaxation away from Capitol Hill. One of his partners in those days was another Texas congressman, Eugene Worley, with whom Johnson played a match at the Army-Navy Country Club in Arlington, Virginia. Johnson complained about how rusty his game was at the time, trying to inveigle strokes from Worley.

"We didn't have much money," Worley later recalled.

> We were playing, I think, for a quarter—a quarter Nassau. So he talked me into a stroke a hole, and sure enough we finish the 17th hole and I'm 50¢ down.
>
> I said, "Lyndon, I ought to play you double or nothing on the 18th and still give you a stroke on the hole." I was trying to get my money back.
>
> He said, "Aw, No."
>
> I said, "Well, why not? What can you lose? You're playing with my money."
>
> He said, "Hell, I didn't work 17 holes just to give it all back to you on one hole." And he didn't.

Vice President Richard Nixon was relatively new to golf when he found himself in a money match teamed with Eisenhower at Cherry Hills Country Club in Denver. Ike, who hated to lose a golf bet, fumed as Nixon's poor play cost them the match.

"Look here," he said to his vice president after the round, "you're young, you're strong, and you can do a lot better than that."

"He talked to me like a Dutch uncle," Nixon said years later.

With Ike's admonition ringing in his ears, Nixon worked hard on his game but also turned to pushing the rules—namely, improving his lie, asking for gimmes, and hitting multiple mulligans. Don Van Natta, Jr., wrote in his book *First Off the Tee* Nixon "embraced the rule-bending as the quickest route to a low score and a modicum of golf course respectability." When playing once with Sam Snead, Nixon followed his errant ball into the bushes. When Snead saw the ball fly cleanly out onto the fairway, he said, "I knew he threw it, but I didn't say anything."

Although Nixon claimed a 14-handicap, most believed he fudged about his game as much as he did the Watergate break-in. Those who played with him thought a 20 or 25 was closer to the truth.

Jerry Ford's wild shots on the golf course, including his ability to bean a spectator 260 yards off the tee, didn't allow him to win many golf bets. During his monologues, Bob Hope made a living off Ford's erratic play.

- "You all know Jerry Ford—the most dangerous driver since Ben Hur."
- "Whenever I play with him, I usually try to make it a foursome—Ford, me, a paramedic, and a faith healer."
- "In one round at El Dorado, the gallery ended up with more dimples than his golf ball."

George H. W. Bush, the 41st president, often didn't have time to bet on golf, because he usually played 18 holes in less than two hours. Some called his game "cart polo." He only bet a few bucks and called the shots when he did wager. A story from business executive Herb Kohler offers a glimpse into Bush's money golf. Before a game at Pebble Beach in 1995, Kohler told Bush his normal game was a $10 Nassau, $2 skins, and Honest John (predicting your score) for $1 a stroke. "Mr. Kohler," Bush countered, "if you play with me, it's a $1 Nassau."

"Mr. President, I accept," Kohler replied.

The elder Bush made a bet with Brad Faxon during the pro-am at the 2003 Memorial tournament, the annual event Jack Nicklaus hosts in Dublin, Ohio. The wager was on their approach shots on the par-5 11th hole. "Mr. Faxon said that he would give him two shots to get inside Faxon's one," Bush's caddie later explained to the news media. "Mr. Bush hit it to 10 feet, and Mr. Faxon didn't even make the green. The crowd was loving that."

The younger Bush plays for bragging rights instead of money. Also, George W. frowns on mulligans, perhaps in keeping with his values presidency. A few do-overs, however, might have helped him on the political front.

—●—

"Ever since Tiger Woods broke onto the scene a few years ago, golf wagering has definitely entered the spotlight, no question," Jeff Sherman said in 1999. Sherman, then the golf oddsmaker at the Resort at Summerlin in Las Vegas, recognized one facet of Tigermania the larger golf public overlooked. All are aware Woods influenced TV coverage after his 1996 debut on the PGA Tour, energized a new generation of golfers, and shifted the endorsement geography with huge deals with Nike, American Express, and others. But he also affected the huge sports betting industry, bringing golf up from the "other sports" category into prime time.

The money Americans bet on sports is on par with the economic output of many countries and a great deal more than the total amount broadcasters spend on sports programming. Industry analysts estimate that Internet betting on the 2006 Super Bowl totaled $500 million, while others bet $100 million in Las Vegas and an additional $4 billion to $5 billion illegally. The 2006 NCAA basketball tournament attracted at least $4 billion in bets. Two-thirds of U.S. workers participate in office betting pools, mostly on NFL and college basketball games. A study showed annual illegal sports betting in America approached $380 billion in 1999. Many experts firmly believe the NFL's rise in popularity is directly attributable to a parallel increase in opportunities to bet on it.

Golf has always been a betting game but mostly among the players. However, men willing to take onlookers' bets also have been around for centuries, especially during the golden age of the challenge matches in Great Britain. Jack Doyle and other bookmakers were no strangers on the PGA Tour. But since the 1960s, when TV sponsors began influencing professional golf's mores, the bookmaker has retreated to Nevada and the United Kingdom. Betting on golf matches became a minor pastime for a few diehards. A phenomenon in the 1990s changed that paradigm—Tiger Woods. Following his dramatic win at the 1997 Masters, Tiger skewed the odds-making process in Great Britain. Before his first professional appearance at the British Open at Troon, eager punters bet so heavily on Woods the bookies had to offer ridiculously low odds to stave off bankruptcy. Just before the tournament, they listed Woods as an extraordinary 5-1 favorite.

"Absurd, but true," said Graham Sharpe, a spokesman for the William Hill Agency, a leading book. "That is certainly the shortest price at our Open since World War II. Not Jack Nicklaus, not Tom Watson in their prime. Not Nick Faldo or Seve Ballesteros. They couldn't have been better than 7-1 or 8-1, if that."

The Open is Britain's largest single betting event, although throughout the year, golf wagering is way behind football (soccer) in total take. As a society, the Brits are keen on wagering, and bookies offer bets on most anything—elections, Elvis Presley's return, and even Tiger's chances at the White

House, which are 1,000-1 by 2020. "Why not?" said Sharpe. "They had a failed actor, so why not a successful golfer?"

The Brits are also cynical of U.S. inhibitions about wagering. "You Americans have funny ideas on gambling," Sharpe said. "Pete Rose, your greatest baseball player, places a few wagers, and he's thought of as a bloody disgrace. Makes no more sense than the way you drive, on the wrong side of the road."

"You've watched baseball?" a reporter asked Sharpe.

"Only on the telly," he said. "So slow, why not lay a few quid down to make it interesting?"

Frank Hannigan, the USGA's executive director during the 1980s, understands the distinction between the two countries regarding betting. "The difference between Great Britain and the U.S. is hypocrisy," he said. "Billions are bet outside the law on the day of our greatest national holiday—Super Bowl Sunday—while the NFL pretends not to like it. Take the gambling out of pro football completely, and what you get is at least a 25 percent drop in ratings."

The PGA Tour is paying attention to the growing interest in betting on its tournaments. "The bigger you get as a sport, the more interest you draw," tour commissioner Finchem said in 2002. "We project our fan base now at 110 million Americans. I just can't spend too much energy worrying about whether they're gambling on us. We're a big-time sport now. If there is an effect, we have to deal with it."

Tiger's impact on golf betting is greatest during the British Open. He severely disrupts the normal ebb and flow of golf wagering during the tournament. Woods shot 67-66 for the first two rounds at the 2000 Open at St Andrews. Scottish bookies stopped taking bets on the tournament winner and instead offered only second-place odds. Tiger won at 19-under, a major championship record.

In 2002, the odds on him winning fell so low, 7-4, sensible bettors pushed back. Instead, they picked proposition bets for the top American other than Tiger, the top Brit, and how many cigarettes John Daly would smoke in 18 holes. At the start of the first round in 2005, bookmakers listed Woods at 3-1 to win. More bets on him pushed the odds to 5-4 by the time he reached the 10th tee. After shooting a 6-under 66, he was 11-10. To seasoned bettors, these wagers were ludicrous. Even Tiger saw no value in betting at those odds. Reporters asked him if he would bet on himself at odds approaching even money. "Probably not—just because I don't think it would be a good business decision, with those odds," he said. "Now, do I like my chances? Yes, I do." Tiger knows that bettors treat value as religion.

The Woods phenomenon has made it simpler for novices to bet on golf; they bet on him to win a tournament. He either does or doesn't. Experienced bettors more often shy away from win bets, however. They like more predicable wagers, those with greater value—longer odds. Matchups between players are favorites, but there are plenty of golf bets to select.

Betting on a golf tournament starts with the odds making. For weekly men's and women's professional tournaments, bookmakers usually post their odds by the Monday before the Thursday start of a 72-hole tournament. "The final field for many events is not decided until the day or two before the tournament starts, as many of the big names, who are exempt for most tournaments, wait until the last minute until deciding to play," explained Andy Clifton, head of communications at Ladbrokes in London.

Ladbrokes employs a team of oddsmakers for several sports, with golf taking the most time because of the number—up to 155—of golfers playing in each tournament. Clifton said the team considers three issues before setting the odds:

Current form. Golfers with recent wins or top 10 finishes receive lower odds, except in instances of a first-time winner, who might suffer a letdown following his breakthrough. The older pros, however, can often win two in a row.

"Horses for the courses." Some players excel at certain venues, others score better on Bermuda than on bent grass, and still others are slow starters or hot weather golfers.

Popular favorites. Clifton said if Ladbrokes put up 10-1 odds for Tiger to win the Masters, "we'd get knocked over in the rush, and Ladbrokes would probably go bust if we took all the money that people wanted to place on those odds."

Jeff Sherman, who is now at the Las Vegas Hilton, follows a similar process. "I keep stats on the golfers, giving them a power rating on each course," he said. "With that as my starting point, I then look at how each has been playing as well as the relative strength of the field. If Tiger plays that week, I have to raise the odds on everyone else."

Sherman offers discrete odds for those he considers the top 49 golfers entered in each regular tournament, and he lumps all the rest into a field bet, usually with odds of 8-1. Other bookmakers post odds for every player. Golf books don't run a tote board or a pari-mutuel system like that used in horse racing, so as money flows to certain players, the bookmaker manually adjusts the odds on those players. In these cases, Sherman raises the odds on players getting no action to give them more value. (Visit Sherman's website at golfodds.com.)

Most every golf book sets odds for the majors, for proposition bets such as Tiger's Grand Slam chances, and for special events, such as Annika Sorenstam playing on the PGA Tour. Some bookmakers, especially Sherman, offer odds for non-tour tournaments during the "silly season," events such as the Shark Shootout, World Cup, and Skins Game.

There are several methods of quoting odds.

Fractional—Davis Love III to win outright: 7-1
American—+700
Decimal—8.00

In the 7-1 quote, betting $1 returns $7 if Love wins. At "+700," someone wagering 100 units gets back 700 units. The "8.00" is the same, but it automatically adds the wager to the return (bet $1, win $7, and get a total of $8 from the bookmaker).

Books offer several types of bets on golf tournaments. The practice helps the bookmakers even out their chances of making money, but the various bets also aids the bettor in hedging against potential losses. Plus, bettors always savor different betting angles. The increased live television coverage of golf worldwide permits a family of wagers unheard of just a few years ago—namely, in-running bets, which allow a bettor to wager on a player during his round. The bet is similar to those offered for a penalty kick in soccer. During the 45 seconds between the referee's whistle and the kick, punters in Britain can try to get down a bet on the kick's outcome.

There will always be variations from one book to another, but here are the most common bets available on golf tournaments.

Outright bet (also *tournament bet* and *to win*). The bettor selects a player to win the tournament. The odds determine the payout. If Phil Mickelson wins the Bob Hope Chrysler Classic and your wager was $5 at 14-1, your winnings would be $70 plus your original $5 investment. Bookmakers had Ben Curtis, a young American ranked 1,269 in the world, at 500-1 to win the 2003 British Open. After his victory, a British betting syndicate took home $347,000. Variations include a bet on a nominated player to finish in a selected place other than winning or to miss the cut.

The year after his win, books listed Curtis at odds ranging from 150-1 to 200-1, the highest odds ever for a defending champion. Ernie Els headed the favorites, and a bettor in the United Kingdom liked Ernie's chances so much that he bet £62,500 (about $112,000) on the South African to win at 8-1. It was reportedly the largest ever golf bet in the United Kingdom. "Him or her has a lot of money to wager," Els said. "But I'm feeling good about this week and I'm glad I've got fans or a betting man that's got a lot of confidence in me." Els lost in a play-off to an unknown, Todd Hamilton. For the second year in a row a journeyman stole the Open from the big dogs. As late as that Saturday night, though, when Hamilton led the tournament by one stroke, one could still bet him as high as 50-1.

A few years ago, new British gaming regulations permitted betting against a player. Called "selling" or "laying" a golfer, the bet was a boon to Scotsmen who have grown weary of betting on Colin Montgomerie to win anything big.

Each way. Betting Vijay Singh each way means you have two bets in one— the first to win and the second to finish in the top four. If Singh is posted at 20-1, you get the first bet at those odds and the second at one-fourth of the winning odds, or 5-1. Betting $10 each way ($20 total bet) gains you $200 if Singh wins, plus $50 for his finish in the top four. If he finishes third, your winnings will be only $50. Some books offer one-fifth of the winning odds for a top five finish.

Match-up (also *head-to-head*). Books offer odds on several pairs of golfers during a tournament. The bet is on who will shoot the lower score of the two—either for one round or the entire tournament—regardless of who wins the tournament.

Many bettors like the Accenture Match Play Championship because of the head-to-head match-ups and the strong international field. Both Las Vegas books and online betting shops see a 50 percent increase in betting during that tournament. Picking the overall winner is tough, even for Tiger, who thinks working the NCAA basketball brackets is easier than those of the Accenture tournament. "I don't see how you can ever win at that, because there's no way you can get every single bracket right because anybody can beat anybody," Woods said. In 2006, he proved himself right. After beating Stephen Ames 9 and 8 in the first round, Tiger lost in the third round to Chad Campbell.

Els played Japanese player Toru Taniguchi in a consolation match for third place in the 2001 Accenture. An astute British bettor correctly assumed Els would be ready to head home and might mail it in during the match. Taking odds of 5-2 on Taniguchi, the bettor cleaned up when the Japanese underdog won 4 and 3.

A professional gambler who asked to remain anonymous—let's call him "Fred"—bets about 20 times a year on golf and always on match-ups, never on outright winners. "The odds are horrible on winner bets. I do it on other sports, but not golf. Anybody can win, just look at Curtis at the British, or Shaun Micheel at the PGA."

Two-ball, three-ball. Although similar to a match-up bet, this wager pits members of an actual pairing against each other. Usually, three golfers play in PGA Tour pairings on Thursday and Friday, so a three-ball bettor selects which of the three players will have the lowest score for that round. On the weekend, two golfers are most often in each pairing, so books offer a two-ball bet.

Insiders suggest finding a three-ball group in a tournament in which one player has no chance and then picking wisely between the other two. For the stout of heart, there are *parlay bets,* similar to those at the track, in which bettors pick the winners in multiple two-ball bets.

Spread bet. This bet is not for the faint of heart or the casual bettor, and not every book offers spreads. The bookmaker selects a range in which a player might finish in the tournament, say between 15th and 20th place, and offers a bet at so many dollars a place. If the bettor wagers $10 a place that the player will finish worse than that range, and the player does, perhaps in 50th place, then the winnings are calculated by the spread between 20th and 50th place. Thus, 30 places times $10 equals a $300 return. If the player gets hot and wins the tournament, then the bettor owes the book $140 (14 places times $10.)

Over/Under. Bettors can wager on whether the winning score falls over or under a total posted by the book. Also, one can bet on a particular player's score. Before Sorenstam played in the 2003 Colonial, a PGA Tour event in Fort Worth, Sherman set the over/under score at 76 ½ for her first round. He lost some money when she shot a 71. When later told of the bookmaker's line, Annika told the news media, "I should have bet on myself."

In-running. Live TV permits bettors to wager during a round, even on a hole-to-hole basis. One online book offers *next hole winner* and *next hole total* (or the total score of all golfers on a hole), and these bets have proven popular with their customers.

Prop (short for proposition). Books offer prop bets when interesting circumstances arise during a tournament.

Darren Clarke, an Irish player with a robust lust for life, saw a wager during the 1997 British Open he liked. It was a prop bet on the number of bogeys players would make in one round on Troon's par-3 eighth hole, known locally as the Postage Stamp. The over/under number was 30. Noting the high wind that day, Clarke took the over. When the field posted 49 bogeys, Clarke won. "It isn't often the bookies make a mistake, but I thought they had on this occasion, so I jumped in," he said later.

During Sorenstam's play in the Colonial, Sherman offered several props on Annika, including one on whether she would make a birdie before she had a bogey. After three straight pars, she birdied her fourth hole. Instead of betting Sorenstam would play poorly, bettors echoed the positive support shown at the tournament. "Everyone took her to do well on just about all of our props," Sherman said. "They all wanted to cheer for her." Sorenstam's entry in a PGA Tour event was a boon to Las Vegas sports books. "We had a great crowd in here this morning," said Chuck Esposito, race and sports book director for Caesars, during the first round.

"Fred," the full-time gambler, saw the Sorenstam issue far differently. "I bet against her, but only after I watched her play at the LPGA tournament in Las Vegas a month before the Colonial. I just didn't think she had a chance. A sports book in Las Vegas offered odds that I though were way too low, not only for making the cut, but also a top 25 finish, and winning. I bet my second-highest total in 2003 against her, wining all but one of a series of bets."

Fourteen-year old Michelle Wie played in the 2004 Sony Open in Honolulu. Sherman set the odds on her wining at 1,000-1 and 15-1 to make the cut. "Fred" didn't wager anything for or against Wie, citing the "home course" advantage she had in playing at Waialae Country Club in her hometown. She almost pulled it off, shooting 72-68, but missed the cut by one shot. She became the youngest golfer to play in a PGA Tour event and proved her talent by posting the same score over 36 holes as Jim Furyk, Chad Campbell, Kenny Perry, Ben Curtis, Darren Clarke, Jeff Maggert, and Stuart Appleby.

Wie played at the Sony again in 2005, and Sherman posted odds of her winning at 500-1 and 3-1 to make the cut. She missed again. She didn't make the cut again in 2006, but her seven birdies in the second round showed that she has game.

The 2003 Irish Open was staged at the men-only Portmarnock Club in Dublin, a situation that led bookie Paddy Power to offer several props. He set odds at 33-1 that a woman streaker would protest the trophy presentation, 50-1 that a female protestor would handcuff herself to the trophy, and 50-1 that one of the participants would withdraw in protest of Portmarnock's membership policy. Hundreds of those fancying a flutter took the novelty bets, but to no avail.

More common props are for holes in one during a tournament, the low score for a round, the highest finish by a Brit or Swede, the most points scored by an individual during the President's Cup, or how many times Sergio Garcia re-gripped his club before hitting the ball (he broke his habit in 2003). The Ryder Cup draws various props, especially when played in Europe and the bookies can really show their flair. During the 2002 event, held at The Belfry in England, one book offered 33-1 odds the German Bernhard Langer would sink a putt to win the cup for the European team. Since Langer missed a 4-footer to lose the cup in the 1991 match played at Kiawah, South Carolina, the bookie called the 2002 prop the "Kiawah Redemption."

For the less ambitious, they can always pursue fantasy golf. Some Internet sites offer substantial prizes, and there are many to choose from. Even the PGA Tour sponsors fantasy competition.

—●—

CHIPS AND PITCHES
Adult behavior. Ladbrokes, the British bookmaker, had a deal with British player Sam Torrance in 2002 that would be unthinkable in Victorian

America. They gave Sam 100 euro each week for him to bet on other golfers, with the proceeds, if any, going to charity. The Europeans are more grown up than we are.

Betting lesson. Mickelson once made a trip to Houston to seek help from one of the game's oracles, Jackie Burke, Jr. During a lesson, Burke challenged Phil to take a pressure putting test—make 100 straight 3-footers. It was a drill Burke did himself every night while he was on tour. Mickelson bet Burke the best dinner in town that he could do it. Phil missed on ball number four and then asked to double the bet. "Man, I can't eat that much," said Burke.

Dormie. A *side* (player or team) is "dormie" when it is as many holes up as there are holes remaining to be played. The USGA maintains the word is a derivation of the Latin word *dormio,* which means "to sleep." If dormie in a match, you can't lose, so the supposition is you can relax and maybe even take a nap for the remaining holes. The earliest written use of dormie was in Scotland in 1851.

Tin Cup. In the 1996 film, actor Kevin Costner plays a West Texas driving range pro who bumbles and bets his way toward the pot of gold at the end of tournament golf's rainbow. As with every other hero in sports movies, Costner's character, Roy "Tin Cup" McAvoy, struggles against adversity and obscurity to reach the pinnacle of his game—in this case, winning the U.S. Open. It's not a coincidence that McAvoy's victory at the Open hinges on a high-risk, high-reward gamble with a 3-wood over water to the 18th green.

The film relies on sports clichés and, in one instance, on an old trick. Following Mysterious Montague's 1933 bat, shovel, and rake caper, McAvoy takes on his rival for both the girl and golf fame for a $400 wager. You know the rest.

8.

Tuesdays on Tour:

The Pros Play for Their Own Money, 1998–2006

Tiger Woods is the face of international golf today. His is a wonderfully expressive face at that, capable of setting sponsors' hearts aflutter with a beaming smile, of staring down competitors, or of revealing the frustrations of championship golf. He is wildly successful, reaping both titles and prize money. He also brings diversity to a game still dominated by whites in America, despite the earlier breakthroughs by Teddy Rhodes, Charlie Sifford, and Lee Elder.

Tiger is also the face of money golf. He does not play for the outlandish sums Bill Walters and Dewey Tomko bet; instead, Tiger bets the $5 Nassaus he knows have been part of the game from the beginning. To him, a friendly wager on the round or even a side bet on how many times he can bounce a ball on his wedge is part of the competition and another way to keep score.

He learned about betting on golf from his father and from other players on the public golf courses in Southern California where he played and practiced as a youngster. He also learned how to fit the size of the bet to the circumstance, to respect the role of wagering in golf, and to pay his debts—although the last part took a few extended lessons.

His competitiveness and fondness for needling friends have resulted in small bets through many parts of his life or at least in those activities he reluctantly shares with the public. As a teenager, he bet another high school golfer $5 on a taco-eating contest. "He ate 12," Woods said. "I ate 14." After losing a bet to Michael Jordan during the holidays, he showed up at the Orange Bowl in early 2001 with bleached hair. In 2002, he and his swing coach at the time, Butch Harmon, each bet Tiger's caddie, Steve Williams, $100 that Williams couldn't run the back nine at the hilly Plantation Course at Maui's Kapalua Resort in less than 30 minutes. Williams, easily the fittest caddie on the tour, ran it in 19:28 and won the money. Tiger won five bucks from financier Warren Buffett by playing one hole on his knees while Buffett played conventionally. Fishing, free throw shooting, Nintendo—they are all ready-made activities for Tiger's competitive instincts. EA Sports, the video game company, not only captured Tiger's swing in its popular *Tiger Woods PGA Tour* game but also got the betting part right. "Back your challenges with wagers before any shot or round," EA says on its website.

His father, Earl, had retired from the U.S. Army by the time Tiger was born in 1975. A Green Beret and a two-tour veteran of the Vietnam War, he met his second wife, Kultida, in Bangkok. The two named their only child Eldrick, an amalgam of their two first names, but Earl nicknamed his son after a courageous South Vietnamese Army officer with whom he had served. Earl raised his son to be a championship player. He obviously succeeded, and he did so without becoming either a Little League parent from hell or the Great Santini. Earl passed away in May 2006.

Modern golf's premier prodigy had game from the start. He shot 48 for nine holes when he was three years old (O.K., they were all par-3s), had two holes in one by age six, and had made 80 straight 4-foot putts at age seven. He won all 30 junior tournaments he entered when he was 11 years old. The TV show *That's Incredible* and talk show host Mike Douglas introduced the child to America.

Until Michelle Wie entered the 2004 Sony Open in Honolulu, Tiger was the youngest person to play in a PGA Tour event, which was the 1992 Los Angeles Open. By then, the phenom had a supporting cast. Team Tiger included his mom and dad, coach Butch Harmon, and a sports psychologist, retired U.S. Navy physician Jay Brunza, who often also caddied for Tiger. His was not a seamless cruise to stardom. Tiger's race was a lingering issue, even though he is only one-quarter African American. "All the media try to put black in him," his mother said when Tiger was 20 years old. "Why don't they ask who half of Tiger is from? In United States, one little part black is all black." Tiger was a little edgy about the matter in TV commercials when he first turned pro, but he has retreated since. "I'm just trying to win golf tournaments, not change the world."

Tiger's string of six straight USGA championships—three national juniors and three U.S. Amateurs—was the biggest thing in amateur golf in 65 years. Those wins brought increased attention to amateur golf. The TV ratings of his third U.S. Amateur final at Oregon's Pumpkin Ridge Golf Club in 1996 were double those of the PGA Tour's World Series of Golf on the same day. Having also won the NCAA individual title the same year, Woods surprised few when he turned pro in late August 1996.

Throughout his extraordinary rise to fame, he bet on his golf game.

"Where'd you get those quarters?" Earl asked a four-year-old Tiger.

"I won them putting."

"Look," said Earl, "I don't want you putting for quarters anymore." The kid did what he was told and began bringing home greenbacks.

Earl toughened up Tiger when they played together by distracting him, jingling coins, throwing head covers, talking, and moving. He made small bets with his son to add a cost to mistakes. "I was determined that he'd never run up against someone mentally stronger than he was," the elder Woods said. He wanted Tiger to have a "dark side, a coldness." Tida spoke plainly about how her son should treat opponents: "Kill them."

Earl also taught Tiger never to offer anyone, especially the news media, any more information than a question required. When Tiger was three, Earl tested him by asking where he was born. "I was born on December 30, 1975, in Long Beach, California." The father suggested that answer was too much information, and Tiger should try again. "I was born in Long Beach, California." If you think Tiger is tongue-tied during PGA Tour question-and-answer sessions, think again.

The following year, *Sports Illustrated* writer Jaime Diaz played a round with Woods. They had no bets until 18, when Tiger offered to play the last hole for some "ABC gum." "I didn't know what that was," said Diaz, "but I knew it could not be much. He was 14."

After Tiger birdied the hole to win, Diaz had to ask, "What's ABC gum?"

"Already been chewed," he said. He played like an adult, but he still liked adolescent humor.

Tiger took his fondness for friendly golf wagers to Stanford. Most of his teammates have a story or two about their competitions. Joel Kribel, who lost to Tiger in a dramatic semifinal match in the 1996 Amateur, recalled their college days. "We had plenty of little money games," Kribel said. "In fact, I probably still owe him a little bit of money." Casey Martin, the young pro whose circulatory disorder has hindered his career, won $180 from Tiger in a putting contest while they were teammates. He cashed Woods's check but also saved a photocopy for his scrapbook.

It was only fitting Tiger ended up in a money game with Jack Nicklaus and Arnold Palmer at the young man's first Masters in 1994. "I'm a college student then; I've got no money," Tiger recalled. "I'm like, 'Ah, how much money are we playing for?' 'Oh, don't worry about it, we'll tell you how much you owe us at the end.'" The 65-year-old Palmer won all the back nine skins with a 20-foot putt on 18.

The two old pros then took Tiger over to the par-3 course for the annual Wednesday tournament there. On the ninth and final hole, both Jack and Arnie stuck their tee shots within three feet of the cup and then stepped back for Tiger's shot. "My iron game was not very good back then," Woods said later. "I'm just hoping to hit land." He did. Palmer congratulated him on the shot and then added, "But I got you on closest to the hole."

The following year, at his second Masters as an amateur, Woods played another practice round with Palmer and Nicklaus. On the par-5 13th, Tiger hit a 3-wood off the tee. Palmer saw him pull an iron for his second shot and nudged Nicklaus, "He's laying up."

"Oh, Arnie," Jack said, "he's not." That's about when the two legends agreed they had seen a new one.

Asked by the news media afterward about the talented college kid, Jack responded, "I was impressed with Arnold the most because he won all the money."

Nicklaus then addressed Tiger's abilities: "You can take all of Arnold's wins in the Masters and my wins in the Masters and add them together, and he should win more than both of us. This kid is the most fundamentally sound golfer I've seen at any age." Given that Palmer won the Masters four times and Nicklaus six, that was a heady prediction.

His U.S. Amateur wins qualified Woods to play in the other majors as well as the Masters. During the summer of 1995, Woods traveled to the United Kingdom for the Scottish Open at Carnoustie and then the British Open at St Andrews. On the trip, he met the reigning British Amateur champion, Gordon Sherry, and the two made a £5 bet on who would have the better record in the two tournaments. This wager was reminiscent of some Bobby Jones made during his career. Sherry won the bet by finishing 10 shots ahead of Tiger at the Scottish and four at the British.

When Tiger turned pro after two years at Stanford, he began the difficult process of attempting to earn enough money on the PGA Tour to get his card before the end of the year. The tour allowed him sponsor's exemptions into only seven tournaments to earn a total equal to that of 125th place on the money list. In his first, the Greater Milwaukee Open, he tied for 60th and won $2,544. "You know, the prize money, that's the paycheck," he said afterward. "That's the money I earned for myself. All the other stuff, my Nike contract and Titleist, and now the All Star Café, to me, that's a bank account."

After tying for 11th in his second tournament, he placed in the top five in the next two tournaments. Tiger won on his fifth attempt, the Las Vegas Invitational, and won again before the year was out. "Here's your PGA Tour card, Mr. Woods."

The novice professional sought advice and counsel about tour life from the veteran Mark O'Meara. The older man took Tiger under his wing and helped the kid set up housekeeping near O'Meara's home in the Isleworth gated golf course community in Orlando. Mark became not only a mentor but also a friend and frequent opponent in money games. Most of their practice sessions at Isleworth or informal rounds around the world are inexpensive, yet cutthroat $5 Nassaus with automatic 1-down presses. The two can obviously play for more money, but the real stakes are larger—needling leverage and verbal fuel for the next game.

The week before Tiger lapped the field at the 1997 Masters, he and O'Meara tuned up at home. Tiger shot 59 that day and $65 changed hands. "It could have been a lot more than that," O'Meara told a reporter. "Tiger could have shot 56 or 57 that day. I didn't play well. I just got smart and stopped pressing him."

Despite his easy-going and affable manner, O'Meara is just the right foil for Tiger. "It might surprise people how competitive Marco is, which is why I love him," Woods said. "We relate to each other as warriors."

O'Meara also taught Woods how to overcome one of the few faults in the young man's game—a "reach impediment." Apparently, Tiger's hand sometimes couldn't reach his wallet when he lost a bet. "He's young," Mark said at the time. "He's got to learn. Fast pay makes fast friends."

O'Meara doesn't wear his competitiveness on his sleeve, plus he is funny and fits in with Tiger's other friends. He often joins in when Tiger plays with Michael Jordan or fellow Isleworth resident, All-Star outfielder Ken Griffey, Jr. "He's one of the greatest guys you'll meet," Griffey said of O'Meara. "You think you're doing okay until the 19th hole, when Mark adds it all up. Then he's cleaned you out. He says, 'You lost four presses, three Omars, two snakes, and a snowman.' I ask him, 'What's an Omar?' He says, 'That's a save from the sand—you know, like Omar Sharif in *Lawrence of Arabia*. Kid, you gotta pay to learn.'"

Tiger Woods and Mark O'Meara are usually in perfect sync on and off the golf course. The two often bet on their practice round matches and sometimes on who has the best score during a tournament. ASSOCIATED PRESS/WIDE WORLD PHOTOS

Knowing the closeness between Woods and O'Meara, reporters approach O'Meara for insights about Tiger that they can't get directly from "Da Man." Mark usually responds, politely offering quotable sound bites. In one example O'Meara encountered a writer for the *Detroit News* in Grand Blanc, Michigan, after the final round of the 2002 Buick Open. Woods had shot a 2-under 70 on that Sunday to win by four shots, his fourth victory in eight starts up to that point.

"You guys just have to understand what we're witnessing right now in the game of golf," said O'Meara. "Certainly Jack has the greatest record and that makes him the greatest player. But in my estimation, Tiger Woods is the actual greatest raw, physical talent that's ever played the game." Oh, and by the way, Mark, the media asked, what did you shoot today? O'Meara smiled and said his 68 topped Tiger's 70, winning the bet they had for dinner that night. "With Tiger, you take what you can get."

There is one notable exception to the Woods-O'Meara betting routine during non-tournament rounds, "cold shafting." Along with several other Isleworth pros, the two try to play early morning practice rounds at tour events. Without warming up, they hit their first shots as early as 5:30 a.m. to dodge the crowds.

"Practice rounds are supposed to be loose and enjoyable and not be stressed out," Tiger said of the routine. "When people are throwing things at you to sign between the green and tee, that's not a relaxing environment. I'm out there to take a look at the golf course, but also to have fun." Members of the "Dawn Patrol," as they call themselves, usually don't bet, and they often skip the first and last holes in a further attempt to escape attention.

The dew-sweeping practice rounds can limit Tiger's playing with other tour regulars before the first round on Thursday. That doesn't stop players from seeking a round with Woods. India's Arjun Atwal, who joined the PGA Tour in 2004, asked Tiger for a game before the HSBC Champions tournament in Shanghai, China, in November 2005. "We put [up] some money because we want to put ourselves under some pressure," Atwal told a reporter. "It's just practice, but we want to practice under pressure." Asked about the size of the bet, he said sheepishly, "I am not going to tell you that. It is against the rules."

Notah Begay III, one of Tiger's college teammates, is a favorite money game opponent. The Native American Begay joined Woods on the PGA Tour in 1999, winning four times until his game tailed off in 2005 and 2006. "He and I go all the way back to junior golf," Woods said of Begay. "I met Notah when I was about 11. In college, Notah and I always played for money, and we had some epic battles. We're great friends. He's like a brother to me."

The two teamed for three matches during the 2000 Presidents Cup at the Robert Trent Jones Golf Club in Manassas, Virginia. They won two of them, both against Ernie Els and Vijay Singh. During an alternate-shot practice round before the Cup matches, Woods and Begay took on Stewart Cink and Kirk Triplett, who also teamed successfully against the internationals. Butch Harmon saw the foursome at the turn and asked if they were going to play a match on the back nine.

"Oh, we've got a match now," Tiger said. "We've got a little money on it." On 18, with he and Begay 1-up, Woods chunked a flop shot into a green-side bunker. He threw down a mulligan but again ended up in the sand. He got the ball on the green on the third try, but by then he and Notah were out of the hole, and they settled for a halve. The bet was a push.

Both Woods and Begay played in the 2003 Funai Classic in Orlando. Before the tournament started, they joined the Sorenstam sisters, Annika and Charlotta, for a friendly round at the Greg Norman course at the Ritz Carlton Golf Club. They threw balls up for partners, with Tiger pairing with Annika. "I swear I didn't rig it," he said later, "the balls just bounced that way." The men played from the tips; the women, the next tee forward. "We had a great time," Tiger said. "Annika and I edged them out for lunch afterward."

Tiger isn't as forthcoming about the stakes when he plays with Michael Jordan, probably because Jordan doesn't need any more publicity about his golf betting. Joel Hirsh, the fine Chicago amateur who has exchanged folding money with Arnold Palmer on the golf course, said the bets are relatively modest for that crowd.

"I qualified for the 1999 Motorola Western Open so I sought out Tiger for a practice round," Hirsh said in the recent interview. "Instead of scheduling a round at Cog Hill, the host course, we played at Medinah Country Club. The PGA Championship was scheduled there the following month, so Tiger wanted to get a round in there." Jordan and former NFL player and NBC TV personality Ahmad Rashad joined them.

"Tiger and Michael played $100 Nassau four ways, and Tiger and I had a separate $100 Nassau, also four ways," Hirsch recalled. "Michael and I had another bet, but I can't remember the amount."

"Tiger's TV commercial that showed him bouncing a ball off his wedge had just been shown, so everyone needled him about the number of takes he needed to pull it off," Hirsh said. "Tiger quickly halted the trash talking when he started bouncing a ball between his legs and around his back. After a minute or two, he flipped it up and hit it 200 yards down the fairway. It was amazing."

Just as Arnold Palmer, Tiger is not opposed to having a gentlemanly wager with a pro-am partner. NFL quarterback Peyton Manning enjoyed a round with Woods at Palmer's Bay Hill tournament in 2005. "Thankfully, I've played in a few pro-ams, so I've kind of gotten over the fear of missing the ball on the first tee," Manning said. The two had a little something on the round, and just as Ben Hogan did to his amateur opponents, Woods stopped giving Peyton tips on the last six holes. "On the last hole, with the match on the line, he nearly holed his shot from the fairway," Manning said. "End of story."

During a practice round in 2003 before Woods's own year-end

tournament, the Target World Challenge, he played eight holes with saxophonist Kenny G. The musician is a member and former net club champion at the host course, Sherwood Country Club in Thousand Oaks, California. Later, as a guest on the weekend telecast, Kenny, a 4-handicap, talked about the game. "He gave me three strokes for the side, but he still won $100." Kenny, a cowinner with Phil Mickelson at the 2001 AT&T Pro-Am, said his round with Woods was one of his golfing highlights.

Like Mickelson, Tiger likes a little spontaneous side bet during a non-tournament round. During the 2000 Bay Hill Pro-Am, Woods found himself under the back lip of a green-side bunker on 18. He was also on the short side of the green, which sloped away from the bunker toward water on the other side. The Bay Hill website warns about the dangers of a shot from that location: "Take a deep breath and fire away."

Tiger's agent at IMG, Mark Steinberg bet Woods $10 that he couldn't get up and down. With only 10 feet of green to work with, Tiger got enough spin on the ball to stop it within two inches of the cup.

Another pro-am story about Woods shows his betting mind. At the 2003 Chick Evans Pro-Am before the Western Open at Cog Hill, a college kid from Miami University, Kyle Healey, caddied for Woods. Healey was the beneficiary of a Chick Evans caddie scholarship and replaced Steve Williams for the day, although Steve walked along with him. On 13, Tiger left his approach shot in the rough, 25 yards from the hole. "He said, 'I don't want to hit this,'" Healey related later. The young caddy volunteered.

"So Tiger takes the bag off my shoulder," Healey said, "and he was cleaning clubs for me. It was a total change of roles. It was pretty funny." Williams and Woods bet Healey $10 he couldn't get down in two. Kyle's chip was 12 feet short, and he missed the putt. Tiger didn't make him pay.

Finally, an unlikely story about Tiger and money golf is funny nevertheless. After talking to Stevie Wonder, Tiger is surprised to learn the blind singer plays golf. Stevie explains his caddie walks down the fairway and yells back, giving Stevie a target. On the green, the caddie lies down with his mouth near the hole, and Wonder putts toward the voice.

"We've got to play a round sometime," the incredulous Woods said.

"Well, people don't take me seriously," Wonder said. "So I play for money and never less than $10,000 a hole."

'O.K., I'm game for that," Woods said after a pause. "When would you like to play?"

"Pick a night."

———•———

"Win or lose, one should always be a gentleman. And always play for money." This was the motto of Lefty Stackhouse, an irascible Texan pro during the 1930s. His advice wouldn't work in another sport, but it has in golf for centuries.

The hysteria in America surrounding sports gambling is founded on the widespread supposition that betting always begets cheating. Many consider the two inseparable. Major League Baseball argued Pete Rose's betting on baseball gave him both the opportunity and motivation to throw a game by how he managed or played. There is no evidence he ever did, but baseball's rules dictated he had to be banned. The NFL suspended Paul Hornug and Alex Karras for betting on NFL games but not for fixing them. Although college basketball has seen real points-shaving problems in the last 50 years, no one has attempted to fix a professional game since the 1950s. But that fact didn't stop the NBA from prohibiting the establishment of a franchise in Toronto until bookies in Ontario stopped offering bets on league games.

There isn't much betting on professional tennis, and no accusations of juiced rackets or other illegal schemes have surfaced. Just in case, however, the Association of Tennis Professionals (ATP) prohibits gambling on anything involved with an ATP event. In 2003, London's *Sunday Telegraph* claimed ATP Tour members were betting on their matches. Most of the suspected players were not the game's stars, but ATP officials examined an October 2003 match between Russian Yevgeny Kafelnikov and Spain's Fernando Vicente. Apparently, bookmakers reported large amounts of money moved to Vicente just before the match. The Spaniard, who had not won a match since the previous June, beat Kafelnikov handily in straight sets. No reported sanctions arose from the allegations, but the ATP reminded everyone penalties for match fixing on the ATP Tour include a $100,000 fine and a three-year suspension.

Given that traditional American moral codes equate cheating with betting and despite widespread betting in the game, how has organized golf remained untainted by scandal? The answer is a social paradox that doesn't fit any other American sports model.

Early golf was strictly a competition between two players or teams. Each put up a stake on the outcome. Alone on the windswept Scottish links and often separated by errant shots, players had no choice but to referee themselves. By the time stroke play came to golf, 400 years after the game caught on in Scotland, there was no turning back on the concept of self-policing. While the presence of other golfers as well as of the gallery added more witnesses to the enforcement process and stiffened the potential cheater's spine, the process was the same.

Nonetheless, cheating occurs in golf today. "The opportunities to cheat in golf are limitless," acknowledged Joe Dey, who was both a commissioner of the PGA Tour and the USGA's executive director. He explained the most common ways to cheat involved moving the ball, scoring incorrectly, colluding with another player, failing to call a penalty, using illegal equipment, and falsifying handicaps. Built into the game, however, are several curbs against cheating.

Integrity. "When you get right down to it, it all hinges on a man's conscience," said Dey. "The integrity of golf is all of golf. If you don't have that, it's no game at all."

Etiquette. "I suspect that golf's comfortable relationship with betting is the result of how proper etiquette is taught along with the golf swing," said Professor Wray Vamplew of the Department of Sports Studies at the University of Stirling.

Teaching. Lee Trevino claims golf will never have a betting scandal because "golfers are raised differently." Trevino, who has played his share of money golf, attributes golf's steadfast integrity to those who teach the game.

Scoring. In a match, opponents keep each other's score.

Ostracism. Players will blow the whistle on a violator. In 1969 Dey referred to this unwritten rule as "Rule 42": "The rule says, 'Thou shall not play with So-and-So.' You'd be amazed how effective it is."

Stakes. The history of golf has proven that with a wager on the line, every player scrutinizes his opponent's behavior. Dewey Tomko and his high-rolling friends aren't the only ones who pay attention to players in the woods or work a toe wedge. A fellow competitor is a "pretty good policeman," Dey maintained.

Parenthetically, Dey also enjoyed a friendly wager when he played. A member of the Creek Club in Locust Valley, New York, he started playing only for a golf ball, but soon he graduated to a four-way, $2 Nassau. He particularly liked a special press at 18 that his group called "the Titanic"—double or quits, sink or swim.

These factors are not completely successful at preventing cheating, at least in one sector of golfing society. In a 2002 survey Starwood Hotels conducted, 82 percent of 401 business executives said they cheated on the golf course. (This statistic was up from 55 percent in 1993.) Moreover, 87 percent reported they also bet when they played, giving pause to the idea that a wager often ensures fair play. Among these same golfing executives, 86 percent admitted to cheating in business. At that time, Enron, WorldCom, and their accounting firms were imploding. In the backlash to their shady business practices and after their criminal prosecutions, perhaps these wayward souls and their peers will start playing it as it lies again.

No evidence suggests tour players follow the surveyed businessmen's lead. Additional forces at work on the tour might inhibit them from cheating.

For starters, professional golfers are well behaved. Some blurt a party word after three-putting but little else. The PGA Tour has by far the highest-rated image in professional sports. *Squeaky clean* is the term the most sensitive judges in modern sports—sponsors and advertisers—use. Professional golfers don't strike, have contract disputes, brawl, or take cheap shots. Name the last PGA Tour player who has been arrested or suspended for abusing drugs or prosecuted for molesting a hotel clerk. Yet professional golfers had been betting for 150 years before Pete Rose pulled on his polyesters.

The early agreements between tour players to split winnings and play-off purses gave the perception of cheating, but only a few surviving stories tell about real monkey business. Sam Snead said the mob fixed the St. Paul Open one year, and Snead's pal Johnny Bulla had a similar tale. He said a player in a tournament in Detroit in the 1930s bet on a competitor and then tanked. "He threw the tournament," Bulla said, "to collect money for losing."

Dave Hill, who won 13 times on the PGA Tour, said a player in the 1960s paid others to shoot a certain score during a tournament round. He also asked Hill on another occasion if Hill could beat so-and-so that day. Hill wrote in his book, *Teed Off,* that a Las Vegas gambler once offered him $2,500 not to post a score better than that of another player. He passed.

Since Hill's time on the tour, all allegations of foul play have involved breaking rules and not attempting to win a bet. Even at that, the subject of cheating on the PGA Tour arises infrequently. Considering the members play about 450 rounds a week and more than 40 weeks a year, the number of reported rules' violations is statistically insignificant. There have been public mea culpas over some incidents, but players usually are circumspect about major allegations. There have been few publicly acknowledged incidents.

Raymond Floyd recalled an instance during the Houston Open years ago when "Player A" clearly hit his tee ball into a swamp. He played a provisional, although he insisted he would find the first. When he did, he had a nice lie in the rough. Floyd said to him, "Hold on. That isn't your ball. There is no way you are going to be allowed to play that. I've walked over this spot three times. How can you find your ball, and sitting up? I'm not blind."

"Well, it's my ball, my number," Player A said. "I took it out of a brand new pack."

"Let's see the other two," said Floyd.

Although he cited this example of blatant cheating, Raymond maintained only a handful of violators played in the old days, and everyone knew who they were.

Hill, a contemporary of Floyd's, said he thought about 1 percent of tour players cheated regularly in the 1970s. He believed most cheating took place on the greens, with players subtly "adjusting" their markers. Hill described one player who hustled to be first on the green, thus giving him the chance to mark his ball more favorably. "He had a long Ping putter, and he would scoop the ball up on the back of the putter as he bent over and tossed a coin down, and by the time his paying partners were on the green, he was putting last instead of first."

Also in the 1970s, the LPGA suspended one of its stars, Jane Blalock, for a year for mismarking her ball. It caused a messy scene, with Blalock's suit against the LPGA prolonging the publicity. She retired in 1986.

Tom Watson, who authored a book on the rules of golf, was involved in two incidents in the 1980s. During the final round of the 1980 Tournament of Champions, he gave a swing tip to his playing partner Trevino. The rules forbid "advising" a competitor, and officials assessed Watson a two-stroke penalty. At the 1983 Skins Game, Watson accused Gary Player of removing a live weed leaf from behind his ball in a bunker. Player vehemently denied doing anything wrong.

"I don't regret what I did," Watson said years later. "I only regret it became a story. We don't need that in golf. We're different. And the proof is, it happens so infrequently."

Vijay Singh's 1985 suspension from the Asian Tour dogged him during his early success on the PGA Tour. A young man keeping Singh's scorecard entered the wrong number for a hole during the Indonesian Open. Singh said in 2004 he had reacted badly with some rough language, plus some debts in Australia exacerbated his image problem. He still maintains he did not knowingly sign a false scorecard.

Also in the 1980s, TV viewers began calling in during tournaments to report violations. Craig Stadler knelt on a towel to keep from staining his pants while he played a shot under a tree, breaking rule 13-3, or illegally building a stance. Fuzzy Zoeller shifted a stepping-stone in a creek to avoid getting his feet wet, which broke rule 13-4 about moving loose impediments in a hazard. Paul Azinger suffered the same fate at the 1991 Doral. The trend reached a crescendo in late 2005 when the LPGA disqualified Michelle Wie after her first tournament as a professional. Sportswriter Michael Bamberger saw her make an illegal drop but reported it the following day after she signed her scorecard. The reaction to Bamberger's handling of the incident was mixed.

Months after the 1997 Trophée Lancôme in Europe, Sweden's Jarmo Sandelin accused Mark O'Meara of mismarking his ball during the tournament. Sandelin had a TV tape of the incident and became a little strident about the matter, to the point that 20 European players apologized to O'Meara for the Swede's allegations. The following year, Lee Westwood accused Sandelin of illegally putting his ball when it had moved after he addressed the ball. No one was willing to say so publicly, but there may have been some payback there.

These are not egregious examples of cheating at golf. Observers believe most violations in recent years have occurred through ignorance of all the rules instead of chicanery. Even then, the numbers are quite small. "I can count on my hand the number of times I've seen guys cheat," Nick Price said in 2003. Watson thinks the sport at the PGA Tour level is "99 percent pure."

"Golfers make and enforce their own rules," said Nicklaus. "We enjoy and appreciate that right." Nicklaus said a few golfers on the PGA Tour have been caught cheating, but "we participants on the tour handled it quietly, and it was taken care of that way."

Today, the PGA Tour expressly prohibits players and caddies from betting money or anything of value at PGA Tour–sponsored events. The PGA Tour Player Handbook states, "A player shall not have any financial interest, either direct or indirect, in the performance or the winnings of another player . . . whether purse-splitting, prize money 'insurance,' financial assistance, bets, or otherwise."

The PGA Tour, however, doesn't view minor betting transgressions to be as serious as breaking the playing rules. Officials disqualified Stadler,

Zoeller, and Azinger. They lost a payday. Conversely, when Al Besselink made a very public wager on himself in 1965, the tour only put him on probation for a year.

At the 1986 PGA Championship at Inverness, the highlight of Payne Stewart's week was calling Bob Tway's winning bunker shot on the 72nd hole. "I was in the locker room watching TV as Tway finished, and was so sure he was going to hole his sand shot on 18 that I bet another player $100 that he would." The tour took no action.

Commissioner Finchem "technically" shook his finger at Mickelson and Weir in 2001, but he took another matter seriously two months later. A security guard barred tour member Jonathan Kaye from entering the contestant's locker room, because Kaye refused to display his PGA Tour badge, which looks like a money clip. Kaye said he had left it in his golf bag. The guard made Kaye fetch his clip anyway. When he returned to the locker room door, Kaye attached the badge to the open zipper of his pants. The tour suspended Kaye, who had also given the finger to a gallery the year before, for the first two months of the 2002 season. NBA-like behavior really gets the tour's attention, much more so than a locker room bet.

The tour has suspended John Daly a couple times for unbecoming conduct. None of his transgressions involved cheating or betting. Losing $12 million in casinos over a four-year period in the 1990s didn't burnish his image, but the tour didn't discipline him for it, either. Just to make sure, however, PGA Tour regulations ban card playing in the tournament locker rooms. That move seems a little over the top.

Organized golf has always tried to keep players from gaining an edge with equipment innovations. The R&A and the USGA began regulating equipment in the 20th century, and today, modern technology brings new developments every few years. The square groove squabble of the 1980s didn't involve cheating, but driver technology sparked a controversy in 2003. Tiger Woods said he confronted a fellow tour member whom Tiger felt was using an illegal driver, one the USGA designated as a "non-conforming" club." The club did not expose itself as flagrantly as Sammy Sosa's corked bat, but the player's unusually long drives caught Tiger's eye. The tour began regular but voluntary testing of drivers in 2004.

In amateur golf, lying about a handicap is the most common form of real cheating. Whether the game is a $2 Nassau or a weekend tournament at the club, golfers cringe upon contact with such varmints. The 1955 Deepdale affair widely publicized handicap cheating, but the incident was neither the start of the problem nor the end.

Golfers have been less than truthful about their skills since the game's beginning. Peer pressure had a way of dealing with early cheaters, especially after the Scots started forming clubs and golfing societies. As competition grew between clubs and golfers from different links, so did the chance for misrepresenting oneself to win the stakes. The handicap system helped ensure fair play, but for the cheater, it simply quantified the scope of his offense: "He said he was a 14, but he was really a 7."

At some point in U.S. golf history, someone used the term *sandbagger* to describe a handicap cheat. Historians suggest the word's origin lies in the age-old practice of adding weight to a bag of produce sold by the pound. Another theory holds that street gang members in New York used socks or small bags filled with sand to deliver a blow behind someone's ear. The assailant struck without warning, just as he might use a blackjack or similar Dashiell Hammett–style tools. This version also maintains sandbagging migrated from the street to golf via poker. When a player holding the nuts wants to lull his opponents into a big pot and bets carefully in amounts not representative of his hand, he is sandbagging.

Sunlight hits handicap cheating occasionally during high-profile pro-am tournaments, especially the AT&T National Pro-Am, formerly the Crosby Pro-Am. Baseball Hall of Famer George Brett won in 1987 with a 17, but he played much better. He did not have an established USGA index, so he asked Fred Couples for the right number. "Oh, I don't know, about 17," Couples said, according to Brett.

Dean Spanos, president and CEO of the San Diego Chargers, won in 1990 with an 11. He helped his pro by 39 strokes over the four days. In 1995, Japanese businessman Masashi Yamada won with pro Bruce Vaughan. Yamada claimed a 15, but he was really a 6 and had previously won the Japan Senior Amateur.

Actor Andy Garcia still plays in the tournament, having weathered a controversy in 1997 when he won with Paul Stankowski. Garcia, claiming an 18, shot a natural 36 on one nine and contributed nine strokes to the team in the second round. Tournament officials cut him to a 10 after that. "Sandbagging is an ugly term," Garcia said.

Dean Knuth, formerly the USGA handicapping director, believes about 1 to 2 percent of golfers are sandbaggers. Asked in 2003 for the odds of a player beating his handicap by eight strokes, Knuth said 1,138-1, or about

54 years of golf for the average player, and 14,912-1 for doing it twice.

At the other end of the stick is a "vanity" handicap, or a reverse sandbagger. Knuth estimates 10 percent of golfers sport a handicap lower than their true skill level and believes it occurs more often with women than men. Two celebrity golfers highlighted the issue of vanity handicaps in early 2006.

Golf Digest published a list of Hollywood's top 100 golfers in December 2005. The magazine listed everyone by handicap, ranking actor Dennis Quaid first and comedian Tom Dreesen third (tied with Matt Craven). Shortly thereafter, while on the *David Letterman Show*, Dreesen claimed Quaid wasn't that good. He even challenged Quaid to a round at $500 a hole to prove it.

The pairing director at the 2006 AT&T Pro-Am showed a sense of humor when he put Quaid and Dreesen together in the same foursome. Quaid played with a 2; Dreesen, a 5. Quaid didn't take the wager, but Dreesen said he beat Quaid by four strokes during the Saturday round, 80 to 84.

—•—

Most of the betting, and none of the cheating, on the PGA Tour happens during practice rounds each week. This custom reflects the game's heritage and further identifies the healthy role a gentlemanly wager has in the sport.

Steve Jones won the 1996 U.S. Open by one shot over Davis Love III and Tom Lehman. He tried to calm his nerves during the final round by talking to himself. "Hey, just play the best you can. Just act like you are out here Tuesday." Jones said that worked because he had played well earlier in the week during a practice round. He and Jeff Maggert had beaten Mickelson and Lee Janzen 1-up.

"We had a little bet going, and it kind of pumped me up," Jones said afterward. Maggert agreed, telling his caddie after the early week round Steve would be tough on Sunday.

Jones also said the previous time he had played a money game during a practice round, he had also won the tournament, the 1988 AT&T Pro-Am. "I played with Tom Watson at Cypress Point against three amateurs: Sandy Tatum, Robert Trent Jones, Jr., and one other guy," Jones recalled. "Tom and I ended up winning that day, and we won a few dollars. They actually paid."

"So now, I think I know what route to take," Jones said after the Open win. "I need some Tuesday games."

Most PGA Tour pros share Steve's understanding of the value of playing for a little something during practice rounds. For some, $5 or $10 will help focus their preparation while others need at least a $100 Nassau to help concentrate. It is a long-standing custom on the tour for players to bet among themselves before the tournament starts. Today's wagering varies some from the action 40 or 50 years ago, however. Three major forces influence betting and talking about it: more prize money, sponsor and tour sensitivities, and the younger players' upbringing.

"Back in the old days when purses weren't so big, a player wanted to make $100 in practice rounds to get him through the week," recalled Dave Hill. He said the custom was not for everyone. "Some guys get so nervous playing for their own money, the greens don't need fertilizing for a year. I never have a great sense of loss if I miss out on a $30,000 winner's check," Hill said in 1977, "as if I blow 100 bucks out of my own pocket."

Jerry Barber is an example of a player who used money matches to learn from the better golfers. Many thought the 1961 PGA champion was too stubborn in overmatching himself in practice rounds, and he frequently lost his bets. "We were gambling pretty hard," Doug Ford said of the diminutive but feisty Barber, "and he was always on the opposite side taking a bath. I asked him why he wanted to keep losing money, and he said, 'You have to pay to go to the university.'"

Some players today bet less than previous generations in reaction to the tour's gambling policy, or at least they are more discreet. Others fear a backlash from sponsors. They are concerned that FootJoy or TaylorMade might cut their stipends if the companies discover a player was throwing away the money by "gambling." One successful tour pro asked a writer to skip a story of winning $3,000 on a practice round, citing a sponsor's possible negative reaction. "Let me give you another about a $20 Nassau," he said.

Now players earn their way onto the PGA Tour by honing their games in college and the pressure-packed Nationwide Tour. They no longer engage in apprentice money games in the caddie yard or in games between hungry club pros at dusty Midwest tracks. As early as the 1980s, Raymond Floyd noticed the difference in the younger generation. "When we were growing up, if you couldn't play for money, you weren't going to beat anybody in a tournament. It was probably as good a training as college is today." Still, the younger set's declining interest in betting has baffled Floyd. "I go out on a tee for a practice round with three boys, and they don't want to play for two bucks or five bucks."

Jim Furyk defies Floyd's generalization. He was a college All-American but sharpened his betting acumen on the Nationwide Tour. In late 2005, Furyk described his money games with David Duval when the two of them were new to the Nationwide. "There were two older players, in their 30s, looking for games on Tuesdays. They paired David and me together, thinking, 'Yeah, we'll take these young guys.' Well, we smoked them seven or eight straight weeks. We never lost, and we were making more money gambling than during the week." Furyk said winning $800 on Tuesday helped since his first Nationwide check was only $150. "It was fun playing against older and more experienced players." There's nothing new in golf.

Tournament preparation is not the only goal during practice rounds. When the players talk about their Tuesday games, it is clear they enjoy themselves. Those are the only fun rounds during the week. Many think the pro-ams are akin to a teeth cleaning, and everyone grinds away during the actual tournament. The practice round is more like our Saturday morning foursome with some yuks, needling, and a gentlemanly wager. Winner buys. It's just regular golf.

The best stories about betting on practice rounds come from the Masters and the British Open. Augusta National's heritage has always included betting on golf. That is clear from Alister Mackenzie's 19th hole, Bobby Jones's fondness for a gentlemanly wager, the Calcutta, and the great tales from Gene Sarazen, Snead, Palmer, Nicklaus, and Woods. British golf is downright founded on the friendly wager. Plus, the betting mood in the United Kingdom is as pervasive as the wind and the gorse at its seaside venues.

The veteran players and former champions enjoy getting together for practice rounds at Augusta National. They also extend invitations to the younger set, especially those playing for the first time, both amateur and professional. Just as Nicklaus and Palmer welcomed Woods, the two old pros invited two Rhode Islanders, Brad Faxon and Billy Andrade, to join them in 1998.

The tournament that year honored Jack for his 40th Masters' appearance and Palmer for the 40th anniversary of his first win. "They received standing ovations on every tee and every green," Faxon said at the time. "It was pretty special. I've played with each of them but never with both at the same time."

Faxon went on to explain how the two legends took advantage of their special status during the practice round. "They let us know that if they won, they'd collect," Faxon said. "If they lost, they said they're not paying. It's as much fun as I ever had in a practice round. We played nine holes and threw seven birdies at them."

Real estate investor and developer Ken Bakst won the 1997 Mid-Amateur, earning an invitation to the Masters the following year. Through good luck and the kindness of Palmer and Nicklaus, he arranged a Tuesday practice round with the two stars. "Fred Funk and I played a $10 Nassau five ways with them," Bakst said. "We won, but no money changed hands. And I wasn't about to ask them for it."

Tim Herron, a four-time tour winner, first played at the Masters in 1996. He joined rookie David Duval for a practice round against Palmer and Zoeller, another former winner. Despite Duval's money match experience on the Nationwide Tour, the youngsters had no chance. "I don't want to say how much we played for," Herron wrote in a diary he kept for his hometown newspaper. "When I gave Fuzzy the check, I put 'Masters Lesson' down in the corner of the check."

By 1998, Herron had a reputation for enjoying playing for challenging stakes. He and Daly teamed to play Mickelson and John Huston. "There was a pretty good amount going," Huston said, "and they doubled the bet on the last hole. They both hit it close, but I holed it out from the fairway for a 2." The next day, Mickelson and Huston played Duval and Daly. Phil made an eagle and three birdies, and he and Huston shot a better-ball 28 on the back nine. One version concerning the money involved has Huston winning a total of $15,000 on the two matches. Another suggests Mickelson won $27,000 over the two days. Either way, the bets were a smidgen higher than the usual practice round wagers at the Masters.

Huston told the news media after the matches he was surprised more players did not want to take on higher stakes, considering the huge amounts of prize money everyone was earning each week. "I think it's the best preparation," Huston said of practice round betting. "It's definitely better than hitting it out of a bunker 100 times."

In 1999, Duval had hit his stride on the tour. He won four tournaments before the Masters and gained the number one ranking in the world that year. He and the money-wise Huston hooked up for a practice round for a $100 Nassau. Duval ran into a Lanny Wadkins–like Tuesday performance from Huston when John shot a 29 on the back nine for a 62. Huston won 10 ways against Duval.

Both the players and the gallery enjoy betting during the par-3 tournament. The club built the nine-hole layout in 1958 and started the tournament in 1960. The course measures 1,060 yards and the course record is 20, shot by both Art Wall and Gay Brewer. It is a perfect event for the friendly wager—no television coverage, knowledgeable fans, and an informal atmosphere.

Sportswriter John Strege reported a match between Palmer and Zoeller during a par-3 tournament. One of their bets was a $1,000 whip-out for a hole-in-one, not a rare occurrence in the event. When Fuzzy aced the final hole, Arnie pulled out his roll and handed Zoeller ten $100 bills as if he were dropping a penny in the ocean.

A few years earlier, Wadkins and Blaine McCallister played in the par-3 tournament, betting $100 for a hole in one. Wadkins hit his tee shot over the green and into the water on eight. He reloaded and made an ace with his second ball. McCallister refused to pay up, saying, "I don't count mulligans."

The crowd loves these sideshows during practice rounds. In one of his frustrating appearances at the Masters, Trevino, who didn't think his game fit the course, started another Masters tradition of skipping balls across the pond at the par-3 16th. When he reached the hole, he noticed the pond between the tee and the green was as smooth as glass. For fun, he intentionally bounced his ball across the water. "That baby took three skips and ran up in the middle of the green, and I 2-putted for par," he said later. Since then, skipping balls on the pond has been a staple of practice rounds at the Masters. It's safe to say it has generated a few bets between not only the players but also the fans.

The gallery at the hole goads the players into doing something fun to watch. "It could get a little boring just seeing guys hit it on the green," Singh said. "I think it's exciting." Price said he "toes in" a long iron and plays a low hook. "That takes talent," remarked Price. "Vijay can do it. He probably practices it—he practices everything else."

In 2005, Els was standing over a putt on the practice green, and he heard one onlooker bet another $1 Els couldn't make it.

"I'll take some of that," Els said to the man. He proceeded to sink it and then collected his dollar.

The caddies at the Augusta National had a tradition of betting on "their man." The club required players to use local men, all African American, until 1983 when Cliff Roberts permitted the first "tour" caddies to work at the Masters. The regulars were a colorful lot, all with nicknames and stories about everything. Most were unknown to the public, with the exception of

Carl Jackson, who comforted an emotional Ben Crenshaw after his second win in 1995.

Ward Clayton tells about the group in his 2004 book, *Men on the Bag*. The old-timers worked hard to out caddie each other and didn't hesitate to back their player with a $3 bet during a round. Willie Peterson, who was on Nicklaus's bag for his five Masters wins, was the most aggressive bettor during the tournament.

"Bet ya my man, Mr. Jack, doesn't make a bogey today," Willie boasted in the caddie shack. "Anybody want some of that?" Many did, knowing what the course set-up could do to even the best golfers in the world. Willie also offered wagers on the number of birdies Nicklaus might make or that he would shoot 69. "That was a foolish bet there, to say his man would shoot in the 60s," said Bennie Hatcher, who started caddying at the club in the 1960s. "He'd bet four or five people and bet them $50 apiece. Nah, he never won. You don't make those kind of bets."

Jackson recalled those days and betting on players in an interview in 2006. He talked about the wagering between caddies and confirmed the Peterson stories, especially how Willie bet with Nathaniel "Iron Man" Avery, Palmer's regular. "He would bet his whole paycheck. He'd bet three grand or whatever, and Iron Man might have caught him on a couple of those bets. Iron Man thought Palmer was the world-beater and Willie felt like Jack was the world-beater, and Willie would bet any man in the caddie house."

Caddies have bet among themselves since they became part of the game in Scotland in the 1700s. An entertaining reversal of that betting role occurs every spring at the Tournament Players Championship. During the Wednesday practice round, players give their caddies a chance to hit onto the island green at 17. Daly started the custom in 1992 when he was playing with Zoeller and Hubie Green. Big John peeled off three $100 bills, pegged them to the ground with tees, and said to the caddies, "I bet you guys can't hit the green." Daly's caddie, Greg Rita, was the only one to hit dry land and picked up the cash.

Tournament officials now place a large jar at the 17 tee, which all the pros fill with greenbacks. The tour contributes a $1,200 Omega watch to the pot, and the caddie closest to the pin takes all. In 2004, 57 of 112 caddies hit the green, with Stephen Ames's brother and caddie, Robert, winning with a shot that was four feet and eight inches from the cup. Robert only took home $1,000 and the watch that year, however. The caddies donated the remainder of the pool—$8,120—to amyotrophic lateral sclerosis

In a practice round before the 1992 Tournament Players Championship, John Daly bet the three caddies in his pairing that they couldn't hit the famous 17th island green at Sawgrass. Since then, caddies take a swing during every Wednesday round. The players stuff money into a large jar, with the caddie closest to the pin winning the pot. Also, the PGA Tour donates a new Omega watch to the winner. MICHAEL COHEN/WIREIMAGE.COM

(ALS) research in honor of Bruce Edwards, Tom Watson's longtime caddie. Edwards died of the disease two weeks after the tournament.

Also in 2004, while waiting for their caddies to hit, Mickelson turned to his playing partners, J. P. Hayes and Tiger, and challenged them to hit left handed to the green while he tried a right-handed swing. Tiger's practice swing looked like a mirror image of normal one, but he sliced his ball into the water. Hayes skulled one short. Mickelson, who does everything right handed except play golf, landed his ball on the green, but it skipped long into the water.

"The popular bet at the British Open is No Bogey [for] $1,000," Curtis Strange told the news media in 2002. "If you go 18 holes without a bogey, the other guys owe you $1,000. It's a difficult bet, because nobody can ever do it on links golf courses."

Watson introduced the game to his fellow players. In 1992 at Muirfield, Watson won £500 each from Wadkins, Couples, and Mark Calcavecchia, roughly a total of $2,700 at the time. He shot a 68, a remarkable score considering the wind was blowing up to 30 miles per hour that day.

"He didn't hit a green for six straight holes," Wadkins said, "but he made 8-footers to save par every time." Couples said Watson wasn't fazed by the others rooting against him.

A popular PGA Tour pro, who asked to remain anonymous, told of playing No Bogey for $1,000. The first player was out after bogeying number two, the second on 12, and the third on 14. "It was the most fun I remember having, those last four holes," he said, "the three of them rooting against me out loud, right to the point of contact. As soon as I hit my tee ball on 18, I offered them a buyout for $975. Nobody took it. I made my par, and they all paid me $1,000. It took a while, but I got a check from every one of them. Somebody's wife wasn't too happy, though."

In 1997, Couples, Love, Justin Leonard, and Tom Kite gave it a go. The wind at Troon was blowing so hard they confidently upped the stakes to $1 million. Couples was the last to stay bogey-free, but he only made it to the seventh hole. At Carnoustie two years later, Calcavecchia, Mickelson, and Billy Mayfair played for $2,000. Calcavecchia said he lasted the longest. "I made it through 10 holes without a bogey. Then I made about six after that."

Calcavecchia is a throwback to the old betting days on tour, and some say he might just skip the practice rounds if no one places a bet. "I need something to make me concentrate," he said. "I'd slop it around and waste my time." His favorite times were at Kapalua, where he organized the play before the old Kapalua International.

"Balls in the air at 7:00 a.m., and if you were late, it was a $100 fine," Calcavecchia said in 2000. "We'd play an eightsome, $100 automatic 1-downs, and half the time on the back nine you'd double up. I remember making a 12-footer on the 18th hole that was worth 6,200 bucks." He said it was a wild affair. "Each of us had our own cart and we're all hauling ass down the hill on the first hole, everybody playing everyone else, guys hitting at the same time. That was the ultimate."

Practice round betting also extends into the two major international team events, the Ryder Cup and Presidents Cup, but in an unusual way. Considering the golfing talent the U.S. team brings to the Ryder and Presidents Cup competitions, many observers have been disappointed with the Americans' uneven play in the past 20 years. Critics say the Yanks don't play well as a team, perhaps through a lack of team practice or because of the Lone Ranger mentality each player adopts on tour. The old hands, however, know the value of a money game in preparing for a tournament.

Before the 1993 Ryder Cup matches, Captain Watson encouraged his players to bet during the practice rounds. Team member Wadkins seconded that suggestion, asking Watson to direct everyone to play $50 Nassaus with automatic 1-down presses. "If a guy says it's against his religion, tell him to get another religion," said Mr. Tuesday.

At the 1996 Presidents Cup, the news media asked Captain Palmer about the relative inexperience of team members Steve Stricker and Mark Brooks. Arnold assured the reporters both men had plenty of experience playing money golf and reminded them such pressure can prepare a player for Cup matches. (Brooks went 0-3; Stricker, 2-2.)

The American side won the thrilling 1999 Ryder Cup at The Country Club in Brookline. Leonard's improbable 45-foot birdie putt sealed the deal, but his team's preparation before the competition didn't inspire too many bets on the U.S. team. On the final practice day, Mickelson and Woods quit after playing alternate shot on the front nine, forfeiting any game they had for the round with Lehman and Duval. On the other hand, four Europeans—Darren Clarke and Lee Westwood playing Jose Maria Olazabal and Miguel Angel Jimenez—had themselves a raucous match for $50 a hole.

Tiger Woods has not sparkled in team competition—10-13-2 in Ryder Cup and 10-9-1 in Presidents Cup through the fall of 2006. He has acknowledged the team's lack of preparation for these events. "You don't get a chance to practice for this at all," he said before the 2004 Ryder Cup matches. "The only thing you can do is probably play some money games with the guys on the team. That's about it."

Prior to the 1995 Ryder Cup, caddie Dan Stojak liked the odds given in Las Vegas for the European team. Stojak, who worked then for American team member Loren Roberts, perhaps understood better than anyone about the American team's lack of preparation. At any rate, word got around Stojak committed the ultimate caddie no-no and bet against his man. He reportedly wagered $1,000 at 3-1 odds that the other side would win, which they did 14 ½ -13 ½.

Roberts said later Stojak gave him three different versions of what happened, at varying times. First he said, "No, I didn't bet on it." Then, "well, yeah, I bet on it, but then I canceled the bet at the last minute." His last version was, "Oh, I sold my ticket. I did bet on it, but I sold my ticket to somebody else." Roberts also told the news media the story came out only after Stojak got into a fight with other American caddies in a bar that Sunday night after the loss. "I guess he was in the bar and started talking. 'Well, I still made money,' and that's how it all came out," said Roberts.

After winning three team matches—two four-ball and one foursome—Roberts lost on the final day to Sam Torrance. That point might have made the difference. Roberts wondered later if Stojak had led him astray, so he fired him; however, Roberts took him back the following year.

Golf Digest surveyed the U.S. players before the 2002 Ryder Cup at The Belfry in England about their feelings about the competition. The questions included one about betting: "You find out that a caddie for the American side has placed a significant (and legal) wager on the European team to win. What would you do?" They answered:

Fire him immediately	66%
Take him by the nape of the neck to the nearest betting parlor and demand that he bet the same amount on the Americans	17%
What kind of odds did he get?	17%

"In a tournament, only two people care about you," Trevino said in 1972, "your caddie and yourself. And if your caddie's betting against you, you're the only one."

—●—

"We always have to have something riding on it," Annika Sorenstam said of golf with Tiger. "I think the bets keep him motivated to beat me. For me, I think it's actually more the pride than anything. I always tell him: 'If I beat you, I can say it.'"

The foremost woman player in the world enjoys a friendly wager on the golf course. If she is betting with men, she asks no quarter. On the first tee for a practice round before the 2003 Colonial, she and her playing partner, PGA Tour regular Jesper Parnevik, were settling on a wager when he asked, "So, how many shots do you want?"

"I told him I'm not here to get any shots," Annika said. "And he didn't say much after that."

In 2004 Sorenstam played in a sixsome on the back nine of a practice round before an annual celebrity tournament, the American Century Championship at Lake Tahoe, Nevada. The group included Donald Trump, Michael Jordan, Ahmad Rashad, and two NBC TV executives. The men were well into several wagers when she joined them on 10.

"I came here to have fun," she told the news media afterward, "but I guess not—I came to the first tee and the bets were all going, they were asking for strokes, and they made me putt 2-footers, so I realized it was serious." Sorenstam easily held her own, shooting a 33. She wasn't sure how the matches turned out but said "I won my bets against M. J., so that's all that matters."

Annika started playing in the PGA Tour Skins Game in 2003. During the 2006 event, following the example of Marlene Bauer Hagge's "almost bet" on Mickey Wright's length in the 1960s, she bet opponent Fred Funk that she could outdrive him at some point. Funk is one of the shortest hitters on the tour, and he is the butt of such weak-shot jokes as "Hey, Mrs. Funk, did your club get caught in your dress?" On the third hole, Annika's 278-yard drive was seven paces past Fred's. The bet called for him to finish the hole wearing a skirt, so Sorenstam pulled from her bag a pink, floral number, knee-length, A-line.

Fred had trouble squatting down to read his putt, and Woods joked he could see up Funk's skirt. "I didn't realize how hard it is to line up a putt with a skirt on," he said, "especially when Tiger's looking from the other end."

The younger players on the LPGA Tour learn quickly about betting customs. Tour officials assign rookies to veteran players. Acting as big sisters, the older pros help the newbies adjust to tour life. Forty-five-year-old Julie Inkster advised 17-year-old Morgan Pressel when the teenager started her rookie year in 2006. At the Safeway International in Phoenix, Arizona, the two played a practice round together for $20, which Julie won. (She also won the tournament.) Asked later what she was learning from Inkster, Pressel said with a smile, "Pay your bets."

Natalie Gulbis joined the tour in 2002 as a 19-year-old. She set an LPGA record for the most money won in one year (2005) without winning a tournament. She is a competitive person who likes a small bet with her friends when practicing. Also at the Safeway tournament, she and Cristie Kerr had a closest-to-the-hole chipping contest, with the loser buying the other a pedicure.

Teenager Michelle Wie has wowed her adult competitors, both men and women, since she won the 2003 U.S. Amateur Women's Public Links

The late Payne Stewart lost his pants in a bet during a 1988 charity fundraiser. He posed afterward with Cindy Figg-Cuurier, who had slipped on his pants. During the 2005 Skins Game, Annika Sorenstam bet the short-hitting Fred Funk that she could outdrive him. She did on the third hole, and the loser had to finish the hole wearing a skirt. LEUKEMIA & LYMPHOMA SOCIETY OF DELAWARE; ASSOCIATED PRESS/WIDE WORLD PHOTOS

Championship. When she advanced to the quarterfinals in that tournament, which was held at Florida's Ocean Hammock Golf Club, she bet her father $300 she would win.

"My dad was like, 'That's way too much,'" she said. "He wanted it to be $100, but I stared him down, and we made it $300." Her father, B. J., told a slightly different version, saying it was shopping money for later in the summer. Michelle was ready for Inkster and her generation when the teenager turned pro in 2005.

In 2006, *Golf Digest* and *Golf for Women* published a survey of 2,262 men and 2,440 women amateur players that examined a variety of golf issues. The poll's purpose was to gauge how each gender responded to the questions. What do men do that annoys women and vice versa, for example. Etiquette and discrimination were other subjects. One of the questions was, "How often do you bet during a round?" The results follow.

	MEN (PERCENT)	WOMEN (PERCENT)
Always/frequently	35	17
Sometimes	28	26
Seldom	23	24
Never	14	33

At the professional level, it seems that men and women bet at about the same frequency, perhaps reflecting the common competitiveness that drove all of them to the top of their sport. At that level, men prefer larger bets, and they talk more about wagering. Winning wagers is like catching the largest fish or hitting the longest home run—a guy thing. The lower percentages among amateur women who bet may reflect the theory that women are less confrontational than men are. A wager certainly involves confrontation: "I bet I can beat you, and here's my $10. Where's yours?"

Money golf seems like the perfect setting for fiction writing. Two or three acts are common to any plot, just as in a $2 Nassau—the front and back nines and then the match. Tension rises and falls through the scenes, or holes, in each act. The dramatic climax falls near the end or at least on the 16th or 17th hole when two evenly matched golfers play. An anticlimatic point might arise if they bet on the bye holes. The characters have a chance to grow and change, especially as the pressure of the bets and the course's challenges wear on them. The characters feature bad guys, or cheaters, and good guys who honor the game by following the rules.

The game can even accommodate a proven literary device, a good "bad" guy. His character appears to speak the truth, but he always holds something back. His edge is not actual larceny but rather a canny insight into a golfer's mind. He's not bad if he shrewdly exposes his opponent's character flaws and then lets those frailties undermine the man's game. Moreover, his hustling skills balance his faults.

Author Lee Gruenfeld created Eddie Caminetti to fill the good bad guy role in the four golf novels he wrote between 1999 and 2004. Writing under the pen name Troon McAllister, he churned out *The Green* first. Then in rapid succession, he followed up with *The Foursome*, *Scratch*, and *Barranca*. A former computer consultant and partner at Deloitt & Touche turned novelist, Gruenfeld always introduces Eddie as a man intent on separating a player from his money. Caminetti then moves on to good deeds, succeeding through his perceptive, hustling wits. In *The Green*, the U.S. Ryder Cup captain names Eddie as one of his picks for the team and suffers the expected second-guessing from the news media. Caminetti inspires his teammates with unvarnished advice and leads them to a victory over the Europeans but not without the usual plot twist at the end.

Eddie turns psychologist in *The Foursome*. As the co-owner of Swithern Bairn, a private golf retreat on a tropical island, he advertises the ultimate in golf vacations. Four golfing buddies, each with a shameful secret, arrive to play Eddie and his team for big bucks. Caminetti takes their cash, but he helps them reconcile their problems through a 36-hole group encounter session.

Scratch has Eddie helping a mad scientist market a miracle golf ball, one that a slumping tour player, who used to be Eddie's caddie, hopes will rejuvenate his game. The friction caused by the new ball, Scratch, and established ball manufacturers led by Medalist (a little thin) takes the reader into the business side of golf. The plot is weak, but Gruenfeld's tongue-in-cheek skewering of PGA Tour event names is fun. The best is the "Nissan Prudential Fruit-of-the-Loom Texaco Waste Management (formerly the Valley View) Open." A close second is the "Verizon Aetna Hairstyles-by-Steffen Bob's Quickie-Lube (formerly Enron WorldCom Tyco Byron Nelson Classic)."

Gruenfeld may have lost some of his momentum by the time he got to *Barranca*. The U.S. president calls on Eddie to solve a Latin American coffee supply crisis by sending the hustler to play golf with the offending dictator, Manuel Villa Lobos de Barranca. Once a caddie to Fidel Castro and Che Guevara, Barranca ends up teaching Eddie a few lessons. You had to be there.

Another novelist entered the field in 2001. John Corrigan wrote *Cut Shot* that year, the first of four books through 2005 starring Jack Austin, amateur sleuth. A struggling PGA Tour player, Austin solves mysteries while trying to keep his tour card. The other books are *Snap Hook*, *Bad Lie*, and *Center Cut*. With more than 600 years of history, golf has a great supply of potential novel titles.

—●—

CHIPS AND PITCHES

Aces win. Many players on the Champions Tour participate in a weekly hole-in-one pool. Each kicks $100 into the pot, and if anyone makes an ace that week, he wins the money. "They don't want us to gamble out here," said Dana Quigley. "This isn't gambling, this is a reward."

It's not gambling. In 2005, South Korean prosecutors charged four golfers with gambling crimes, which carried potential two-year prison sentences. They had bet a total of 1.4 billion Korean won (US $1.3 million) over 18 months and 32 matches. A Seoul judge acquitted the golfers. "In gambling," he ruled, "luck plays a critical role to decide the game. In golf games, it is the players' competence, not luck, that decides the game."

Minus his plus fours. The late Payne Stewart played in the 1988 Leukemia Classic, a fund-raiser in Wilmington, Delaware. He was paired with three LPGA players: Cindy Figg-Currier, Deborah McHaffie, and Chris Johnson. He offered to play against their best ball and then asked what they wanted to bet. "Why don't we play for your knickers?" one suggested.

"That's fine," Stewart said. "My knickers against your shorts. Whoever loses takes them off on the 18th green and gives them to the winner." Payne lost 2-down, stripped to his skivvies, and posed for pictures. He quipped, "I'm glad my shirttail was long."

Pay up or Els'. During a 1999 recreational golf trip through Ireland with friends and family, Ernie Els and one of his playing partners kept a tab going on their bets. On the last hole of the last course, Ballybunion, Els, and fellow South African Johann Rupert had $8,500 riding on the outcome. "As far as my own money, it was by far the most I'd ever played for," Els told *Golf Digest* in 2006. "That's still the most nervous I've ever been on a golf course." Els won but let his friend off the hook because Rupert supplied the aircraft for the trip. "I'll tell you, it's a different feeling when you're playing for your own cash."

Playing for your own money, sorta. Former NFL quarterback Steve Bartkowski organized the 2005 Big Stakes Match Play Golf Championship. He wanted a tournament where the golfers played for their own money. Although 64 two-man teams competed for the $3 million first prize, only one team ponied up its own money. All the others had sponsors, so 62 players were still trying to make a putt for someone else's cash.

The two golfers who paid their own way were club pros from Utah, James Blair and Steve Schneiter. Both excellent golfers, each has played frequently in sectional PGA tournaments, and both earned their way into the PGA Championship through good finishes at the Club Pro

Championship. They made it to the Big Stakes semifinals and split $400,000, which included their $100,000 ante. "It was as good a shot that we were ever going to have," Blair said. Californian David Ping and South African Garth Mulroy won the $3 million. After paying their sponsors, the two winners took home $725,000 each.

In 2006, Bartkowski agreed to join with Las Vegas hotel mogul Steve Wynn to produce the follow-on to the Big Stakes event, the Ultimate Game at Wynn Las Vegas. They skipped a 2006 tournament and are planning for a June 2007 event at the Wynn Las Vegas Golf Course and Country Club.

Shades of Montague. Comedian Tom Dreesen, who thought actor Dennis Quaid's handicap was a vanity plate, discounted the pressure at the AT&T Pro-Am. He told *Golf World* magazine in 2006 money games at his club are the real test. He plays at Lakeside in Los Angeles, the site of Bing Crosby's match with Mysterious Montague. "We play skins," he said. "You get to the 18th hole and we are in an eightsome or a ninesome and all the skins are out and you have a [3-footer] and your knees are knocking. There might be $3,800 of your money riding on it, and those other seven guys, they're not wishing you well. They're putting the horns on you."

Special delivery. At the 2005 British Open, Darren Clarke and Davis Love III played a practice round in which Love won £100. Later in the week, Love used his Sharpie to write the sum on a golf ball, then took his wedge, and pitched it down the practice tee to where Clarke was hitting balls. Fast pay makes fast friends, as Mark O'Meara said.

One more Clarke story: "Darren has to be the world's best recreational golfer," said David Howell, a fellow European PGA Tour player, in 2006. "I had to cut down what we were betting because I was losing 300 or 400 quid a week."

9.

BETTING GAMES:

FEAR THE SNAKE, AVOID THE WOLF, CHASE THE RABBIT

MONEY GOLF IS NOT JUST ABOUT TIGER WOODS and Annika Sorenstam. Millions of other golfers around the world play for their own money. Many are just folks playing in the trenches of the game, golfers who are known only to their friends and families. A few pique the public interest or even attract the attention of the golf news media because of their off-course personalities. What virtually all players, including Tiger and Annika, have in common is their attitude toward money golf. Although a handful of those millions bet large amounts of money on their games, everyone else keeps money golf in the right perspective and the bets in their comfort zone.

The vast majority of players also realize betting on golf is not necessarily about the money but rather a part of the game. On a perfect day, you cheerfully accept the losers' money and then spend it all buying them lunch. The money stays at the golf course. And to be sure, the golfing gods won't let you win the next week. The game has a way of balancing winning and losing over time.

Any golf course will accommodate a gentlemanly wager on a match. Some have acquired reputations for being especially receptive, with the links at St Andrews and Musselburgh leading the way in the United Kingdom. In the States, many private venues—including The Country Club, Lakeville in Long Island and Lakeside in Hollywood, Seminole and La Gorce in Florida, Ben Hogan's Shady Oaks in Fort Worth, and Augusta National—have welcomed a friendly bet over the years. The favorite public tracks include Reilly's Pankapoag and Jenkins's Goat Hills, Lee Trevino's Tenison Park in Dallas, and Western Avenue in Los Angeles.

There is one place, however, where betting on golf fits like a new glove— El Paso Country Club. Just about everyone there plays golf for money, whether they're famous PGA Tour players, cotton farmers on a rare day off, young flat bellies, or aspiring assistant club pros. Golfers there play a variety of betting games, and a couple stories about money golf at the club provide a good introduction to the various games available to golf course bettors.

El Paso Country Club opened in 1906 and relocated at its present site in 1925. At 6,781 yards from the back tees, the sun-baked course is a relatively short par 71. It is enough of a test, however, to host the Western Refining College All-America Golf Classic. The annual 54-hole tournament attracts the best collegiate golfers, and past winners include Davis Love III, David Duval, and Woods.

Two weekly money golf events are highlights at the club, the Wednesday and Friday games. "They get the most attention," said head pro Mark Pelletier, "but people play for money everyday around here." The Wednesday games are more relaxed, but on Fridays, the superintendent cuts the cups in corners of the greens and sets the tee markers for the maximum yardage.

Good players abound at the club, with 100 men carrying single-digit handicaps; almost half of them have 5s or less. Joining them occasionally are PGA Tour winner and El Paso resident J. P. Hayes, local club pros, and LPGA Tour veteran Kristi Albers, who also lives in El Paso. The pro shop staff always participate in the games, but they can't bank on winning the money. "If you're playing out of the shop, and you shoot only 69 you're toast," said former head pro Cameron Doan, now at Preston Trail in Dallas.

Pelletier said the usual format is a two-man quota. Points are awarded for the better-ball score on each hole, much like the modified Stableford scoring system that rewards eagles and birdies. The winning team most accurately predicts its score for the round. Each of the 10 or so regular teams kicks in $10. In addition, there are payouts for anyone who shoots net par 71 or better, $10 bets on Wednesday for low medal ($20 on Friday), and a Big Team bet for low net and gross between foursomes. Players make plenty of side bets, and some foursomes will often play games like Wolf and Las Vegas among themselves. (Details follow, but the wolf can play alone or with a partner against the rest of the foursome, and Las Vegas is a four-ball game.) Pelletier added the club is very strict on handicaps to forestall sandbagging.

Rich Beem, the 2002 PGA Championship winner, started his journey to the PGA Tour at the club. He was an assistant pro at El Paso in 1997 and

1998, and he played in the weekly money games to hone his skills and prepare for the 1998 Q School, the PGA Tour Qualifying Tournament. Now a club member and an occasional player on Fridays, Beem earned his card on the first try and joined the tour in 1999.

With not much in his pocket compared to the members, Beem learned to play under pressure. One club regular talked Beem into a match for $100 a hole, pretty steep for an assistant making $350 a week. Another member bankrolled Beem, who went on to win $2,400 from all the bets in the game. But another time, Rich lost $500 to $600 playing Wolf. "We showed no compassion," John Butterworth said with a half smile. A fellow club member and Beem's accountant, Butterworth continued, "There were times when Rich lost two or three or $400. Maybe we'd say 'You can pay me later.' But he always had to pay."

Doan did not regard Beem's betting as inappropriate but rather as helpful in his golfing development. "Oh, I think it's a great story. It shows he thought he could get it done. That belief is by far the most important thing when it comes time for the nut cutting." Beem certainly believed in himself when he faced down Tiger to win the PGA in 2002.

—●—

Golf bettors can choose from plenty of games. Some are as simple and classic as Payne Stewart's swing. Others, to further stretch the metaphor, have as many moving parts as a hacker's triple-looped lunge. The list's length might be daunting to a beginner, but golfers have been inventing betting games for centuries. Actually, the following games are just the most common ones played. There are dozens of others as well as at least two variations for every one included here.

Because of the large number of possible games, prefacing the list with betting advice from golf betting gurus seems best. Their cautions and reminders will hopefully guide less experienced money golfers through the thickets of betting games. The experts who contributed material for the following categorized nuggets and proverbs form an eclectic group. Included are golf greats Sam Snead and Doug Sanders; Donald Trump; Dr. Richard Coop, a psychologist and mind coach to tour players; the editors of *Golf Digest*; gambler and gamesmanship consultant Gary Moore; golf writer Guy Yocum; and "Action" Al Williams.

Manners

- Always pay promptly.
- Be a good sport.
- If someone doesn't pay up, don't play with him again.

Negotiating the Bet

- Know ahead of time which bets you want to offer.
- If dealing with a first-tee betting artist, ask for more than you will accept.
- Don't make lock bets because you won't be very popular. Seek an edge, but don't get greedy.
- Bet with your head, not your pride.
- Avoid games with too many bets.

Bet Size

- If the winner buys after the round, make sure the bet will handle dinner and drinks.
- Don't try to raise the size of existing bets with reluctant bettors. Introduce new bets to raise the stakes.
- Don't play friends for a lot of money; they won't be friends long.
- Never wager to hurt a friend.
- Never bet outside your comfort zone.
- Never play for more than what's in your pocket. IOUs are lame.
- When playing your boss, keep the bet small. If you win, don't ask him for the money.
- If an opponent is having a bad day and not joking about it, don't needle him.
- Keep the size of the side bets to less than 20 percent of the overall bet.
- Be a gracious winner.

Presses

- Never give an opponent back-to-back double-or-nothing presses. Tell him, "Get out the way you got in."
- If you are aggressive, try for a bet when you can press any time.
- If your opponent declares a press on one of his stroke holes, decline it. Stupid is as stupid does.
- If you agree to a bet with an automatic 2-down press, make sure you have the edge in the match or, at worst, have enough money to cover the loss.

- Offer your opponent the chance to start 2-up instead of getting strokes on two holes. That way you can start a press on the first hole if you are playing automatic 2-downs.
- If playing poorly, lay off the presses.

Pressure
- Pay attention to how your regular opponents play the last three holes.
- Don't play anyone who has a backer for the stakes. He will feel less pressure.

Partners
- Pick the best player, and if you are playing away, pick a club member.
- Don't fight with your partner or apologize for a foozle. Always encourage a partner.
- If you are an aggressive player, pick a steady player, and vice versa.
- Pick up a partner who enjoys betting.

Cheating
- If you see someone break a rule, call it then, not back in the clubhouse or behind his back.
- Don't play with people who cheat regularly.

Gamesmanship
Dos
- If you outhit your opponent from the tee, pause by his ball as if it is yours. He will be deflated when he realizes that it's his.
- Let the other guy find his stray ball. He will lose his focus.
- Tell him you have never seen a backswing like that.
- Walk fast to your ball and act impatient as he catches up.
- Root for his ball even though it is clearly headed for the water.
- Ask "Who's away?" when it's clearly him.
- Praise your opponent after a few holes. "You're hitting it great, a lot better than a 14."

Don'ts
- Accept another man's bet. Modify it somehow, and make a counteroffer.
- Jangle coins, rip Velcro, zip zippers, or walk to the next tee when your

opponent is still putting.

- Remind an opponent about hazards or give swing advice.
- Make an opponent putt tap-ins.
- Show pleasure when he hits a bad shot.
- Question his handicap or argue over strokes.
- Wear a cowboy hat. It doesn't intimidate.

STRANGERS

- Don't trust a stranger to throw up the balls on the first tee. He might manipulate the toss and stick you with the load (poor player).
- Don't gamble with a stranger, and consider everyone a stranger until you've played with him at least a dozen times.

HUSTLERS

"Never bet anyone you meet on the first tee who has a deep suntan, a 1-iron in his bag, and squinty eyes," warned Dave Marr, the late PGA golfer and revered television announcer. In addition, Snead offered the following advice to those wishing to stay out of a hustler's grasp.

- Beware of anyone who simultaneously asks for fewer strokes and a larger bet.
- Unless you are impervious to pressure, resist unexpected side bets or do-or-die wagers on chips or putts; the edge usually favors those who offer the bet.
- Stick to simple bets, usually Nassaus. Too many bets can be distracting.
- Think twice about accepting a bet from a guy with a good suntan. Think again if there are three of them.
- If in doubt about a handicap, check the calluses on his hands.
- If you are caught in the middle of a hustle, cut your losses and go quietly.

—●—

For the completely uninitiated, you can keep score in a golf game several ways. Some betting games are best suited for one or another scoring method, so it's best to know the difference. The use of masculine pronouns in this section is not meant to slight women golfers; it just simplifies sentence structures.

SCORING

Medal. The lowest aggregate score for a prescribed number of holes wins the match, playing either gross or net with handicaps. If played net, players can compute scores hole by hole ("across the card") or on the differential handicap holes. (For example, if player A is a 15-handicap and B is a 20, then B gets strokes on the differential holes, which would be handicap holes one through five.) A match between two golfers is a *singles* game, played either gross or net. A *better-ball*, or *four-ball*, match is between two teams, either gross or net.

Match. The player or team winning the most holes wins the match. Play either gross or net.

Match and medal. Play only one game but with separate bets for each method of scoring.

Foursomes. (*alternate shot, Scotch, modified Scotch*) Play is by teams only, with team members alternating driving, one on odd holes, the other on even, and then playing alternate shots until holing out. In a modified version, both drive and then pick which ball to start the alternate-shot sequence. (Also called "greensomes.") Scoring in tournaments is usually medal, but match play is most commonly played between two teams.

Stableford. Players accumulate points for specific scores on each hole, and the winner accumulates the most points. This system is for medal play events. The original Stableford scheme recognized bogey as the standard score and granted zero points for double bogey, one for bogey, two for par, three for birdie, and four for eagle or better. The modified Stableford system is the most common today. Doubles or worse yield a minus three points; bogey, minus one; par, zero; birdie, two points; eagle, five; and double eagle, eight.

Bisques. In either medal or match play, each player takes his handicap strokes whenever he wants rather than on specified holes. A 12-handicap gets 12 bisques, and he can take all 12 on one hole or one at a time on any hole of his choosing. The player must announce on the tee if he is playing a bisque.

No Alibis. (Also *Criers and Whiners*) Instead of applying normal handicaps, each player can use a number of mulligans equal to three-quarters of his handicap. This game is played gross only.

Three against four. A game for seven players, three play better ball against four. The group of three starts 2-up to compensate for the missing player.

COMPLETE ROUND BETTING GAMES, CLASSIC

These are the oldest and least tricky for an 18-hole round. Play them either gross or net and in either singles or four-ball games, unless noted. Players should always set the bet's value before starting the match, especially for games where the bets grow in number or size through the round. A push means neither side wins, as in a halve or tie.

Chicago. (Or Quota). Played gross (after handicap adjustment) and medal, one or more groups can play the game. Players (or teams) ante an agreed amount into the pot, and each player gets a quota of points equaling 39 minus his handicap. A 10 has a quota of 29 points; a 20 gets 19. Thereafter, players earn points for specific gross scores: one for bogey, two for par, four for birdie, and eight for eagle or better. The player who exceeds his point quota by the most points wins the pot. If no one does, the player closest to the quota wins. Some play Chicago within other games.

Low Ball. (Also $1 a hole, or $10, or whatever). This straightforward game is for singles, four-ball, or foursomes play. Players first set the bet for each hole, with the low or better ball winning the wager for each hole. The payout is on the differential of holes won between sides at the end of the round. (If player A wins five holes and B three, and they halve ten, then B pays A two betting units.)

Low ball and low total. This four-ball match play game awards one point on each hole for the low better-ball score and another for the low team total. Ties don't carry over, and the payout is based on point differentials between teams.

Nassau. This is normally a match play bet. Golfers can, however, play it medal by scoring each nine separately. Played either in a singles or four-ball game, there is one bet on the front nine, a second for the back, and a third for the match—that is, $2, $2, and $2. A *press* adds another bet for the remainder of the nine. Players must agree at the start that a player can decline a called press or that it is automatic when one side is either one or two strokes down for the nine. *Variations*: *Four ways* stipulates one bet unit on the front, two bet units on back, and one unit on match. (Four ways can also mean one bet on each nine and two on the match.) *Six ways* involves one bet on the front, two on the back, and three on the match. Double or nothing presses on the last hole often have their own names—*Aloha*, *Titanic*, and *Get-Even*, for example.

Robbins (Sixes, Round Robins). A game for a group of four, Robbins requires players to change partners every six holes. Toss balls to pick the teams on the first hole. The individual who wins the most holes after playing on three teams wins the bet. Medal play, gross or net.

Skins. This old match play game is for two, three, four, or and even eight golfers. Players set the value of the skin in the beginning, and whoever wins a hole wins a skin. If two tie on the hole, all tie, and the skin carries over to the next hole. A 2006 *Golf Digest* survey indicated that 39 percent of the respondents claimed skins to be their standard game, while 32 percent favored a Nassau.

Wheel. Usually a fivesome game, one two-man team, players A and B, form the wheel. The game matches the wheel against each of the other teams in the group: CD, CE, and DE. Scoring is by net better ball for each match between the four teams. Wheel is usually a Nassau, but players can use other bets. Better bring your A game if you are the wheel. *Variation:* One player is the wheel alone. Play up to an eightsome if you've got the game and deep pockets.

COMPLETE ROUND GAMES, TRICKED UP

Bobby Jones. Each golfer plays his second shot from the location of his opponent's tee shot. The bet is usually a Nassau, but other wagers will do.

Bridge. In this four-ball game, the team with the honor bids what it will score on that hole. If both team members think they can par the hole, their bid would be eight on a par-4. The other team can call the bid or call and double the bet. The bidding team can redouble, just as in the card game. If the bidding team matches its bid, the opponents pay one betting unit; if the bidders score one shot lower, the bet doubles. *Variation:* Use limited bids—1-over par for the team with a combined handicap of 19, 2-over for handicaps between 20 and 29, and 3-over for 30 and greater. Play as a side bet, also.

Chairman. A game for groups of three, the first player to win a hole becomes the chairman. He loses the chair after losing a hole, with ties carrying over. If the chairman wins the hole, he wins a point. The payout is on the points differential between players.

Choose 'em. Another game for three, the designated player rotates each hole. After all players drive, the designee chooses a partner to play better ball against the third for that hole. The payout varies with the agreed-on bet.

Fairways and Greens. Players set the value of a point on the first tee. Then they win one point for each fairway hit and another for each green in regulation. Birdies or better earn two points, usually on par-4s and 5s only. The point differential at the end determines the payout.

Instant replay. Play is gross only, with each player getting a number of "do overs" equal to his handicap. Use a Nassau or another bet.

Lakewood golf. The game permits distractions, short of touching a player or his ball, when any player is hitting a shot.

Nines (also Nine point). In this game for three, each hole is worth nine points. The winner of a hole gets five points; second, three points; and last, one point. If two tie for the low score, divide the points four-four-one; if two tie for the worst score, divide five-two-two. If all three tie, then divide the points three-three-three. Pay on the points' differential at end.

Pick up sticks. Usually a match play singles game, the winner of each hole takes one of the loser's clubs out of play. To return a club to play, the opponent must win a hole. Use half handicaps or gross between evenly matched players, and play a Nassau.

Rabbit. Each player in a group of three or four players antes an agreed amount to the pot. The first player to win four holes (four rabbit legs) outright wins the pot. Halved holes are pushes with no carryover. Play either gross or net. *Variation:* The rabbit is "loose" on the first hole. The first player to win a hole outright holds the rabbit. Lose a hole, lose the rabbit. Whoever holds the rabbit on nine and 18, wins the bets for each nine.

Six, Six, Six. A four-ball game, teams play better ball for the first six holes, foursomes (alternate shot) on the second six, and team aggregate on the last. They place one bet on each six and then another for the match.

Sixteens. Similar to *Nines* and *Twelves,* the winner of a hole gets seven points; second place, five points; the next, three; and last, one. For ties, add the number of points for those places and then divide the total by the number of tied players. A game for four players.

String. Each player starts with a length of string, say 12 feet, or a length scaled to handicaps. Each player can use a portion of the string to move a ball any length, be it two inches or two feet, until the string is gone. Carry scissors to trim the string after each use, but don't run with them.

You can use this game also as a side bet within another game. *Variation:* Use for putts only. Need a 3-footer? Cut off three feet of string.

Twelves. In this game for four players, the winner of the hole gets six points; the next place, four; next, two; and last, zero. If two players tie for the low score, allocate the points five-five-two-zero; if three tie, four-four-four-zero; all tie, three-three-three-three. If two players tie for highest score, divide the points five-five-one-one; if three tie, six-two-two-two.

Vegas. In this four-ball game, each team creates a two-digit number from the scores of its members on each hole. The low score on the team is always the first digit. If the players on team A shoot a three and a five, for instance, their score for the hole is 35. Team B has a three and a four, yielding a 34. Team B wins one point after subtracting its 34 from their opponent's 35. If one player shoots 10 or more, reverse the order of scores; so a 10 and a five become 105 instead of 510. A birdie flips the opponent's score (or *flippin' the bird*). If team A has a birdie two and a four, their score is 24. Team B's 34 flips to 43, earning 19 points for team A (43 minus 24). This game is for high rollers.

Weekender. (courtesy of *Golf Digest's* David Owen) Multiple groups of four play this game at net best ball. Draw teams from a hat, and have each team contribute $10 to the pot. Half the pot goes to the winning team and half to the skins winners. Divide the skins' portion by the total number of skins won that day. (Be sure to carry over all skins from halved holes.) Mulligans on the first tee, no side bets, and no gimmes. Strokes are given off the lowest handicap—that is, subtract the lowest handicap from everyone's handicaps to determine the resulting handicaps. Players get no more than one stroke on each hole and no strokes on par-3s. Play off ties on the putting green with creative tie-breaking rules—for example, throw or kick the ball or putt with your eyes closed. In 2006, Owen wrote his group prints their own scorecards with extra spaces for all the bets, just like the gang at Palmer's Bay Hill club. The card also lists the group's local rules—one extra stroke for wearing shorts after November 1, a guy named Harry isn't allowed to keep score, and no one gets strokes on par-3s.

Wolf. (Also Pig, Captain, Hawk) In this game for a group of four, each player is the wolf on every fourth hole. (Flip for wolf on the first tee.) The player losing the most bets through 16 is the wolf on 17 and 18. The wolf picks a partner on each hole, but he can make his pick at various times: before everyone hits their drives; after the wolf hits his drive, but before the others do; before the wolf's selected partner drives; or after all drives. *Variation:* The lone wolf picks no one, and then plays against the other's best ball at double the bet. If the wolf declares he is playing alone, the bet triples.

Side Bets (Trash, Garbage)

These bets can accompany any full round betting game. Players should set the betting unit's value at the start of the round, but spontaneous betting amounts are not completely unwelcome. Losers pay one betting unit to the winner, unless otherwise noted.

Arnies. (Also *Sevies*) The winner must score par or better on a hole without being in the fairway (par-4s and 5s only).

Barkies. (*Woodies*) Par a hole after hitting any part of a tree. *Double Barkies* for hitting two trees, and it doubles the bet.

Bingo, Bango, Bongo. (*Bingle, Bangle, Bungle* and other similar alliterations). There are three bets or points on each hole: Bingo—first on green, no matter how many strokes; Bango—closest to hole after everyone is on the green; and Bongo—first to hole out, regardless of score. *Variation*: Bingo—first on the green in the fewest strokes; Bango—same; and Bongo—lowest net score on the hole. Payout is on point differentials at the end of the round. Match or medal play.

Birdies. A birdie (or better) wins a bet. The 2006 *Golf Digest* poll showed the favorite side bet is for birdies.

Bogey. The first player with a bogey is the Bogeyman until another player bogeys a hole. (If two or more bogey the hole, the first in the hole breaks the tie.) The Bogeyman pays each opponent one bet unit after his bogey and each hole thereafter until another player becomes bogeyman. Ties push. *Variations*: The Bogeyman owes double to an opponent who birdies a hole. The Bogeyman then owes double the bet on succeeding holes until another player bogeys.

Boo! (**Noonan!**) The higher handicap player gets an agreed number of times during a round that he can yell "Boo!" or "Noonan!" during his opponent's swing. (*Hint:* Noonan was a character in *Caddyshack.*)

Chuck wagon. Whoever loses the hole before the snack bar buys.

Crenshaws. Making par with one putt.

Disasters (Bong). Players earn points for bad shots: out of bounds, in a hazard, lost ball, out of a bunker and into another, 3-putt, whiff, and others. Opponents pay the player with fewest disaster points.

Do-or-Don'ts. This one is a basic call bet—such as "I bet that you can't get up and down"—for any sticky situation.

Flaggies. Tee shot on par-3 within the length of the flagstick to the hole.

Froggies. Scoring a par after skipping a shot across water.

Greenies. (*Bobs, Blue-plate specials*) The player closest to the pin on par-3s wins the bet or half if it is team play. Ties carry over. *Variations:* If no one shoots a par, the bet is returned. If a player birdies, the bet doubles. If one player wins all Greenies, the bet is doubled for a *Carpet.* If there are Greenies on every hole, then the player with most Greenies but fewest strokes wins the bet.

Hammer. This bet usually happens in a singles game, with a low-ball bet on each hole. Player A hammers B when B appears to be in trouble or when A is in good shape after a shot. If B rejects the Hammer, play continues for the original bet. If B accepts, the bet doubles, and the Hammer passes to B after the shot. If B hammers A on the next shot, the bet quadruples. The Hammer must be accepted or rejected immediately and before the next shot. *Variation:* In *Air Hammer,* Player A must call a Hammer when the ball is in the air, either his or B's, and B must accept or decline before it hits the ground.

Hogans. A player wins a bet for shooting par or better with the ball always in the fairway (par-4s and 5s only). The winner must reach the green in regulation to qualify. This side bet is a version of Fairways and Greens.

Honest John. Each player writes out his predicted score and then gives the slips to the pro shop. The player with the score closest to his prediction wins the pot. A double bogey or higher on 17 and 18 disqualifies a player. This stipulation prohibits padding the score to meet a prediction. (If a player predicts a score way over his handicap and then shoots it, don't play with him again.)

Jacks. (*Nicklauses*) The longest drive wins on par-4s and 5s. In a variation a player must par the hole to win.

Leslie Nielsen's Specials. Comedian Nielsen offered these side bets in his *Stupid Little Golf Book.*

- *Weenies*—shortest drive

- *Whoopsies*—ball closest to the center of the adjacent fairway
- *Topsies*—shortest fairway wood shot
- *Turfies*—biggest divot
- *Obies*—ball farthest out-of-bounds
- *Washies*—first to the ball washer

Moles. If your ball is still in the bunker after one shot, you pay your opponents. After two shots, you pay double.

Municipals. Parring a hole from an adjacent fairway.

Murphy. A player wins the bet if he calls a Murphy on himself and then gets up and down from off the green. If he fails, he pays his opponents. *Variation:* If an opponent calls Murphy after a shot, the player must play it again. The number of allowed Murphies per round equals the handicap differential between players.

One-hole press. The press expires on the hole it's made rather than after the nine. It's similar to the Hammer.

Oozle-Foozle. The player who hits the green and is closest to the hole wins the *Oozle* bet. If he then 3-putts, he forfeits the Oozle bet and pays opponents the *Foozle* bet.

Pavins. The bet calls for making par with the shortest drive.

Putts by the yard. Players set a value for a yard of putting before the match. Opponents pay the player who sinks the longest total yardage of his putts during a round. One pace is about a yard. *Note:* Don't step on someone's line when you pace off the putts.

Sandies (Omars, Gritties). Any player who gets up and down from a green-side bunker wins the bet. *Variations:* A *Super Sandie* doubles the bet if a player pars from a fairway bunker. An *Exotic Sandie* quadruples the bet for a par via both fairway and green-side bunkers.

Scruffies. A player can elect to call a Scruffy on himself after a horrible tee shot. If he pars the hole, he wins the bet. He pays for bogeys or worse. A birdie doubles the bet. Opponents must first agree the shot was bad enough to qualify for a Scruffy.

Splashies. (also *Titanics, Whalies,* and *Fishies*) The bet covers making par after hitting a ball into the water.

Snake. The first player to 3-putt gets the snake and pays the bet. He passes it on to the next player who 3-putts. The Snake holder keeps paying others until someone else 3-putts. The holder of the Snake on nine and

18 pays the agreed-on amount to the others. *Variation:* The bet doubles after each Snake.

Snakes. The last player on a hole to 3-putt pays each opponent. *Variation:* Every 3-putt pays.

Thirty-twos. Player A bets Player B that B will 3-putt; B can accept or decline bet.

If B accepts and 3-putts, he owes A two bet units. If B 1 or 2-putts, B wins three bet units from A, hence the name Thirty-two. *Variations:* On tough holes, make the bet for fairways and greens. With a *Paul Bunyan*, a player calls a Thirty-two when on the tee facing a narrow, tree-lined fairway. *Lawrence of Arabia*: Bet an opponent he can't avoid a bunker, say on a long par-3. *Davy Jones*: Can't avoid a water hazard.

Total putts. The player with the fewest putts during the round wins the bet.

Umbrella. This is a four-ball game with six points available on each hole. One point is awarded for the ball closest to the hole in regulation, one for the low score, one for the fewest putts, and one for a birdie. The last two points go to the low team's score. If one team wins all six points, the bet doubles.

Watsons. (*Ferrets*) Chip-ins from off the green, regardless of the score on the hole. In a Super Ferret, a player holes a bunker shot, and the bet doubles.

Yardages. (*By the yard*) Each player wins points for the length in yards of the holes he wins (390 points for a 390-yard hole). Losers pay on the point differential after each nine. Try to keep the point's value low—that is, 5¢ or so—because these points add up fast.

PUTTING GREEN GAMES

Eleven. Five points for holing a putt and one point for closest to the hole. The winner must total 11 points exactly. If a player exceeds 11, he must start over.

Horse. Just as with the basketball game, a player hits to the hole of his choice. If his opponent can't equal or get closer, the first gets an H. If his opponent does better, he has the honor and gets to pick hole. The first player to spell *horse* wins the game.

Low putts. Gross score, nine or 18 holes. Rotate who selects the hole, and no gimmes.

Pullbacks. First, set a value of the bet for the overall game as well as determine whose putter will be used for the pullback distance. If Player A leaves a putt short, he must pull it back from the hole, using the designated putter, before hitting his next putt. He also pays player B one betting unit outside the regular per-hole bet.

Seven points (Seven up). This game is for two to eight players, and the winner is the first to seven points. Anyone who sinks a putt when all others miss gains two points. One point goes to the player closest to the hole when no one else makes the putt. A three-jack loses three points. The honor on each hole goes to the highest point winner on the previous hole. Play stymies, and if two tie, all tie, except when someone 3-putts.

Three Points. One putt per player per hole. Players win one point for closest to the hole, two points for closest to the hole and past the cup, and three points for holing a putt. Play for any number of holes.

—●—

CHIPS AND PITCHES

Pressure putting, part 1. NBC TV teamed with the Sports Psychology Lab at Arizona State University to examine who chokes under pressure. Lab technicians measured the heart rate, brain activity, and anxiety of 10 mid- to high-handicap amateur golfers in three situations. In the first, they had to hit 20 putts, all five feet with no break, and in the second, they had to hit the same putts with NBC cameras running. In the third situation, golfers hit the same putts on camera but with a bet on the outcome. If they exceeded the number of the putts that they sank in the first stage, NBC would give them $300. If they did worse, they had to pay $100. All of their heart rates doubled from stage one to three, and all had the same anxiety levels. Five won the bet, and five lost. The brain activity of the better putters was greater and more widespread, suggesting to the researchers the winners processed information better under pressure.

Pressure putting, part 2. NBC TV golf analyst Johnny Miller thinks choking is part of the game. Criticized by some PGA Tour players for his unvarnished assessments of their gagging on Sundays, Miller contends handling the pressure with money on the line is the game's most interesting part. "When you have a $2 Nassau with six presses going, and you've got a 3-footer in front of the clubhouse with everyone watching, it's all about whether you can make that putt. That is why golf is a great game."

Side bets. Several clubs offer their members a chance for a side bet during their weekend rounds. At the Golf Club at Eagle Mountain near Phoenix, players can bet $50 of their own money that they can hit the green on a designated par-3. If they do, they win $100 of merchandise in the pro shop. Wichita Country Club in Kansas has done the same, reportedly leading to increased golf club sales, lesson bookings, and shop revenue.

Retired CBS TV producer Frank Chirkinian co-owns the private Emerald Dunes Golf Club in West Palm Beach, Florida. Twenty-two-year PGA Tour veteran and Director of golf Lee Rinker installed a practice mat on the clubhouse's back porch, which overlooks the 18th green. His staff encourages members to try the 84-yard shot to the green for $20 a pop. Closest to the hole wins the pot.

SELECTED BIBLIOGRAPHY

FOR INTERESTED READERS, listed below are particularly valuable sources on golf's unique relationship with betting. Private sources, such as author interviews and unpublished materials are not included because they are not available for public use.

BOOKS

Barkow, Al. *Getting' to the Dance Floor: An Oral History of American Golf.* Short Hills, NJ: Buford Books, 1986.

———. *The Golden Era of Golf: How America Rose to Dominate the Old Scots Game.* New York: Thomas Dunne Books, 2006.

———. *Golf's Golden Grind: The History of the Tour.* New York: Harcourt Brace Jovanovich, 1974.

———. *The History of The PGA Tour.* New York: Doubleday, 1989.

Brown, Cal. *Masters Memories.* Chelsea, MI: Sleeping Bear Press, 1998.

Browning, Robert. *A History of Golf: The Royal and Ancient Game.* London: A & C Black, 1955.

Burnett, Jim. *Tee Times: On the Road With the Ladies Professional Golf Tour.* New York: Scribner, 1997.

Callahan, Tom. *In Search of Tiger: A Journey Through Golf With Tiger Woods.* New York: Crown, 2003

Campbell, Shepherd, and Peter Landau. *Presidential Lies: The Illustrated History of White House Golf.* New York: Macmillan, 1996.

Chew, Robert Z., and David D. Pavoni. *Golf in Hollywood: Where the Stars Come out to Play.* Los Angeles: Angel City, 1998.

Clavin, Tom. *Sir Walter: Walter Hagen and the Invention of Professional Golf.* New York: Simon & Schuster, 2005.

Clayton, Ward. *Men on the Bag: The Caddies of Augusta National.* Ann Arbor, MI: Sports Media Group, 2004.

Cousins, Geoffrey. *Golf in Britain: A Social History From the Beginnings to the Present Day*. London: Routledge & Kegan Paul, 1975.

Darwin, Bernard. *James Braid*. London: Hodder and Stoughton, 1952.

Darwin, Bernard, Henry Cotton, Henry Longhurst, Leonard Crawley, Enid Wilson, and Lord Brabazon of Tara. *A History of Golf in Britain, Part II*. London: Cassell & Co, 1952.

Davies, Pete. *Davies' Dictionary of Golfing Terms*. New York: Simon & Schuster, 1980.

Esquinas, Richard. *Michael and Me: Our Gambling Addiction . . . My Cry for Help!* San Diego: Athletic Guidance Center, 1993.

Fleming, Ian. *Goldfinger*. New York: McMillan, 1966.

Frost, Mark. *The Grand Slam: Bobby Jones, America, and the Story of Golf*. New York: Hyperion, 2004.

————. *The Greatest Game Ever Played: Harry Vardon, Francis Ouimet, and the Birth of Modern Golf*. New York: Hyperion, 2002.

Geddes, Olive M. *A Swing Through Time: Golf in Scotland 1457–1734*. Edinburgh: HMSO, 1992.

Glenn, Rhonda. *The Illustrated History of Women's Golf*. Dallas: Taylor, 1991.

Grimsley, Will. *Golf: Its History, People & Events*. Englewood Cliffs, NJ: Prentice-Hall, 1966.

Hagen, Walter, and Margaret Seaton Heck. *The Walter Hagen Story*. Ann Arbor, MI: Sports Media Group, 2004.

Hamilton, David. *Golf: Scotland's Game*. Kilmacolm, Scotland: Patrick Press, 1998.

Herd, Alexander. *My Golfing Life*. London: Chapman & Hall, 1923.

Hill, Dave, and Nick Seitz. *Teed Off*. Englewood Cliffs, NJ: Prentice-Hall, 1977.

Hope, Bob. *Confessions of a Hooker: My Lifelong Love Affair With Golf*. New York: Doubleday, 1985.

Hutchinson, Horatio G. *Fifty Years of Golf*. New York: Scribner's Sons, 1919.

Johnston, Scott. *The Complete Book of Golf Games*. Memphis: Mustang, 2000.

Joy, David, comp. *The Scrapbook of Old Tom Morris*. Chelsea, MI: Sleeping Bear Press, 2001.

Kahn, Liz. *The LPGA: The Unauthorized Version: The History of the Ladies Professional Golf Association*. Menlo Park, CA: Group Fore Productions, 1996.

Kirkaldy, Andra. *My Fifty Years of Golf*. London: T. F. Unwin, 1921.

Labbance, Bob. *The Old Man: The Biography of Walter J. Travis*. Chelsea, MI: Sleeping Bear Press, 2000.

Leighton, Beach. *Mr. Dutch: The Arkansas Traveler*. Champaign, IL: Sagamore, 1991.

Macdonald, Charles Blair. *Scotland's Gift: How America Discovered Golf*. London: Tatra Press, 2003.

Mair, Lewine. *One Hundred Years of Women's Golf*. London: Mainstream, 1992.

McAllister, Troon. *Barranca*. New York: Rugged Land, 2004.

———. *The Foursome*. New York: Broadway Books, 2000.

———. *The Green*. New York: Broadway Books, 1999.

———. *Scratch*. New York: Rugged Land, 2003.

McDaniel, Pete. *Uneven Lies: The Heroic Story of African-Americans in Golf*. Greenwich, CN: American Golfer, 2001.

Nielson, Leslie, and Henry Beard. *Leslie Nielson's Stupid Little Golf Book*. New York: Doubleday, 1995.

O'Conner, Tim. *The Feeling of Greatness: The Moe Norman Story*. Indianapolis, IN: Masters, 1995.

Owen, David. *Hit & Hope*. New York: Simon & Schuster, 2003.

———. *The Making of the Masters*. New York: Simon & Schuster, 2003.

Palmer, Arnold, and James Dodson. *A Golfer's Life*. New York: Ballentine Books, 1999.

Penna, Toney. *My Wonderful World of Golf*. New York: Centaur House, 1965.

Peper, George, ed. *Golf in America: The First One Hundred Years*. New York: Harry N. Abrams, 1994.

Plimpton, George. *The Bogey Man: A Month on the PGA Tour*. New York: Penguin, 1983.

Pottinger, George. *Muirfield and the Honourable Company*. Edinburgh: Scottish Academic Press, 1972.

Price, Charles. *A Golf Story*. Chicago: Triumph Books, 1986.

Reilly, Rick. *Missing Links*. New York: Broadway Books, 1996.

———. *Who's Your Caddy?: Looping for the Great, Near Great, and Reprobates of Golf*. New York: Doubleday, 2003.

Rodriquez, Chi Chi, and John Anderson. *Chi Chi's Golf Games You Gotta Play*. Champaign, IL: Human Kinetics, 2003.

Rosaforte, Tim. *Tiger Woods: The Makings of a Champion*. New York: St. Martin's Press, 1997.

Salinger, Pierre. *With Kennedy*. New York: Doubleday, 1966.

Sampson, Curt. *The Eternal Summer: Palmer, Nicklaus, and Hogan in 1960, Golf's Golden Year*. New York: Villard, 2000.

———. *Hogan*. Nashville: Rutledge Hill Press, 1996.

———. *The Masters: Golf, Money, and Power in Augusta, Georgia*. New York: Villard, 1998.

Sanders, Doug, and Russ Pate. *Action of the First Tee: How to Cash in On Your Favorite Sport*. Dallas: Taylor, 1987.

Sarazen, Gene, and Herbert Warren Wind. *Thirty Years of Championship Golf*. London: A & C Black, 1950.

Sifford, Charlie. *Just Let Me Play: The Story of Charlie Sifford, the First Black PGA Golfer*. With James Gallo. Latham, NY: British American, 1992.

Sommers, Robert T. *Golf Anecdotes: From the Links of Scotland to Tiger Woods*. New York: Oxford University Press, 1995.

Snead, Sam, and Al Stump. *The Education of a Golfer*. New York: Crest, 1962.

Snead, Sam, and Jerry Tarde. *Pigeons, Marks, Hustlers and Other Golf Bettors You Can Beat*. New York: Golf Digest, 1986.

Stowers, Carlton. *The Unsinkable Titanic Thompson*. Redwood City, CA: Palmer Magic, 1982.

Strege, John. *Tiger: A Biography of Tiger Woods*. New York: Broadway Books, 1997.

———. *Tournament Week: Inside the Ropes and Behind the Scenes on the PGA Tour*. New York: Cliff Street Books, 2000.

Towle, Mike. *I Remember Ben Hogan: Personal Recollections and Revelations of Golf's Most Famous Legend From the People Who Knew Him Best*. Nashville: Cumberland House, 2000.

———. *I Remember Bobby Jones: Personal Memories and Testimonials from the People Who Knew Him Best*. Nashville: Cumberland House, 2000.

Trevino, Lee, and Sam Blair. *The Snake in the Sandtrap and Other Misadventures on the Golf Tour*. New York: Holt, Rinehart and Winston, 1985.

———. *They Call Me Super Mex*. New York: Random House, 1982.

Ussak, Rich. *Golfgames: More Than 120 Side Games From Tee to Green*. Chicago: Contemporary Books, 1999.

Van Natta, Don. *First Off the Tee: Presidential Hackers, Duffers, and Cheaters From Taft to Bush*. New York: Public Affairs, 2003.

Vardon, Harry. *My Golfing Life*. London: Hutchison, 1933.

Venturi, Ken, and Michael Arkush. *Getting Up & Down: My 60 Years in Golf*. Chicago: Triumph Books, 2004.

Willi, Jay. *The Hustler's Guide to Golf: Great Golf Betting Games and How to Win Them Every Time*. Kansas City: Andrews McMeel, 1998.

Wind, Herbert Warren. *The Story of American Golf: Its Champions and its Championships*. New York: Simon & Schuster, 1956.

Wodehouse, P. G. *The Golf Omnibus*. New York: Wings Books, 1973.

NEWSPAPERS AND PERIODICALS

American Heritage, 2005

Associated Press, 1999–2003

Atlanta Journal–Constitution, 1995–2006

Augusta Chronicle, 1933–2006

Avid Golfer, 2003

Black Enterprise, 1994–2003

Boston Globe, 1985–2006

Chicago Tribune, 1988–2006

Daily Oakland Press, 2005

Denver Post, 1993–2006

Detroit News, 2002

European Intelligence Wire, 2002–2006
Forbes, 1994–2006
Fortune, 2004–2006
Golf Digest, 1950–2006
Golf Magazine, 1983–2006
Golf World, 1999–2006
Guardian, 1996–2006
Houston Chronicle, 1985–2006
Huntsville Times, 2003
Knight Ridder/Tribune News Services, 1994–2003
Los Angeles Times, 1985–2006
New Orleans Times–Picayune, 1998–2006
New York Times, 1872–2006
Publishers Weekly, 1999–2006
San Diego Union, 1965–2006
San Francisco Chronicle, 1989–2006
Sporting News, 1993–2006
Sports Illustrated, 1962–2006
St. Louis Post–Dispatch, 1992–1995
Time Magazine, 1937–2006
USA Today, 1992–2006
Wall Street Journal, 1999–2006
Washington Post, 1904–2006
Washington Times, 1997–2006

WEBSITES

http://www.bet365.com
http://www.cfo.com
http://www.cigaraficionado.com
http://www.golfobserver.com
http://www.golfodds.com
http://www.golftoday.com
http://www.golfweb.com
http://www.pgatour.com
http://www.pokernews.com
http://www.usga.org
http://www.wikipedia.org

INDEX

About the Author

Michael K. Bohn is the author of two other books—*Nerve Center: Inside the White House Situation Room* (2003) and *The Achille Lauro Hijacking: Lessons in the Politics and Prejudice of Terrorism* (2004). As a freelance writer, he regularly contributes to a group of newspapers in Virginia.

He appeared in a 1999 Discovery Channel documentary on submarine warfare during the Cold War. Bohn helped develop and appeared in two BBC Television documentaries about crisis management in the White House, one in November 2002 and another in April 2003. Also, Mr. Bohn appeared in a July 2003 special, "The White House at War," a joint ABC News/New York Times/Discovery Channel project. He is a featured contributor to the German public television documentary "The Palaces of Power."

A career naval intelligence officer, Mr. Bohn served at the White House twice. During 1970–72, he was a military social aide to President Nixon. He helped manage White House social events ranging from afternoon coffees to Tricia Nixon's wedding. During the second Reagan administration, Mr. Bohn was the director of the White House Situation Room. He organized the flow of critical information into the White House and National Security Council throughout the Middle East kidnappings and international terrorism of the mid-1980s. He wrote daily summaries of world events for the president, vice president, and senior White House officials.

Bohn earned a bachelor of arts and a master's degree in political science from Texas Tech and is an honors graduate of the Naval War College. He is married with two sons. He is a member of Mount Vernon Country Club in Alexandria, Virginia, where his once respectable handicap is increasing along with his belt size and age.